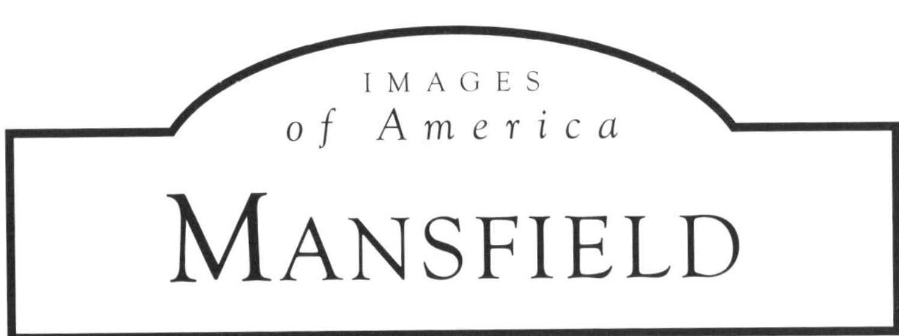

IMAGES
of America

MANSFIELD

Mansfield Historical Society

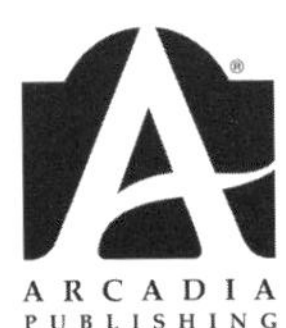

ARCADIA
PUBLISHING

ISBN 978-1-4671-6271-5

Published by Arcadia Publishing
Charleston, South Carolina

Printed in the United States of America

Library of Congress Control Number: 2025948842

For all general information, please contact Arcadia Publishing:
Telephone 843-853-2070
Fax 843-853-0044
E-mail sales@arcadiapublishing.com

Visit us on the Internet at www.arcadiapublishing.com

IMAGES
of America

MANSFIELD

On the Cover: The 1908 Mansfield municipal band included, from left to right, (first row) Roy Ault (director), Henry Buttrell, Jake Hobson, Hayden McElvany, Harry Lipscomb, Ed Dalton, Ned Man, Brit Buttrell, Elmo Davis, Marcus Timms, and Claude Ellis; (second row) Bishop Timms, Oscar Smith, Raymond Thomas, Earnest Rosier, Willie Wade, Sam Darwin, Hodges McKnight, Cleo Wilson, Joe Hobson, Jim Yates, Dick Caldwell, Bill Darwin, Bob Carroll, Robert Timms, Alley Wade, and Dick Holland. (Courtesy of the Mansfield Historical Society.)

Contents

ACKNOWLEDGMENTS

The Mansfield Historical Society is grateful to all who provided pictures, stories, and support as this endeavor took shape. A special thanks goes to the staff of the Mansfield Historical Museum for their assistance. All of the pictures and stories came from the archives of the Mansfield Historical Society and are housed at the Mansfield Historical Museum unless otherwise noted. We apologize for any inaccuracies or omissions; everyone worked diligently to provide you with the most accurate information possible. The book committee was composed of Marty Thomas, Jessica Baber, Linda Leddy, and Karen Leach.

INTRODUCTION

What and where is Mansfield, Texas, formerly known as Mansfeild? This city is primarily situated in the southeastern corner of Tarrant County, with portions extending into both Johnson and Ellis Counties. While some Caddo Native Americans called this area home, most Indigenous peoples in the region were nomadic.

In 1845, a Texas Ranger outpost was established approximately six miles north of what would later become downtown Mansfield. As far as frontiers go, this area was considered relatively safe, which attracted individuals eager for land ownership.

The first settlers were farmers who cultivated grains, like corn and wheat. Soon after these settlers' arrival, Julian Feild and Ralph Man established a steam-powered mill that produced meal and flour to supply the Confederate army. This development contributed to Mansfield's prosperity, and the community that formed around the mill adopted the name "Mansfeild," derived from the mill owners' last names. Over time, various misspellings led to the widely accepted spelling "Mansfield."

An intriguing side story about the mill involves a whiskey-making operation, either housed within the mill or in a nearby building. Despite Mansfield's prohibition on the sale of alcohol, the resourceful distillers circumvented this restriction by setting up a saloon called Brooklyn just across the railroad tracks and outside the city limits, where they sold their products. This establishment attracted many visitors.

The city of Mansfield also attracted citizens who were thirsty for knowledge. In 1870, Dr. John Collier founded the Mansfield Male and Female College. One of Dr. Collier's prerequisites for establishing the school was that the community must be platted, as he believed it would provide a suitable environment for the college. The *Fort Worth Democrat* newspaper ranked the institution as the "first place among educational establishments in the state."

Mansfield continued to experience steady growth due to its stable economic foundation, its newly established center of higher education, and a land survey that facilitated the sale of land parcels. Many of the new families were seeking fresh beginnings in Texas following the Civil War.

By the late 1800s, it was clear that Mansfield was here to stay. Fraternal organizations like the Masons and Odd Fellows were established in the 1870s, which contributed to the community's development. Then, in the early 1880s, a group of visionary businessmen in Mansfield raised $5,000 and provided land rights-of-way to persuade the railroad to route its tracks through the town. This was a significant step in Mansfield's growth, not only for passenger rail service but for farmers who could now ship their goods to other markets. The railroad helped cotton to become king in Mansfield.

By 1890, Mansfield was incorporated with a population of 518. As more houses were built, a business district began to emerge on both sides of Water Street, now known as Main Street. The town saw the establishment of banks, new churches, a growing city government, and expanding schools. Daily passenger and mail service to Fort Worth began, and by 1900, the population had reached 700.

Although the Mansfield Male and Female College closed in 1887, education was still very important to the residents of Mansfield. After the closure of the Mansfield Male and Female College, the Mansfield Academy was established. Many small schools also operated out of private homes. In 1909, the Mansfield Independent School District was formed, taking over the academy buildings. A rock gymnasium was built in 1940 as part of a Works Progress Administration project.

Significant improvements followed, including a water system, telephone lines, brick and concrete sidewalks on Water Street, and an electrical plant. In 1910, an ordinance was passed to limit automobile speeds to 10 miles per hour. One of the most appreciated improvements was the installation of a sewer system in 1926.

During that time, Memorial Hall, located at the corner of Broad and Water Streets, was the hub of community life, serving as a center for civic activities, a library, and city government offices. However, as progress continued, Memorial Hall was eventually torn down to make way for a new city hall.

During the 1930s, the Texas Highway Department aimed to bypass small towns while constructing new highways. The residents of Mansfield fought hard to ensure the highway passed through their town, even relocating a lumberyard and several houses to make it happen. The highway was completed in 1940, marking a milestone comparable to the railroad's arrival in the 1880s.

In the 1950s, Mansfield served as a marketing, service, and transportation center for the farms in southeast Tarrant County. However, as the population grew, city services improved, including the paving of streets.

Mansfield remained a quiet town until the 1970s, when it began to experience growth, mirroring the expansion of the Dallas-Fort Worth metropolitan area. New housing developments were built to cater to commuters to Fort Worth and employees of new industries in Mansfield. The city developed award-winning parks, hospitals, schools, and city services, growing from a population of 418 in 1890 to an estimated 87,000 by 2025.

As Mansfield grew, many newcomers settled in the area, prompting longtime residents to worry that the town's history might be forgotten. In response, the Mansfield Public Library received a grant in 1982 to preserve the history of Mansfield and its surrounding communities. The library collaborated with the Mansfield Historical Society, which was chartered in 1985 to unite those interested in the area's history. This organization collects and preserves photographs and printed materials that illustrate Mansfield's past. Unless otherwise stated, the images in this book come from the Mansfield Historical Society's collection. In 2002, the historical society opened the Mansfield Historical Museum, which allows visitors to learn about the history of the town and the men and women who built it.

Throughout Mansfield's history, many heroes—often unsung—have worked hard to improve their community. While this book includes many of their stories, numerous others could not be featured due to space constraints.

Now, it is time to explore some of the people and places that have made Mansfield a wonderful place to live.

One

Early Days

The first wave of settlers to Mansfield arrived in the rolling Cross Timber country of north central Texas in the 1840s. Primarily of Scotch-Irish origins, these pioneer farmers came for the most part from the southern states, following the frontier as it shifted west of the Mississippi.

The beginnings of a community probably existed around 1856. Julian Feild purchased 540 acres in the area. Ralph Man and Feild completed their three-story brick gristmill sometime before 1859. It was located on Walnut Creek at the crossroads that would become the center of Mansfield. The mill, which produced flour and meal, was the first built in North Texas to utilize steam power.

Feild opened a general merchandise store at the same time as the mill. He built a log house for his family, which also served as an inn for travelers. By 1860, the nucleus of the future city existed. The first post office was established that year with Feild as the postmaster.

During the Civil War, the Man and Feild Mill supplied meal and flour to Confederate troops, hauling it as far as Shreveport, Louisiana, and Jefferson, Missouri. The small community around the mill was unique in that it prospered throughout the Civil War. The community took on the name Mansfeild, a combination of the names of the founders. Repeated misspellings over the years resulted in the acceptance of the conventional spelling of Mansfield.

In 1870, the town was platted. With its stable economic base, the establishment of a local school, and a land survey that facilitated selling parcels, Mansfield enjoyed steady growth. The population was 249 in 1880. With the arrival of the railroad in the 1880s, growth continued. Mansfield was incorporated on August 23, 1890, with a population of 418.

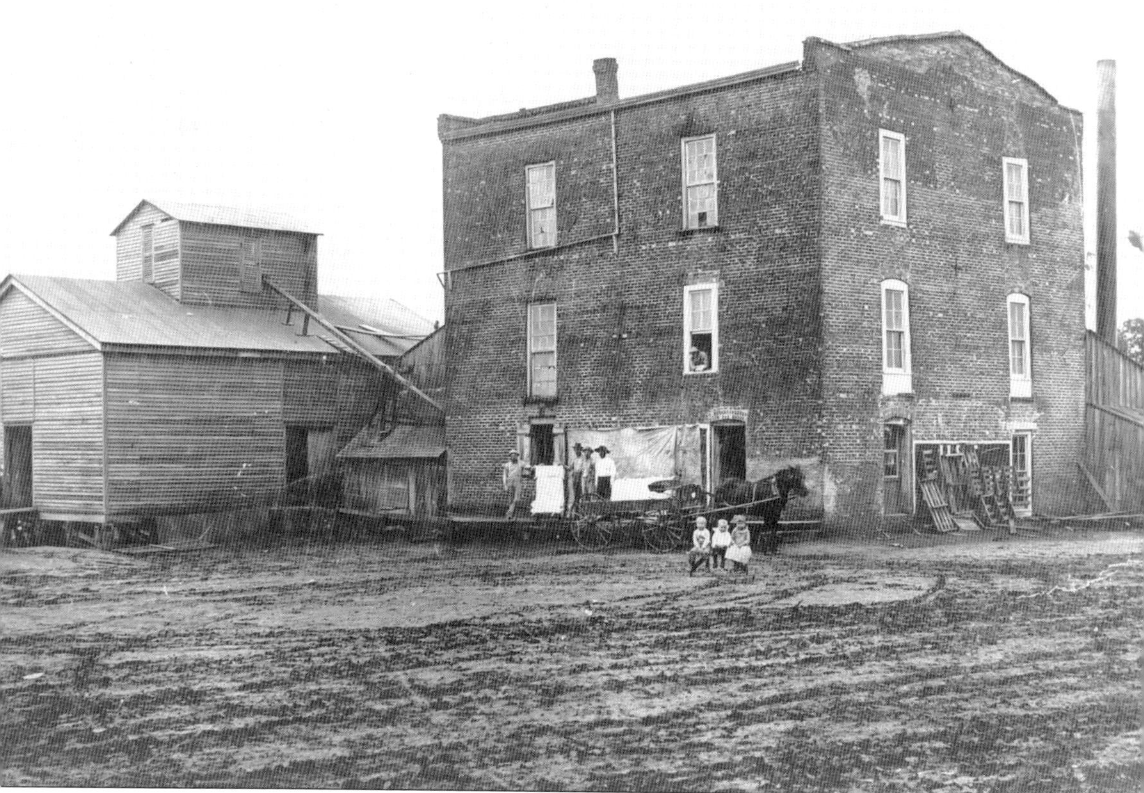

When Ralph Man and Julian Feild moved to the Walnut Creek community, they utilized a small, preexisting mill. However, the business quickly outgrew the building. So, Man and Feild built a new gristmill located at what is now the southeast corner of Main and Broad Streets sometime around 1859. While it produced flour and meal, the mill was significant for being the first one built in North Texas to utilize steam power, and it enjoyed patronage as far south as San Antonio and as far north as Oklahoma. During the Civil War, the Man and Feild Mill supplied meal and flour to the Confederacy, hauling it as far as Shreveport, Louisiana, and Jefferson, Missouri. Due to the mill's success and the important role it played in developing the community, the town was named Mansfeild, a combination of Man and Feild's surnames.

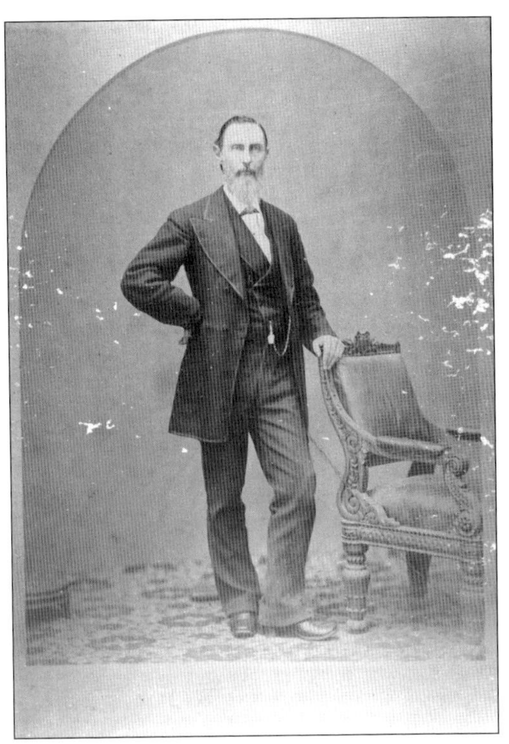

Julian Feild was one of the founders and namesakes of Mansfield, the place where he and Ralph Man established a wheat and corn mill that brought workers to the community in 1859. He lived in Mansfield with his wife, Henrietta Boisseau, and family for several years before moving to Fort Worth. Feild later married Ida Major in 1885 and moved to San Diego, California, before his death in 1897. The image below contains a unique collage comprised of 14 photographs of the Feild family, including Dr. Richard Alexander Feild and Dr. Julian T. Feild, two of Julian Feild's sons, in the larger ovals on top and Henrietta Boisseau Feild on the bottom center right and Julian Feild on the bottom center left.

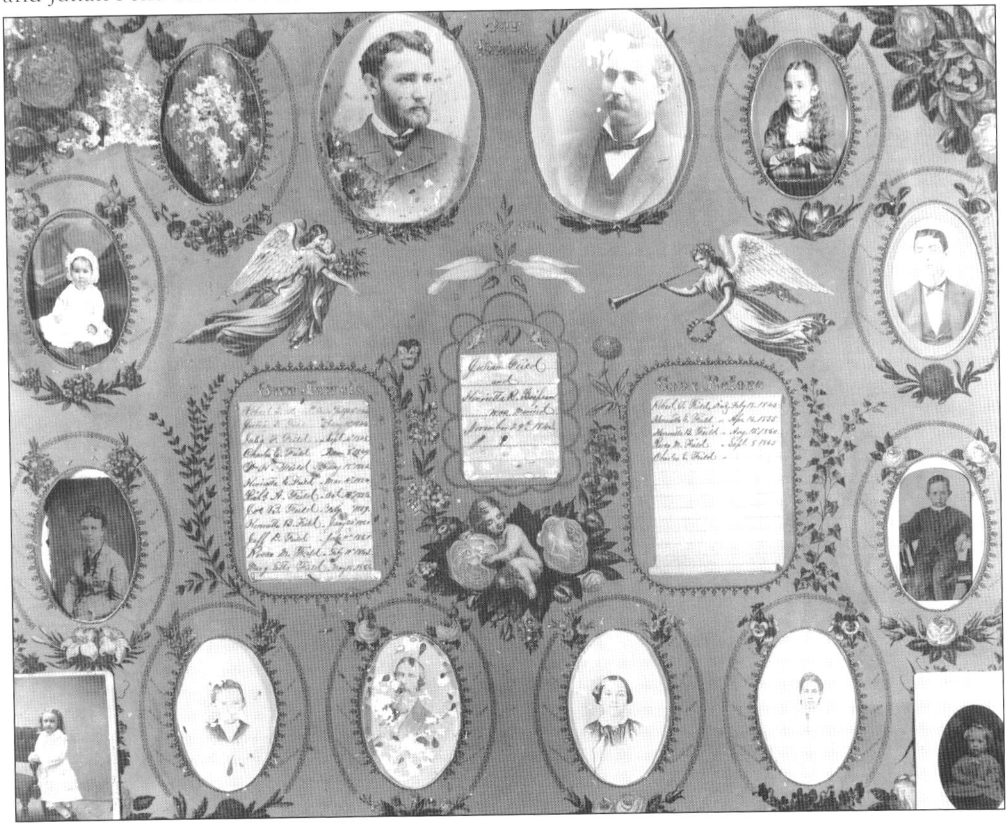

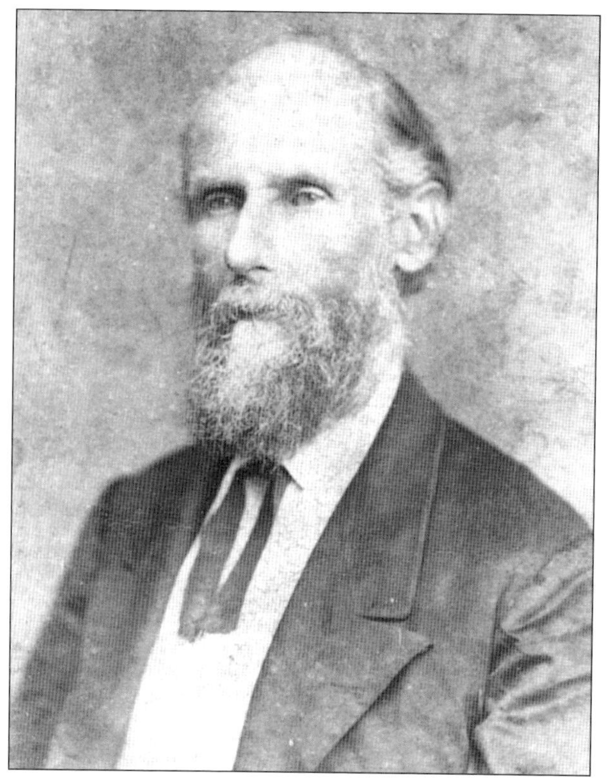

Ralph Sandiford Man was born in Charleston, South Carolina. He left Charleston at age 22 to move west. He met his future business partner, Julian Feild, in Harrison County, Texas, around 1850. Man and Feild moved to the Walnut Creek community, and by 1859, they had constructed their wheat and corn mill in a brick, three-story building. Man married twice, once to Julia Boisseau in 1863 and again to Sarah Stephens after Boisseau died in 1868. Man had six children. He lived the rest of his life in the Mansfield community and was involved in the Cumberland Presbyterian Church, giving three acres of his land to the church to use as a cemetery. Man died in 1906. The photograph at left is of Ralph Man. The photograph below is of his home, built in 1865, which is now the Man House Museum.

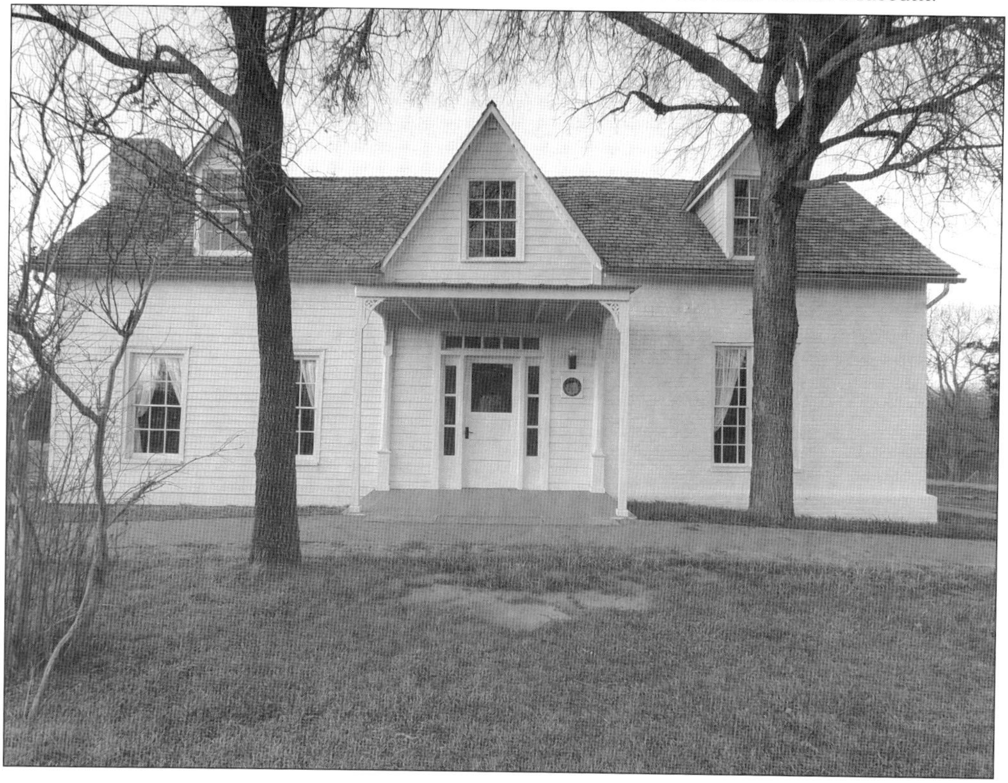

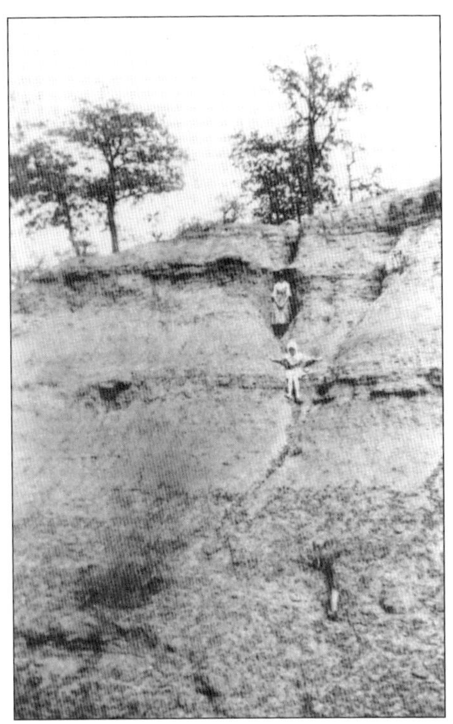

Walnut Creek was integral to the founding of Mansfield, as it provided the water necessary for the personal and industrial growth of the town. This area along the creek is known as Red Bluff, a natural formation along the Walnut Creek, named for the red dirt sandstone of which it is made. Today, a fence keeps visitors safely along the trail, but the bluff once served as a popular picnic spot, "lovers' hangout," and field trip destination for local science classes. The photograph at right shows young people climbing down the face of the bluff. Seen below is the same group at the base of the bluff on the bank of the creek.

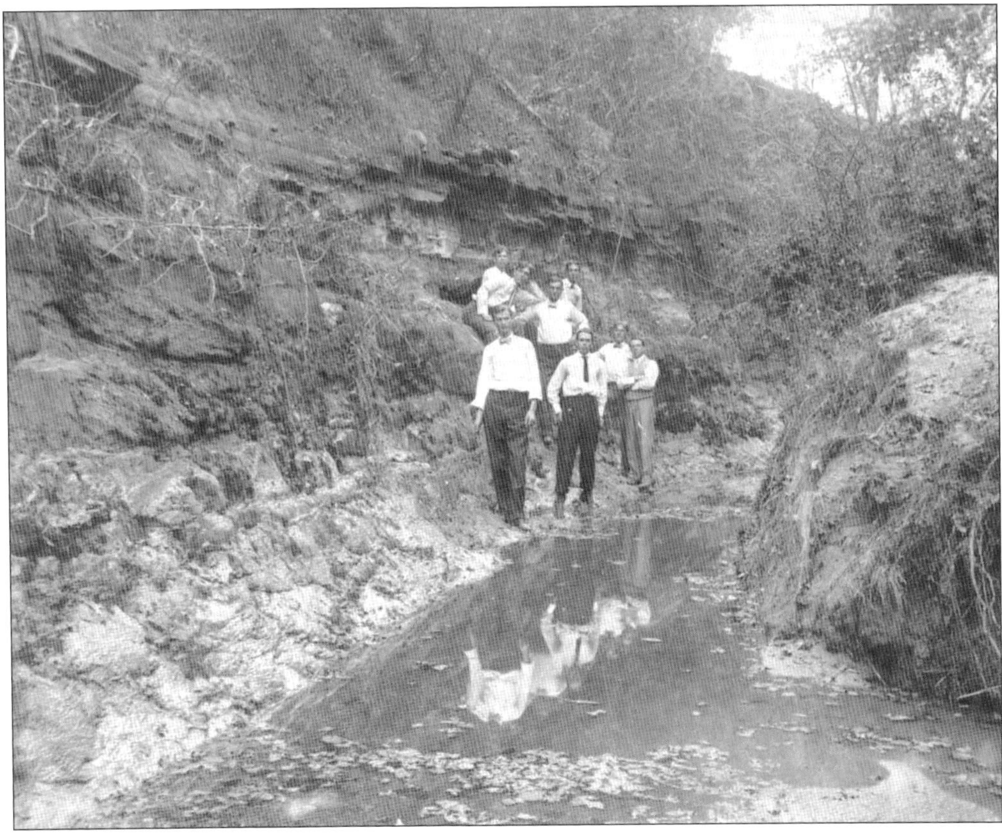

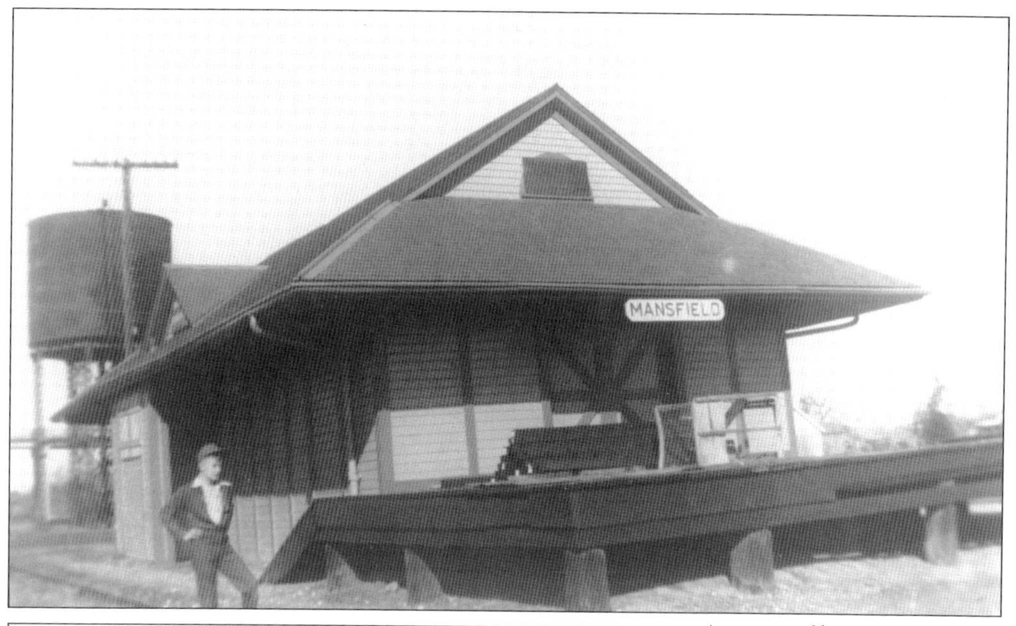

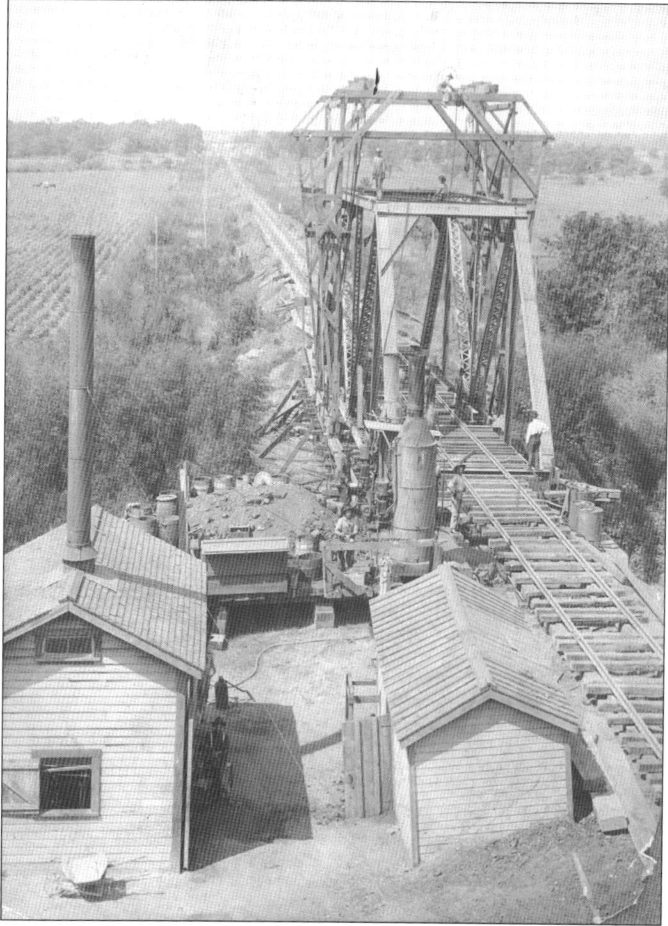

A group of businessmen helped raise $5,000 and donated right-of-way land to encourage the Fort Worth & New Orleans Railway to route its track through Mansfield. The railroad began operating in Mansfield in 1886. The photograph above shows W.E. Marshall standing in front of the passenger depot that stood at the corner of Smith and Depot Streets until it was demolished in 1950.

Built in 1885, this Pratt through truss steel railroad bridge, located near Cardinal Road and crossing Walnut Creek, is one of the oldest surviving bridges in Tarrant County. This image shows the bridge undergoing renovation in 1906. In the foreground is the water pump house located on North Street.

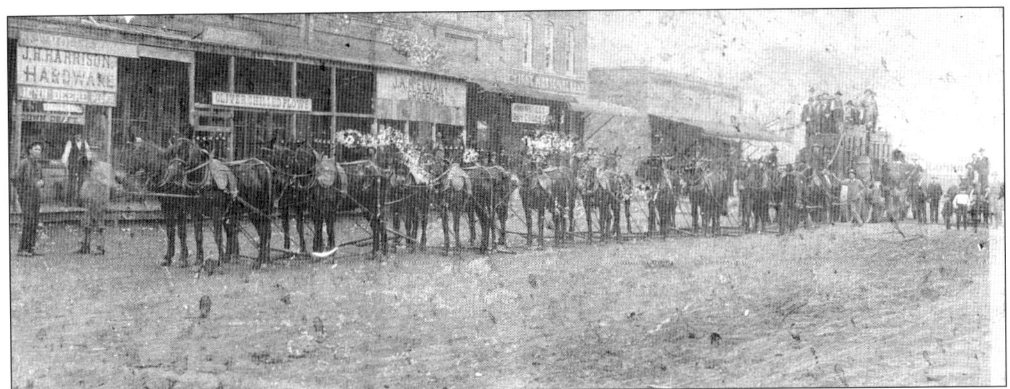

This photograph, taken in 1905, shows a 20-mule team on Water Street (now Main Street) in downtown Mansfield advertising "20 Mule Team Borax." Several businesses from the time can be seen in the background, including J.H. Harrison Hardware, Oliver Chilled Plows, J.A. McElvaney Groceries, Mansfield Dry Goods, and First National Bank.

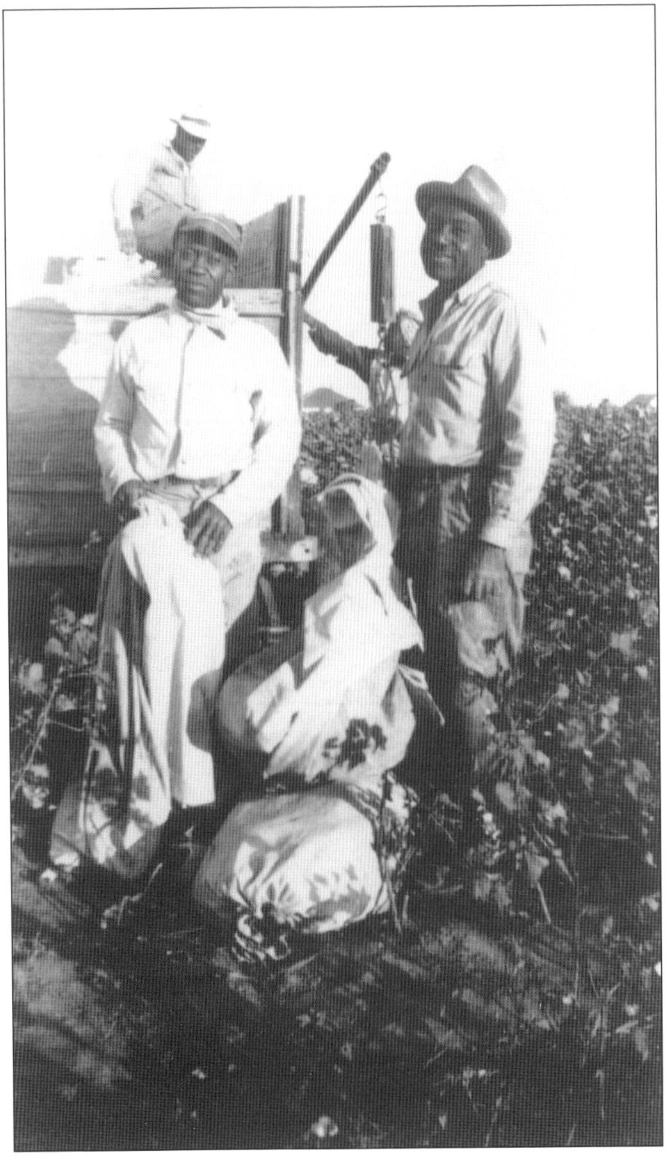

The Mansfield area produced premium cotton. At the time this photograph was taken, people picking cotton filled the bag they carried, took it to a wagon for weighing, put the cotton in the wagon, and went back out to begin the process again. Workers were paid by the pound, and a fast worker could pick 300 pounds each day.

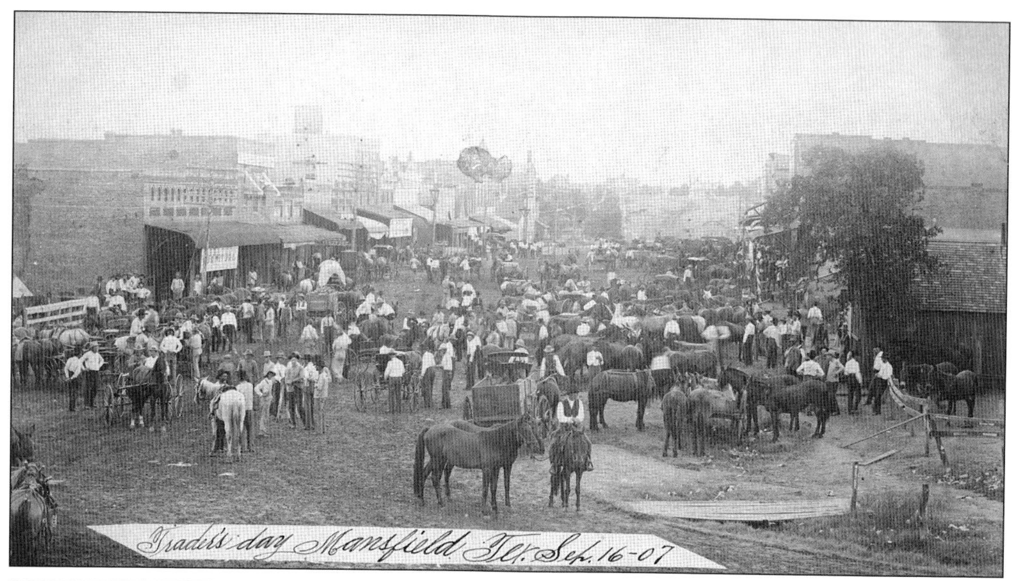

On the third Thursday of each month, early Mansfield residents gathered on Water Street to buy, sell, or trade. This photograph of Traders' Day was taken in 1907 from the north end of the street, facing south. The tradition faded away as tractors and cars replaced horses, mules, and buggies.

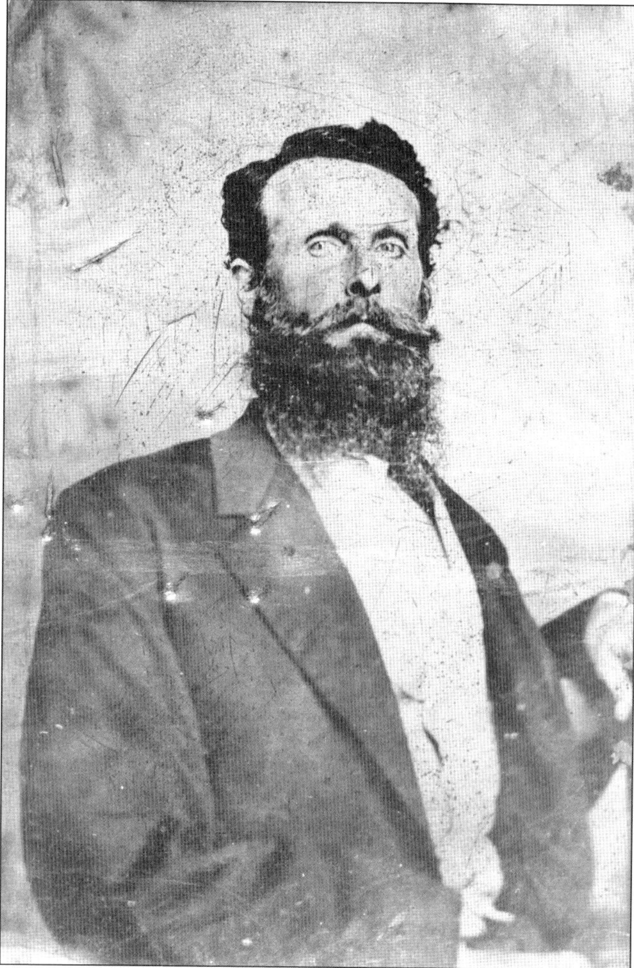

Dr. Duff Green Hodges was Mansfield's first doctor. He traveled to Texas with his family in 1859 in a covered wagon. He saw no roads or doctors over a large stretch of land, so he settled here. He visited his patients on horseback and dispensed medicine from his saddlebag. Dr. Hodges donated land for Mansfield's first church and school. He also donated land to entice the railroad to Mansfield. Dr. Hodges died of exposure at age 39.

Two

HOME LIFE

Though Mansfield was originally just another vast field in Texas's rolling plains, Ralph Man and Julian Feild saw the area as a potential space for a sprawling town. With Man and Feild building their mill in the area around 1860, records show that by the 1870s the land was surveyed to facilitate the selling of parcels of land to interested western settlers. By 1890, about 400 settlers officially chartered their small town as Mansfield.

With Mansfield's official establishment and continued population growth came local homes, churches, schools, and businesses. Homes came in different sizes and shapes; farmers, doctors, and local businessmen built unique city houses, country homes, shared homes, mansions, and cabins. As city services improved through the early 20th century with a new water system, telephone lines, an electric light plant, and a sewer system, more western travelers brought their trades, started local businesses, and built homes in Mansfield. Thus, the town shifted from a small farm community to a town with a booming business district with rare goods to share with Mansfield's interested neighbors.

Religion played an important role in the lives of the early residents of Mansfield. Many early church efforts began in homes until a congregation established enough members to build their own chapels. These buildings provided ample space for worship and functioned as the primary space for Mansfield's social scene; early residents' limited social life often consisted of the few social gatherings provided through a church's picnics and revivals. Accounts from this era highlight these gatherings as a source of entertainment for the community. Newspaper reports convey that many Mansfieldians viewed church picnics and revivals as an opportunity to showcase their singing, cooking, or oral storytelling talents. As the decades rolled on, churches continued to be the center of the community by bringing people together.

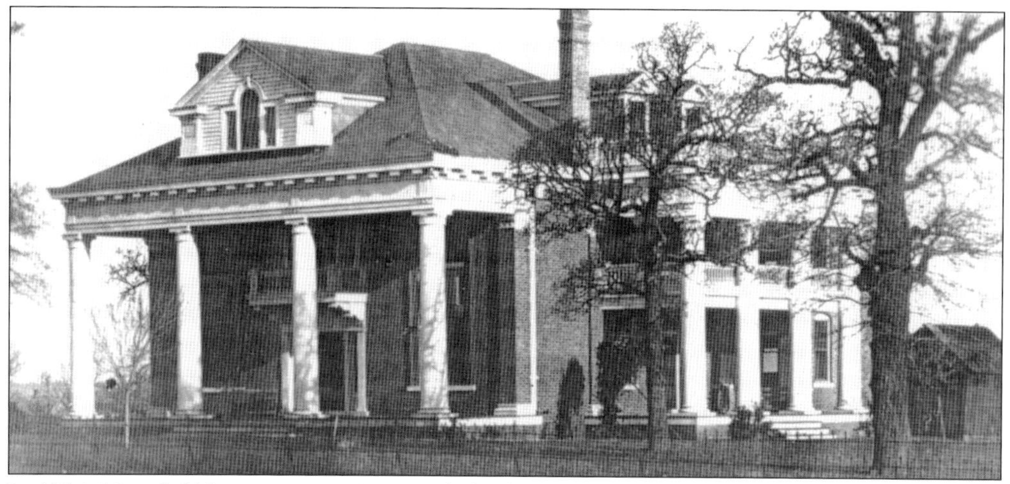

In 1904, Mansfield businessman J.H. Wright built a 16-room, brick home for his family. In 1944, the home was sold to Ira Gibson and later to Agnes Kirk White, who ran a nursing home called White's Sanatorium from the home. In 1966, a fire destroyed the second floor of the home. A smaller second floor was reconstructed.

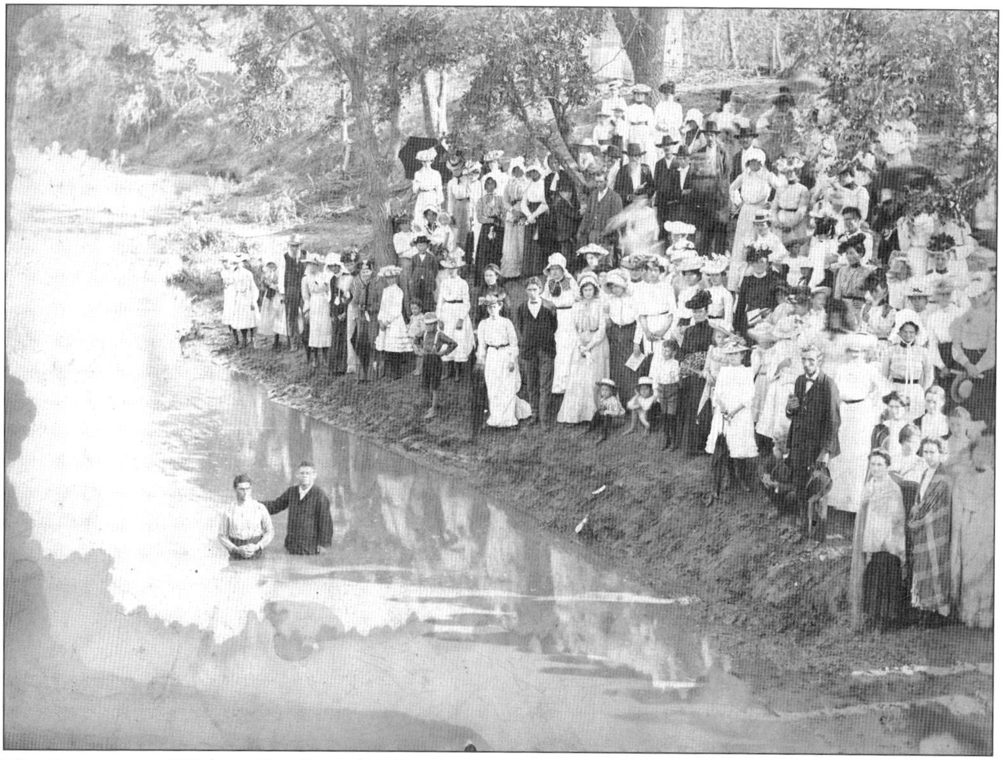

This baptism in Walnut Creek took place in Jacob Back's pasture around 1900. These baptisms often took place in front of the entire congregation, with everyone dressed in their Sunday best, and regularly utilized local bodies of water. This photograph shows previously baptized believers on the right, wrapped in blankets.

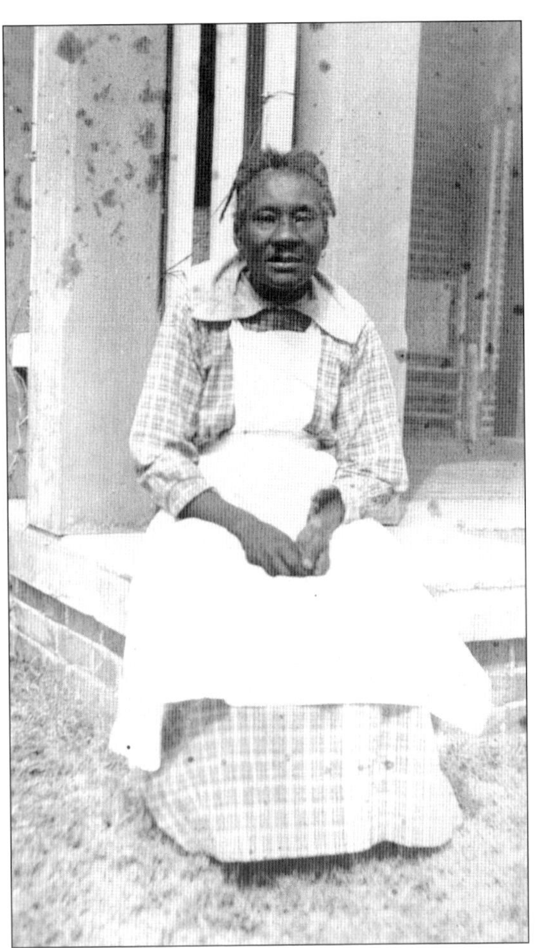

Sofy Moody Nolan and her husband, Ben Nolan, were pioneer settlers of Mansfield in the 1800s. The couple had five children. Sofy was a midwife who delivered many Mansfield babies. She also removed warts from people's faces and made a liniment used for rheumatism. Additionally, Sofy worked for Sarah "Sallie" McKnight. The Nolans were a close-knit family and were dedicated members of Bethlehem Baptist Church.

Built around 1890, the Wright-Malone-Farmer House at 305 West Broad Street has been home to many Mansfield families through the years. The building was originally located at 302 West Broad Street, but over a three-day period in 1904, it was rolled on logs across the street to where it stands today, so the Wright family could build a new home on the original location.

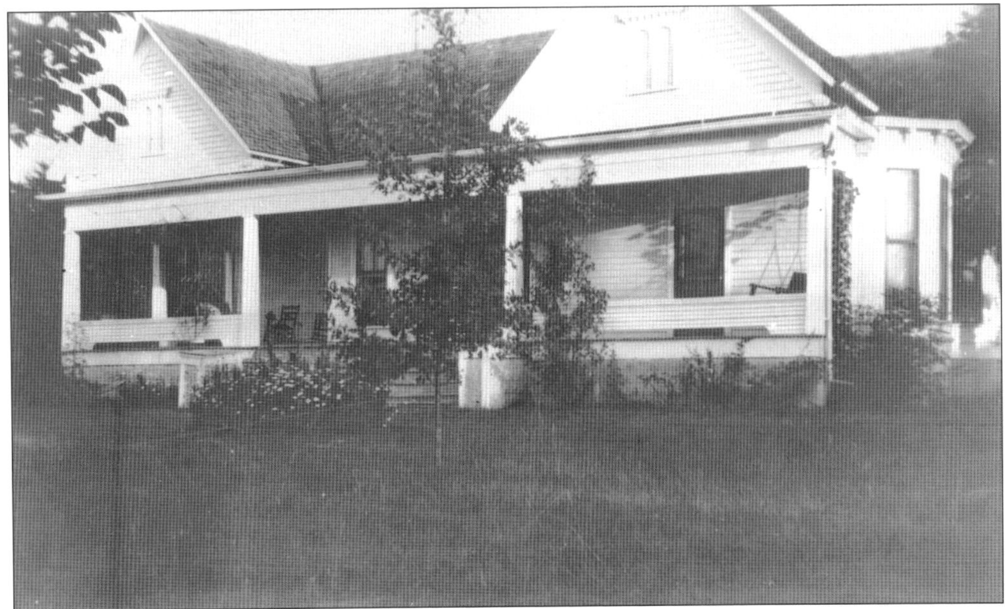

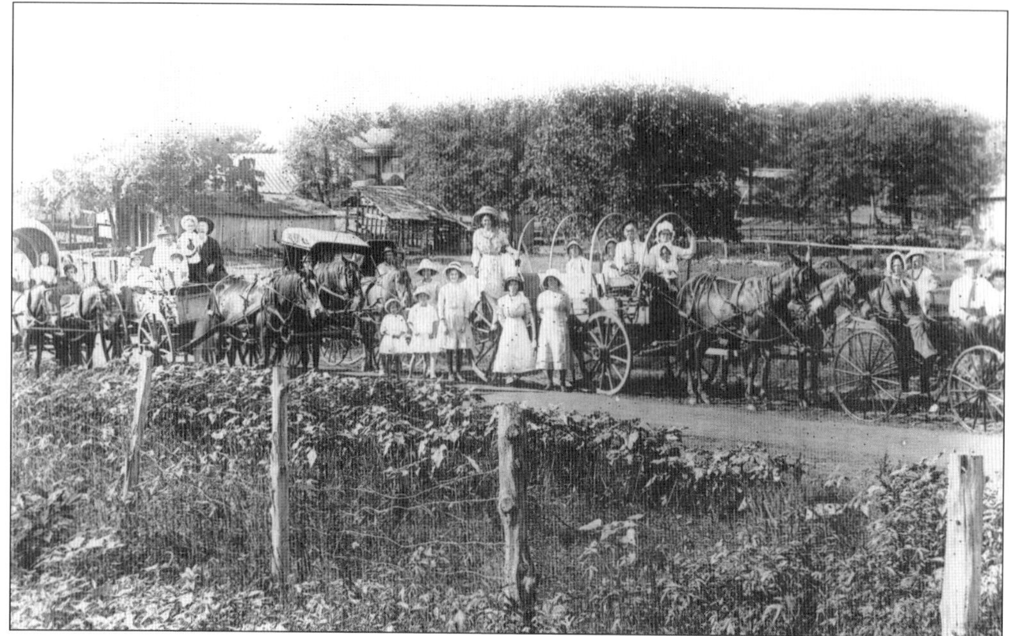

The Cumberland Presbyterian Church was founded in 1854, with the eight members regularly meeting in their homes before they gained an official building. When they gathered for socials, such as the all-day picnic pictured above, congregants spent the whole day sharing food, fun, and fellowship. By 1868, the church needed its own building, which was proving difficult with the current costs of lumber. Word came to those in charge that a nearby saloon was being torn down, and they had the building shipped to their location. A place of worship was erected in an oak grove overlooking Walnut Creek. It is believed the church site was donated by Dr. Duff Hodges. The church, pictured below, served as an interdenominational house for Methodists, Baptists, Presbyterians, and the Church of Christ until each congregation found its own home.

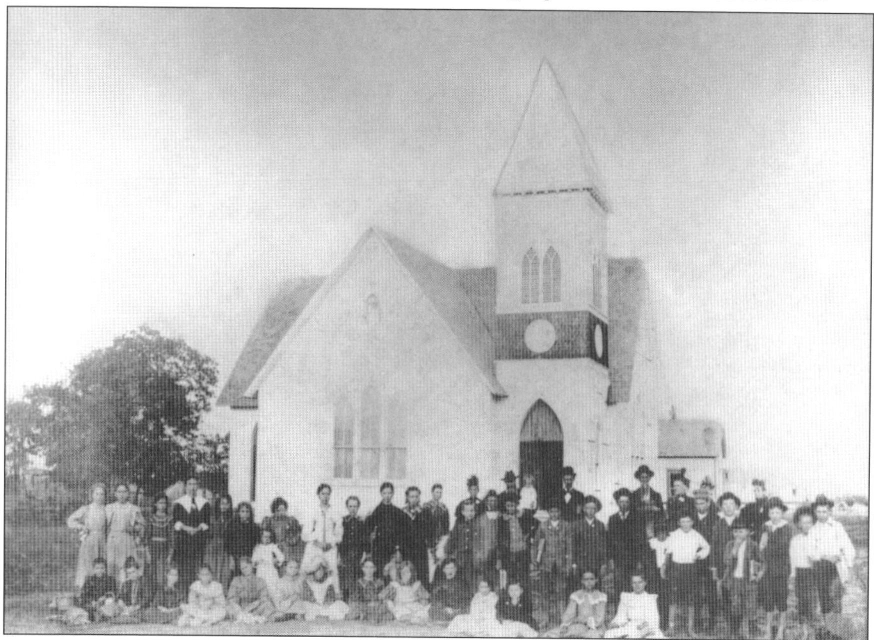

Hezekiah "Khi" Balch married Mattie Kate Boswell on April 20, 1902, at the Boswell home in Mansfield, around the time this photograph was taken. They were a devoted couple; Katie wrote volumes of poems and songs about her love for Khi. Together, they had six children and were happily married for 25 years.

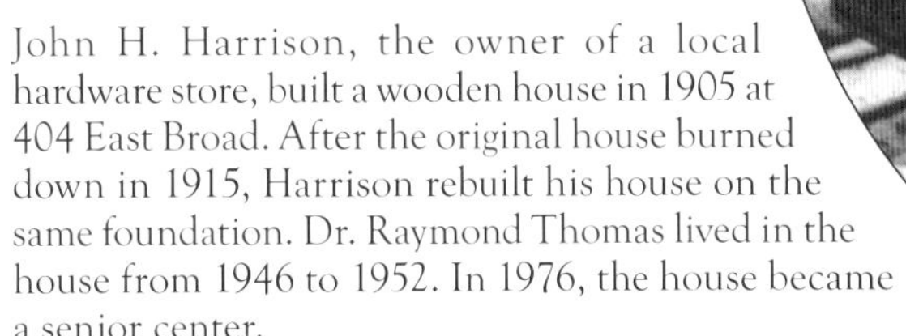

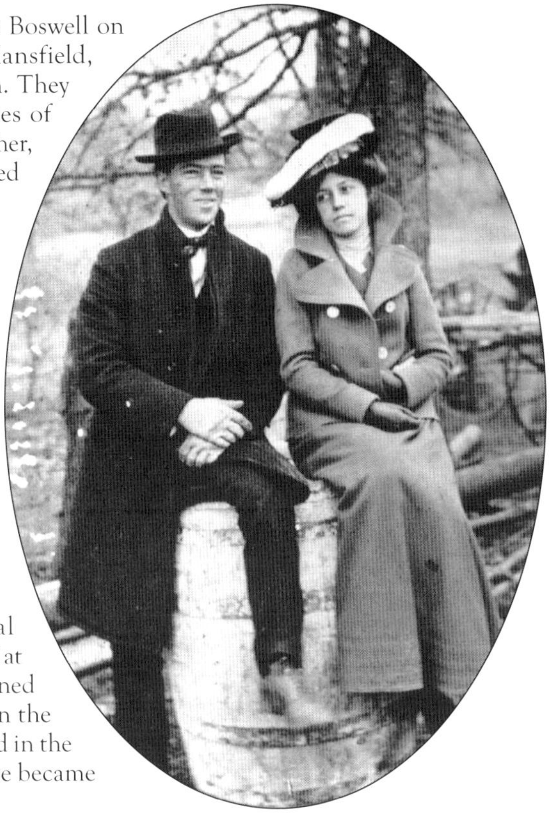

John H. Harrison, the owner of a local hardware store, built a wooden house in 1905 at 404 East Broad. After the original house burned down in 1915, Harrison rebuilt his house on the same foundation. Dr. Raymond Thomas lived in the house from 1946 to 1952. In 1976, the house became a senior center.

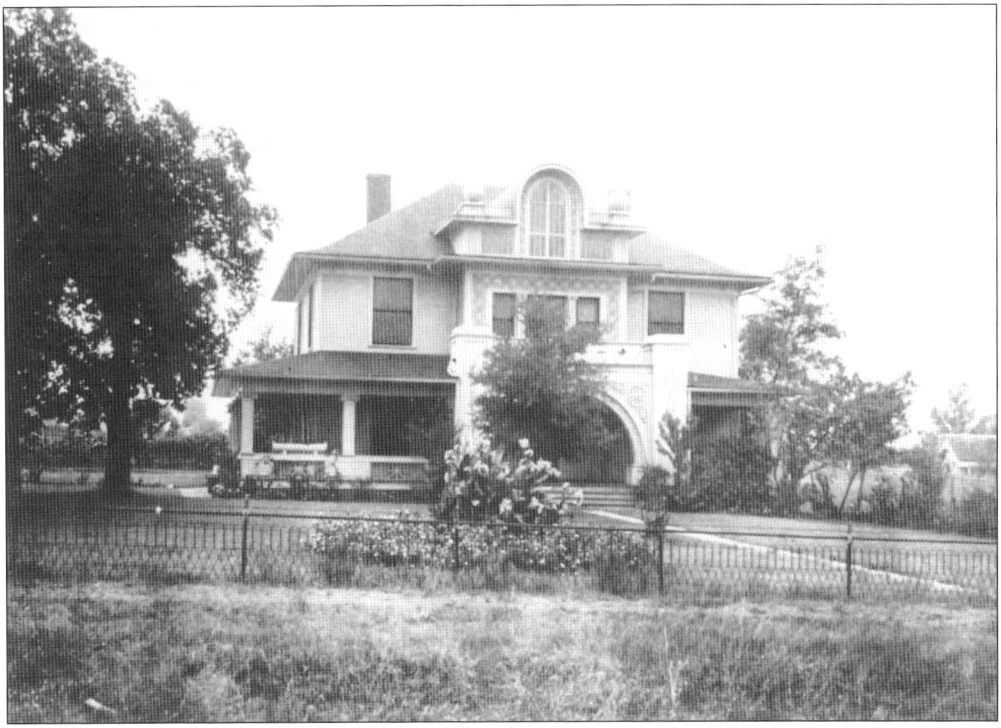

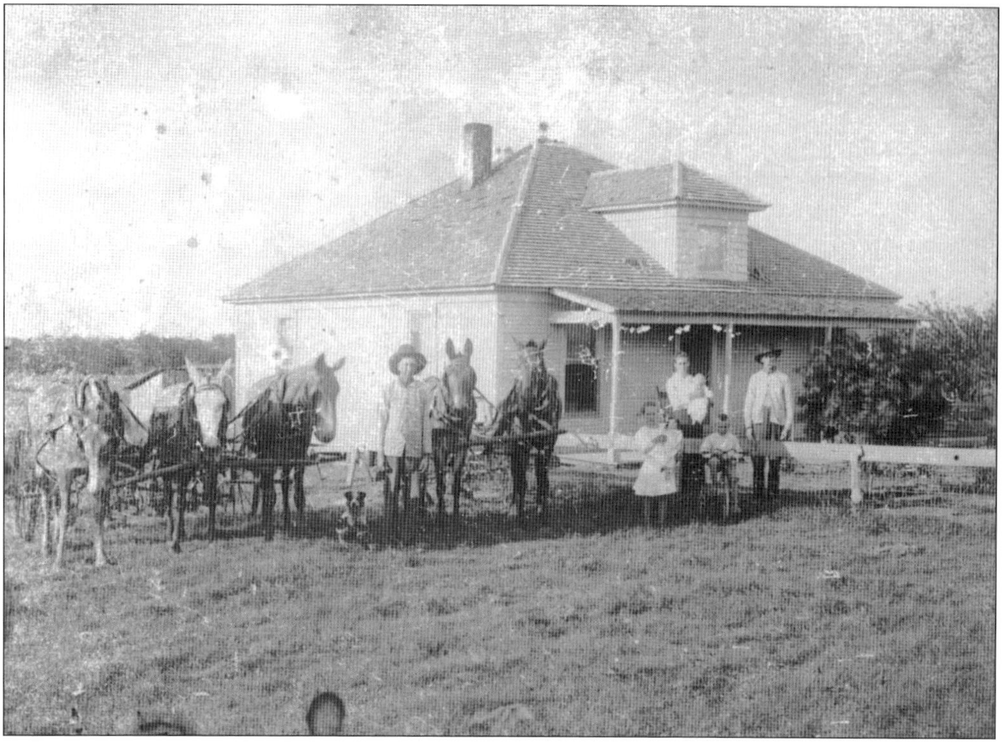

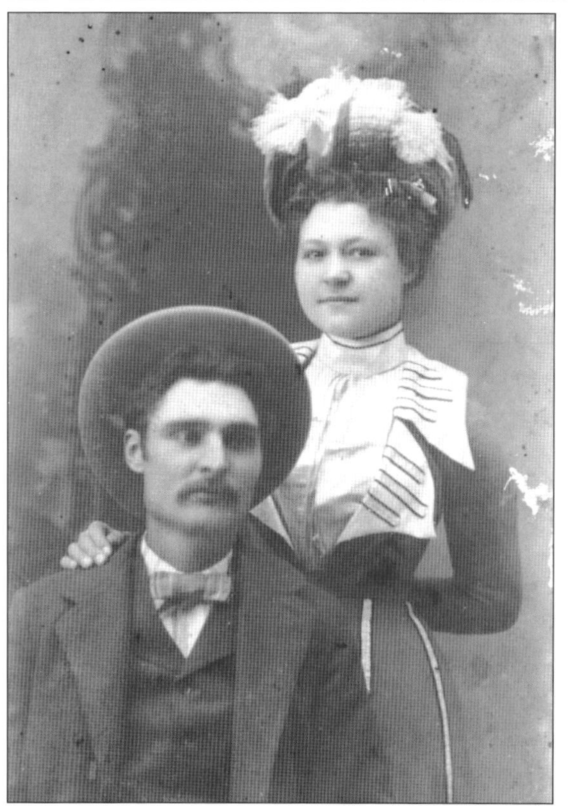

Richard and Frances Bratton, one of Mansfield's pioneer families, established themselves in Mansfield in 1852. They arrived in the area in a covered wagon and became highly respected among early settlers. The couple had 12 children and lived on a farm a few miles outside of Mansfield. The Bratton family played an important role in the development of the community, and the family has continued to live in and around Mansfield for six generations. The photograph above shows the Bratton family home with members of the family. The photograph at left is of Henry Ward Bratton, the grandson of Richard and Frances Bratton, and his wife, Sarah "Aunt Sally" Joyner Bratton.

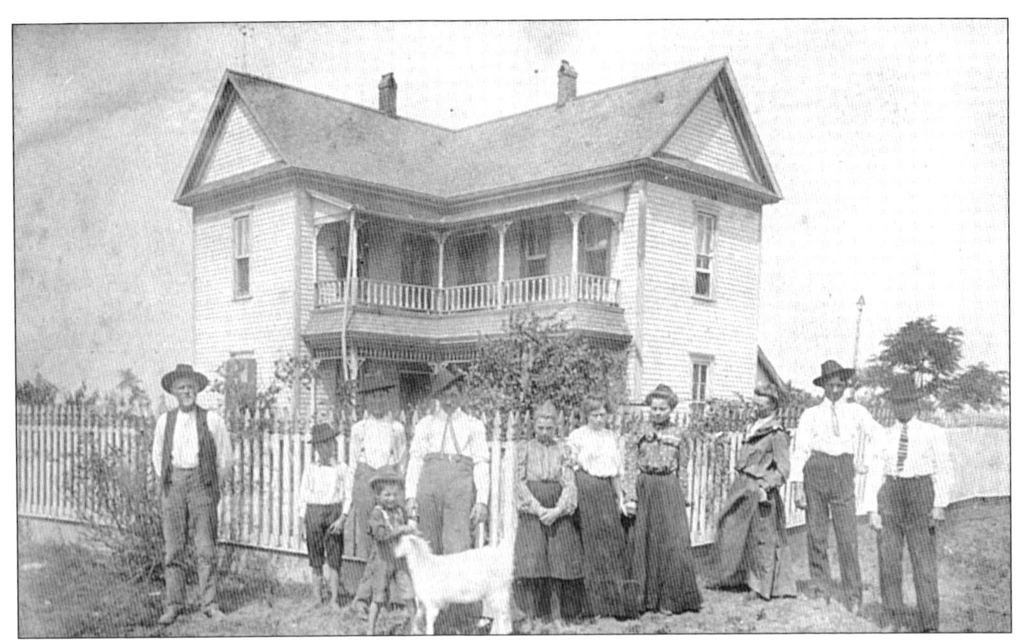

Martin Ballweg was born in Germany in 1843 and came to America with his parents and two brothers in 1852. They settled in Wisconsin. Ballweg and his wife, Anna, moved to the Mansfield-Cedar Hill area with their family in 1883. The couple had 12 children, many of whom are pictured here in front of the family home in 1902. They were founding members of the Catholic Church in Mansfield. Some of their descendants still live in Mansfield today. The farm was well known and recognizable for having its name painted on the roof of the barn. The family eventually owned over 700 acres of property.

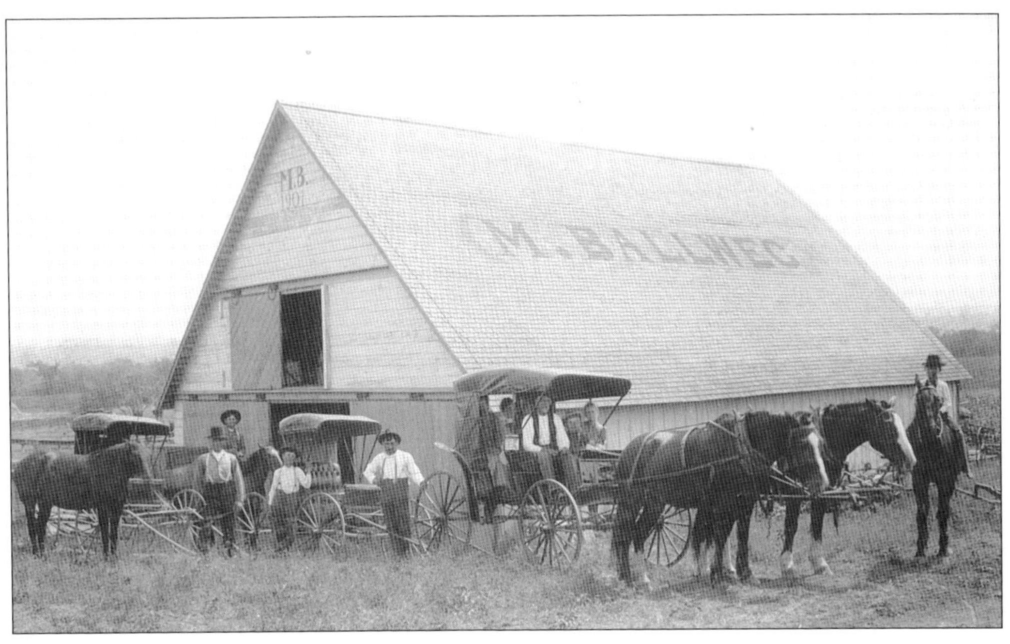

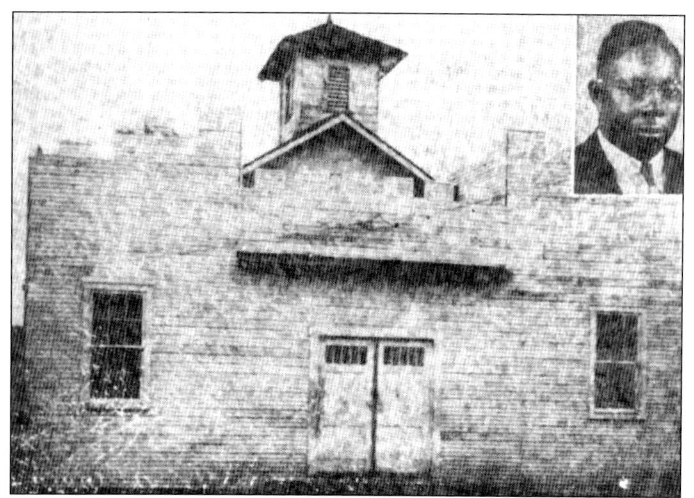

Bethlehem Baptist Church was established in 1819. The church, which began meeting in homes, served the Black community in Mansfield. Rev. Green Medlin organized the congregation and served in the role of preacher for 22 years. By 1892, the church met at the local Black school, and in 1896, a church building and a parsonage were constructed. The congregation continues to thrive today.

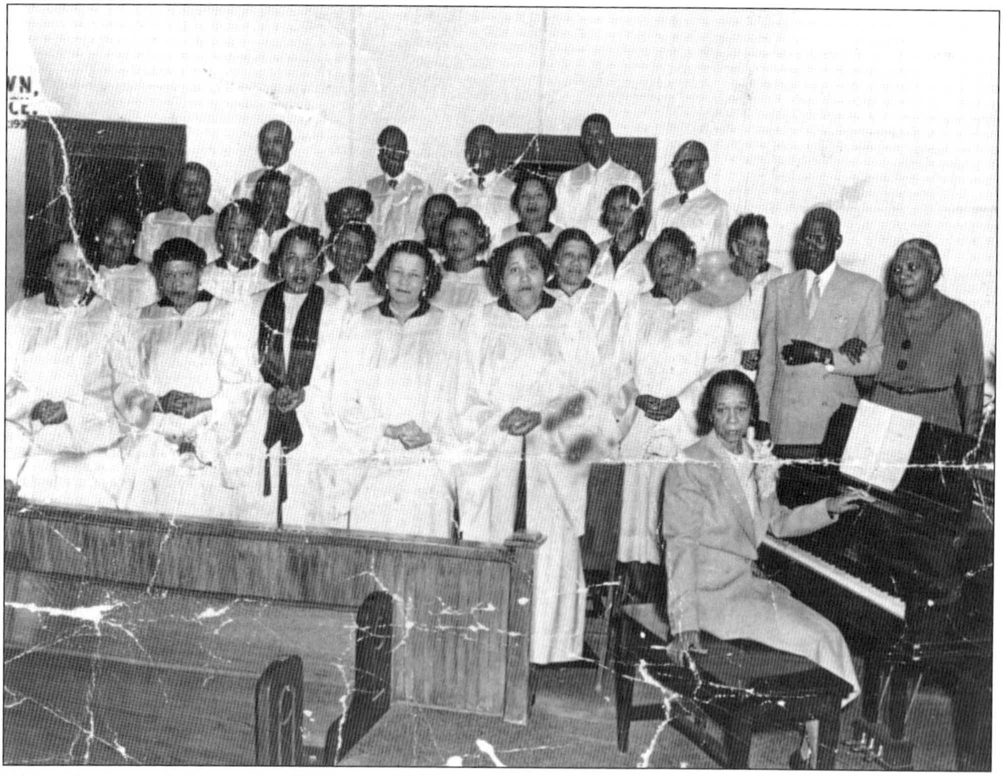

This photograph from the 1950s or 1960s is of the Bethlehem Baptist Church choir. Seated in front of the choir is Rev. L.E. Billingslea. Among the 19 choir members pictured are Gladys Lawson, Mildred Briscoe, Elnora Jackson, and Louise Hawkins as well as members of the Lawson and Bennett families.

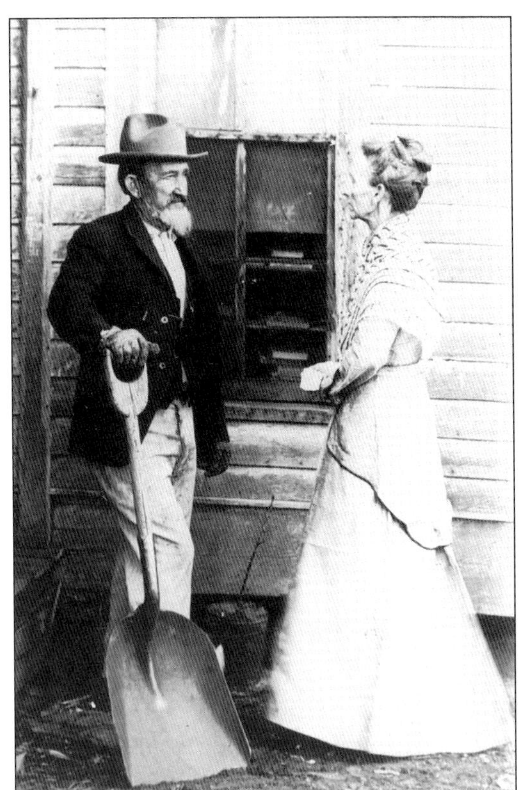

The Emmons family left Cork County, Ireland, in 1790 and went to Southampton, England. While there, they became friendly with the Chorn and Blessing families and eventually all three families immigrated to the United States, where they all ended up in Mansfield. Elijah Simeon Emmons married Sarah Conelia Goodnight, thought to be the niece of Charles Goodnight, the famous Texas frontiersman. Together, they raised five children. Elijah, a farmer, developed peanuts as a major crop in southeast Tarrant County. He also developed a mobile peanut thresher. He is pictured at right with his wife, and below, he is seen with his horse, Henry.

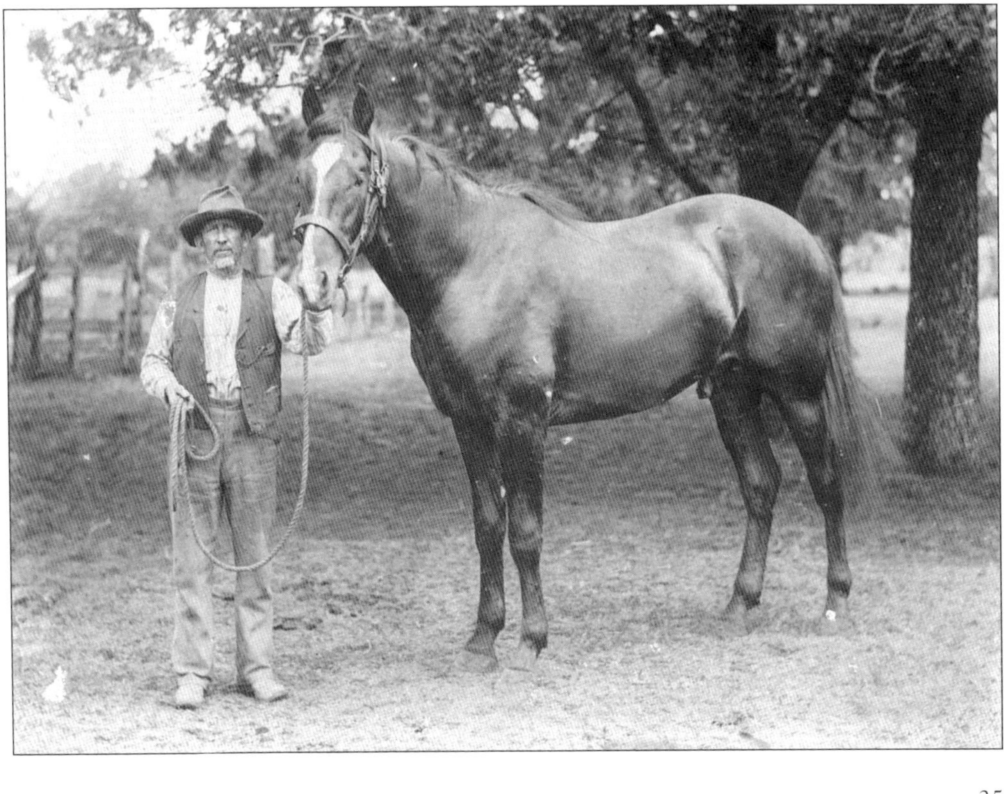

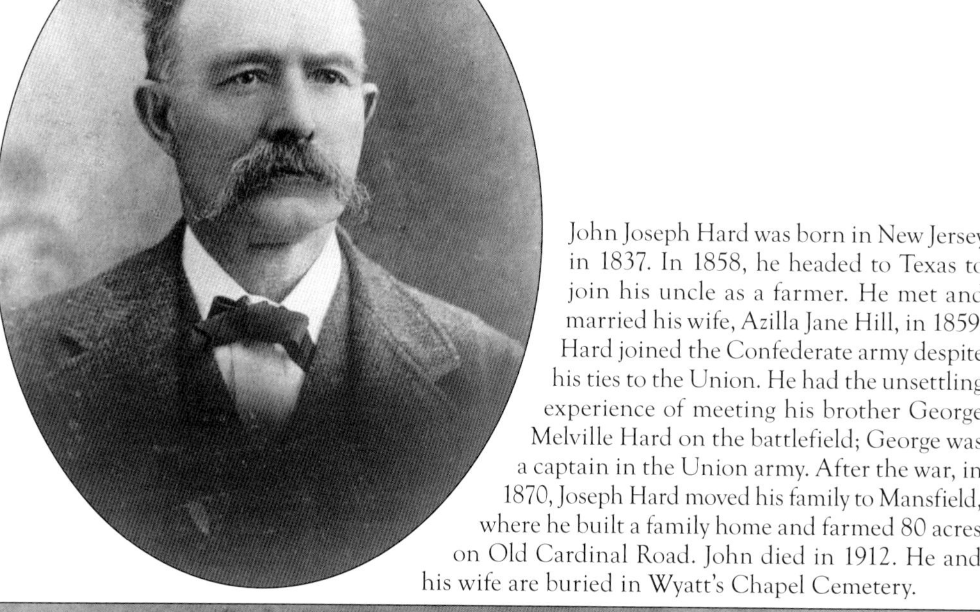

John Joseph Hard was born in New Jersey in 1837. In 1858, he headed to Texas to join his uncle as a farmer. He met and married his wife, Azilla Jane Hill, in 1859. Hard joined the Confederate army despite his ties to the Union. He had the unsettling experience of meeting his brother George Melville Hard on the battlefield; George was a captain in the Union army. After the war, in 1870, Joseph Hard moved his family to Mansfield, where he built a family home and farmed 80 acres on Old Cardinal Road. John died in 1912. He and his wife are buried in Wyatt's Chapel Cemetery.

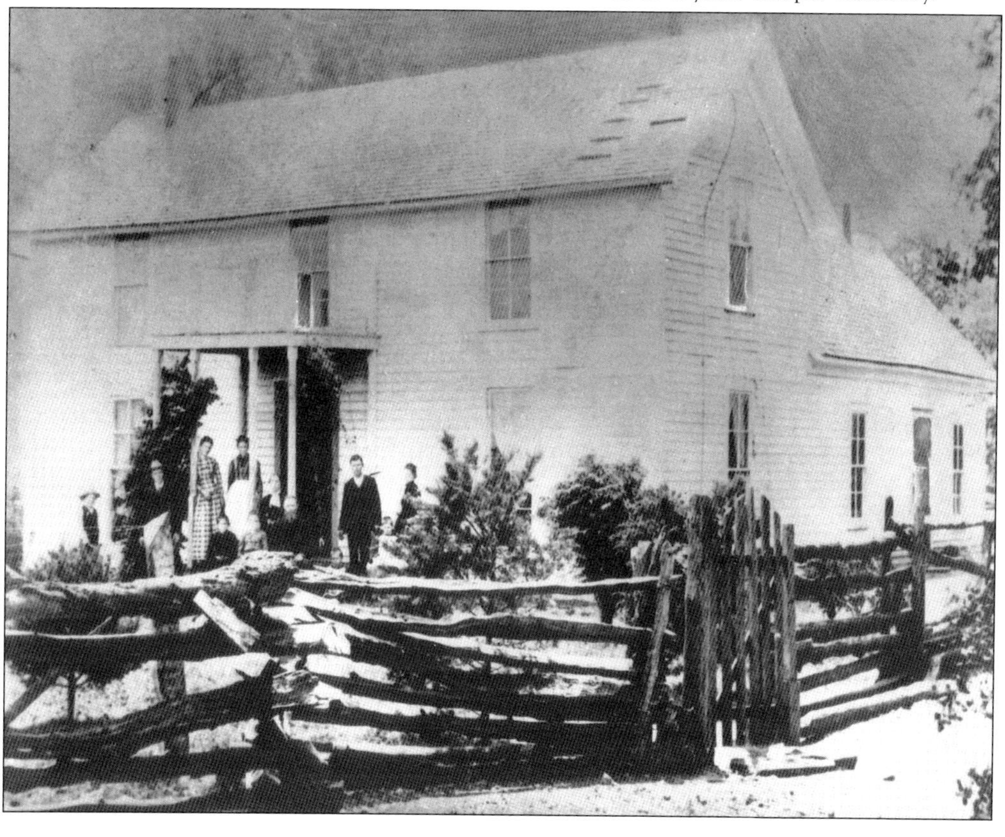

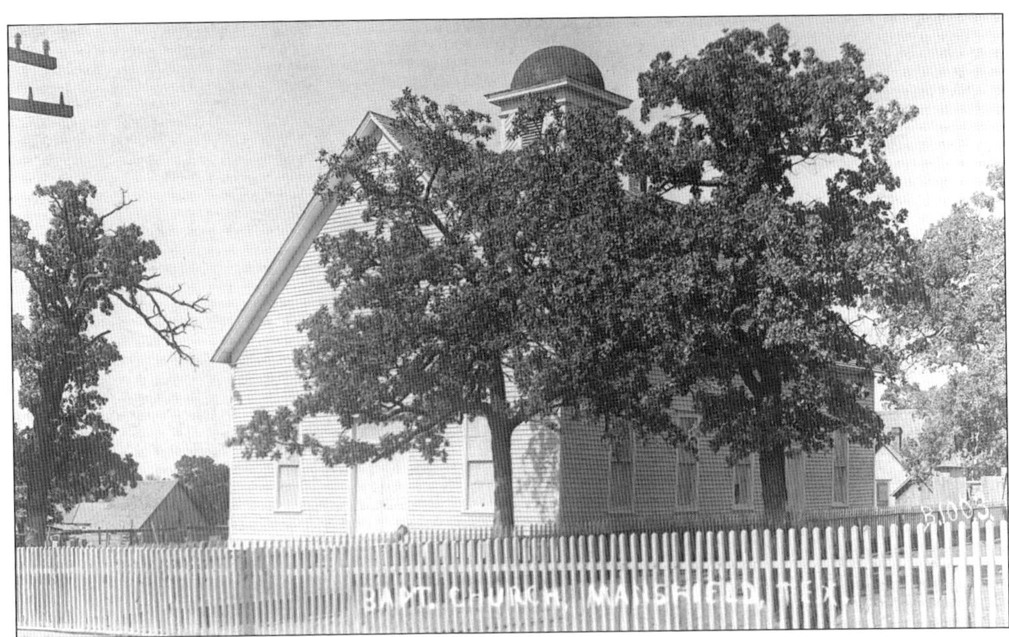

Members of the Baptist faith in Mansfield first met every fourth Sunday of the month in the Presbyterian church, as they had no building of their own. Eventually, the congregation built a small, wooden church themselves in 1890, which included their members hoisting the bell and installing it in the belfry.

Ed Lewis came to Texas in the early 1900s, finding initial work as a sharecropper and chauffeur for Dr. William McKnight. Lewis married Eliza Nolan, and the two had four children: Benjamin, Ruby, Bernie, and Hattie. In 1922, Lewis bought a house and worked hard on his farm while Nolan worked as a cook. Pictured here in 1940 are Ruby, Hattie, and Bernie Lewis with their cousin Ysletta Briscoe.

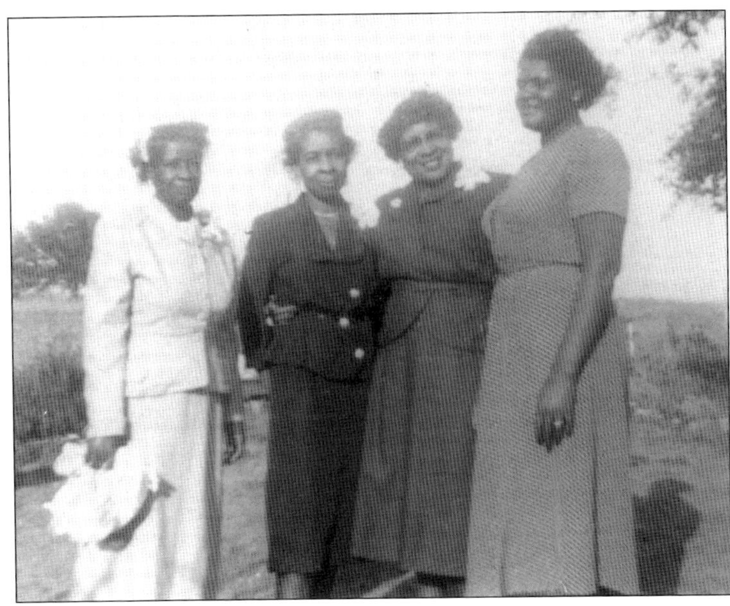

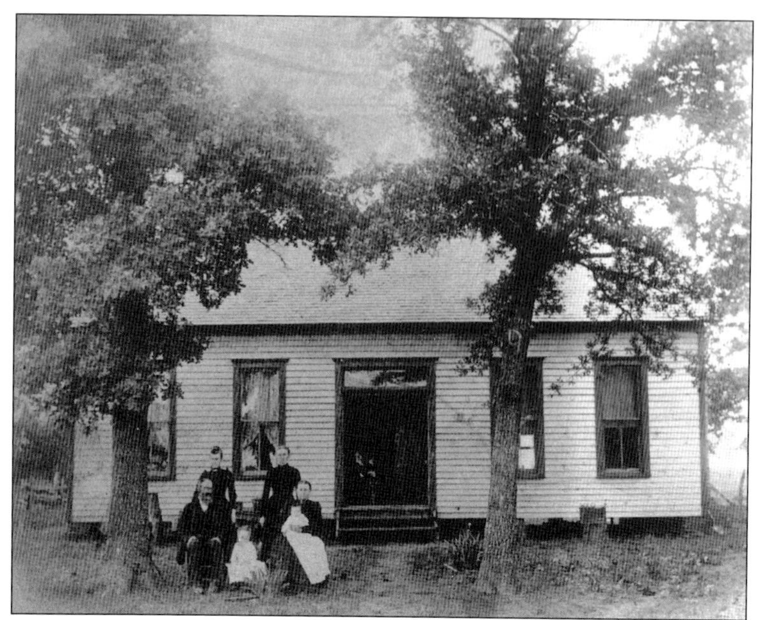

Samuel Hook came to Mansfield because of his friendships with Ralph Man and Julian Feild. He made the bricks used to construct North Texas's first steam-powered mill. During the Civil War, Hook fought at the Battle of Appomattox and was shot through the jaw. Hook treated himself by putting his jaw in a spring to let the water clean it. He later wore a beard to hide the scars.

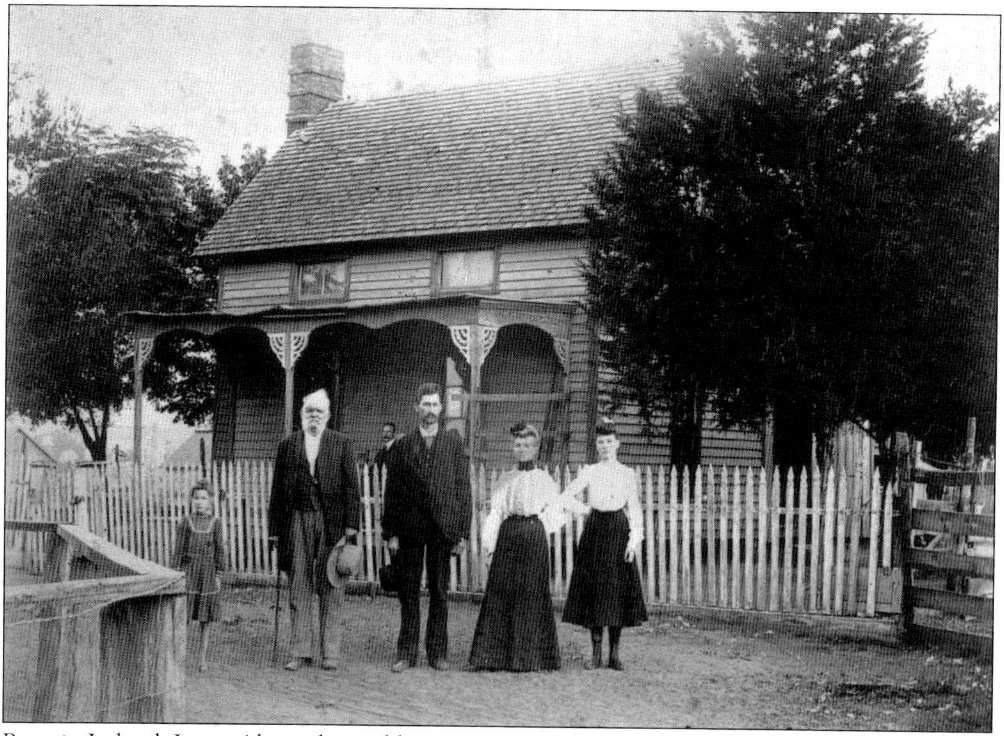

Born in Ireland, James Alexander and his wife, Lavinia Pendergrass, moved their family to Texas after the Civil War. The Alexanders camped at a French settlement in Dallas County called La Reunion Colony while James scouted for a permanent homestead. After several moves, they settled into a house at 103 Van Worth Street, Mansfield, Texas, built in 1870. James was the first justice of the peace in Mansfield.

Charles "Charlie" Moody was the grandson of Nathan Moody, an enslaved person brought to Mansfield. Charlie, who was born in 1879, worked as a farmer and married Emma Brinson in 1896. The couple had nine children: Elizabeth, Lena, Charlie Jr., John Henry, T.M., Roy, Eugene, and Susie. Charlie died in 1949.

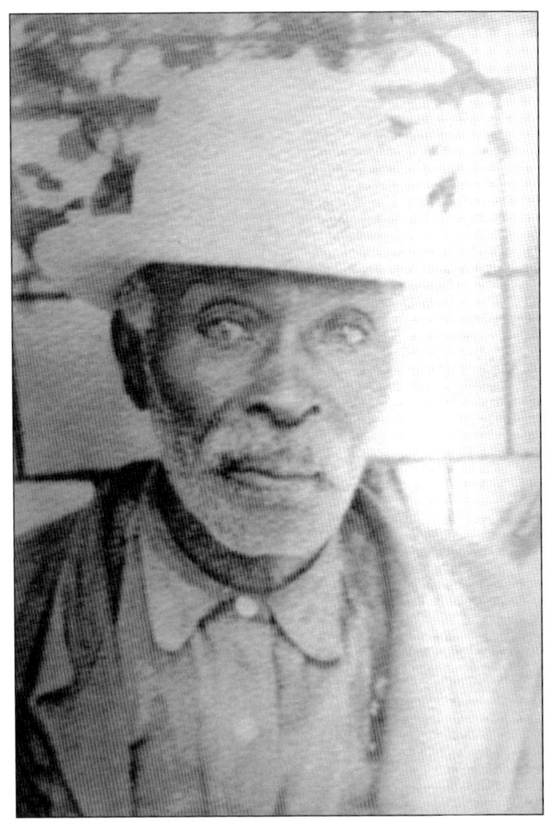

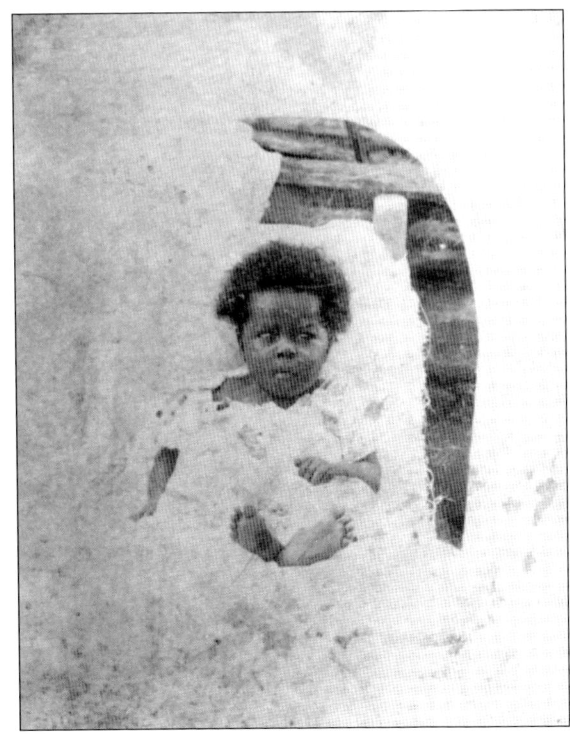

Pictured here as a baby, Charlie Moody's daughter Elizabeth Moody was born in 1897. She attended the Mansfield Colored School. After graduating, she attended Prairie View University, where she received a degree in teaching. She came back to teach at Mansfield, where she taught her two youngest siblings. She went on to marry Wesley Bean. She left teaching and worked at the All Church Home for Children for 15 years.

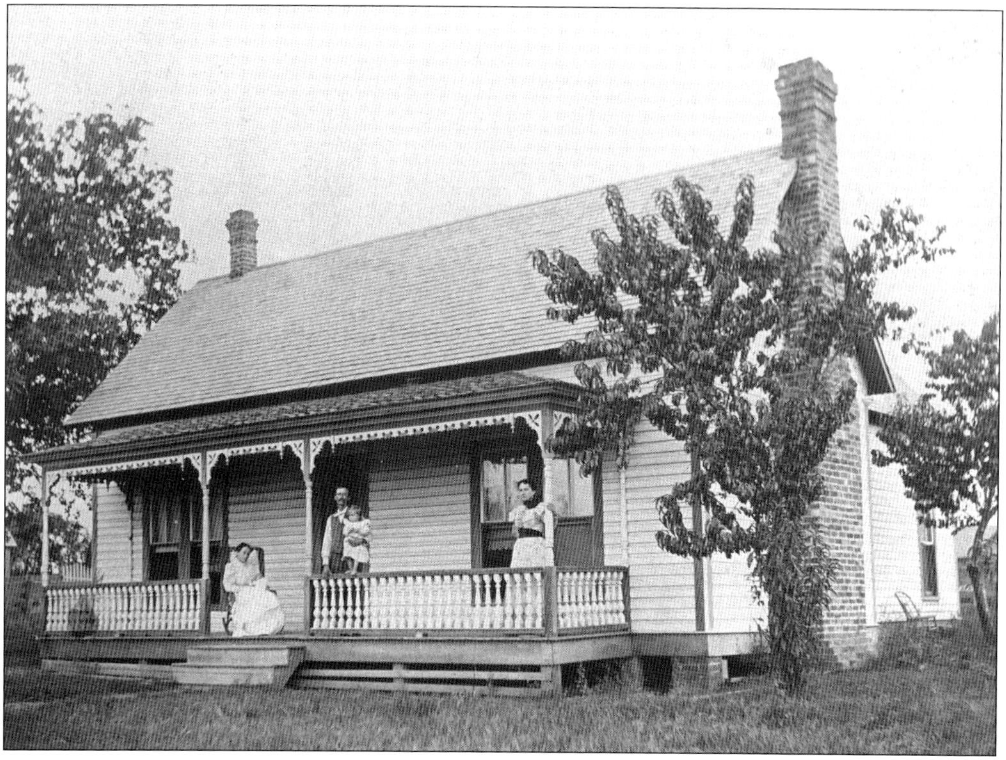

In the early 1880s, Rev. Andrew Hayter built a home located at 306 East Broad Street. Hayter was the pastor of the Cumberland Presbyterian Church. The house is considered the church's first parsonage. The home was later owned and remodeled by the Witherspoon family. Pictured are, from left to right, Mary Doughty Witherspoon with infant Ann, Mr. Witherspoon with Ellen, and Annie Doughty. The photograph was taken on the day of Ann's christening.

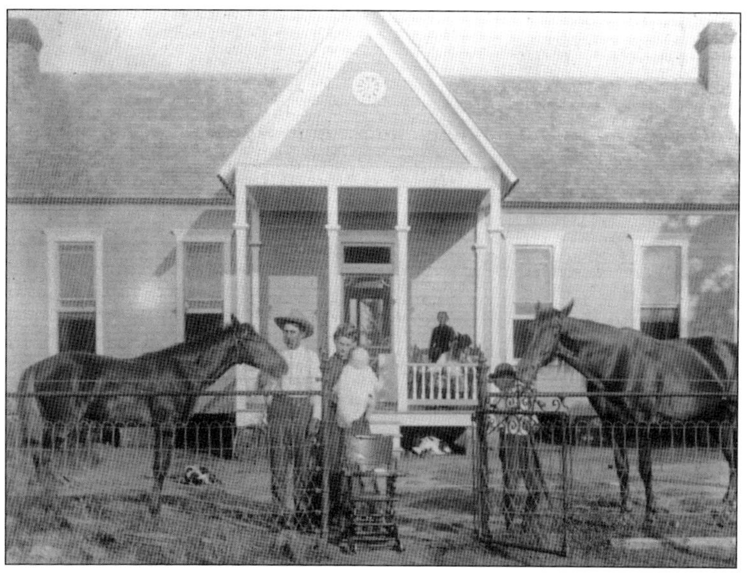

Shown here are three generations of the Poe family, one of the early families in Mansfield. From left to right are (first row) William Silas Poe Sr.; his wife, Maggie Lee Poe; baby William Silas Poe Jr.; and son Jay Poe; (second row) Henderson and Nancy Poe. The family is pictured outside their home, which was rebuilt after a fire destroyed their first house.

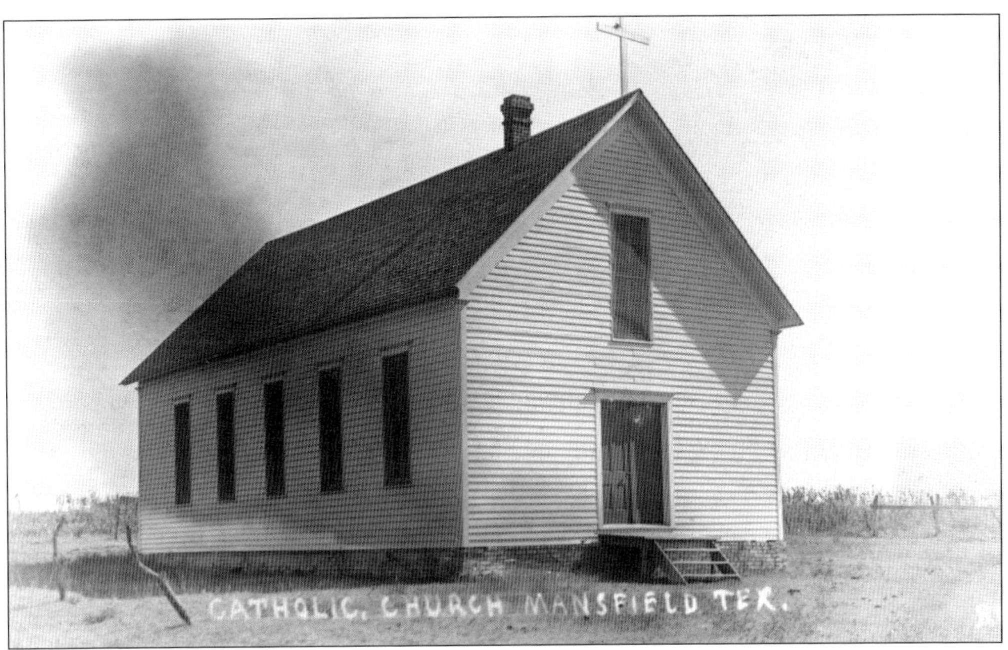

Catholics in Mansfield first met in the Moriarty family's home in 1897, where a Waxahachie priest arrived every month for services. Some years later, they constructed a small, white-framed building and dedicated it as St. Joseph Catholic Church. This photograph of St. Joseph Catholic Church was taken around 1900.

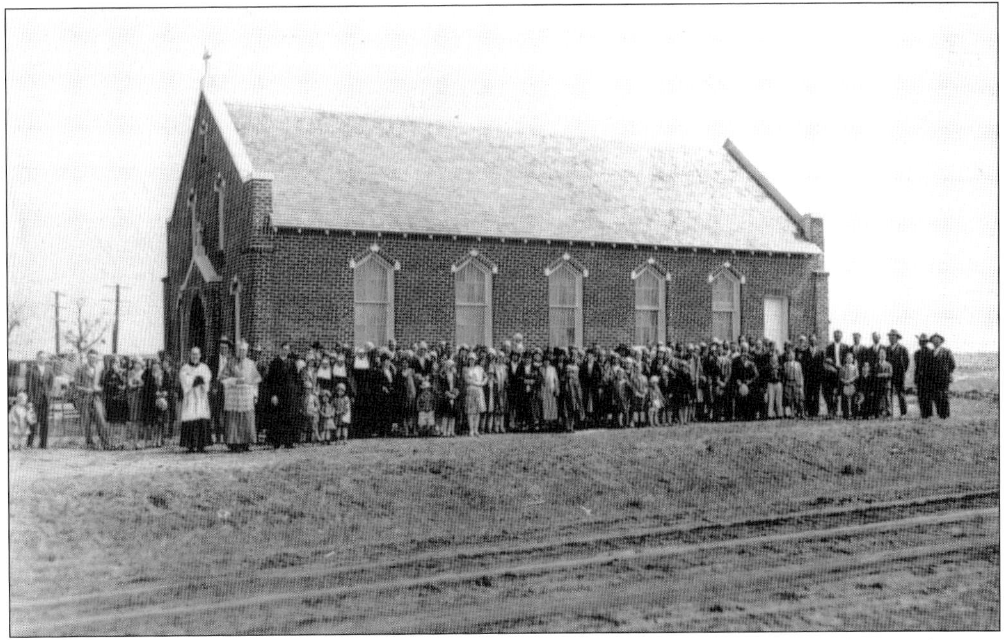
A new building was erected in 1929 and dedicated as St. James Catholic Church to replace St. Joseph. The new building was made of red brick. However, the congregation outgrew the building and another was needed. The current building was constructed and dedicated in 1971 as St. Jude Catholic Church. This photograph of St. James Catholic Church was taken at the dedication ceremony in 1929.

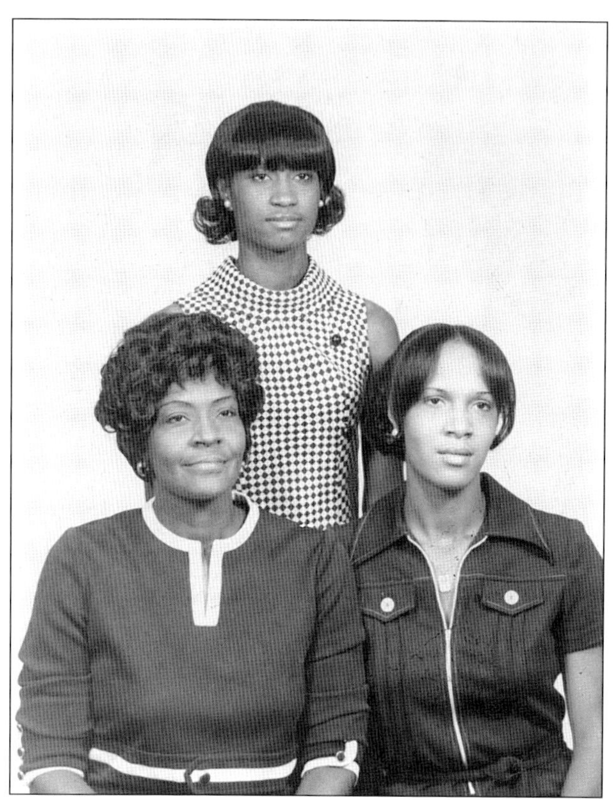

This is a 1960s photograph of, from left to right (first row) Louise Hawkins and Ora Lee Hawkins; (second row) Brenda Hawkins Norwood. Twins Brenda and Ora Lee graduated in the first integrated class of Mansfield High School. Brenda went on to become the first Black person hired by the Mansfield School District after integration, first as a paraprofessional and then as a teacher. In 2021, an elementary school was named in her honor. (Brenda Norwood.)

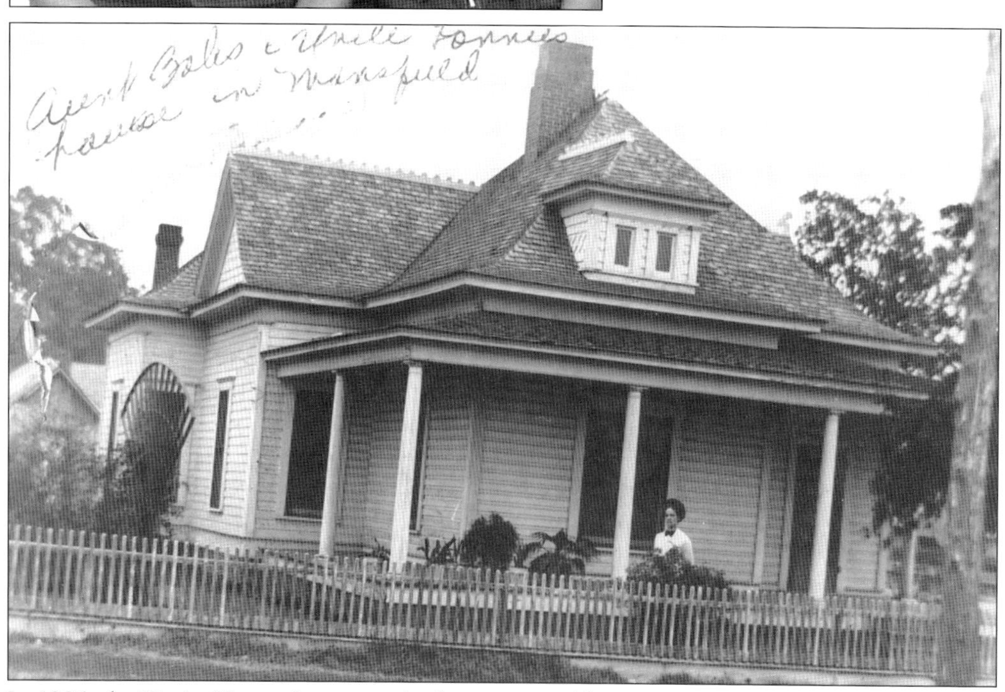

In 1906, the Kizziar-Haynes house was built as a marital home for Alonzo and Bobbie Spearman Kizziar. Alonzo Kizziar owned a dry goods store in Mansfield. Sadly, he died soon after the home was completed. His wife sold the property in 1916 to the Hayes family, who lived there until 1955.

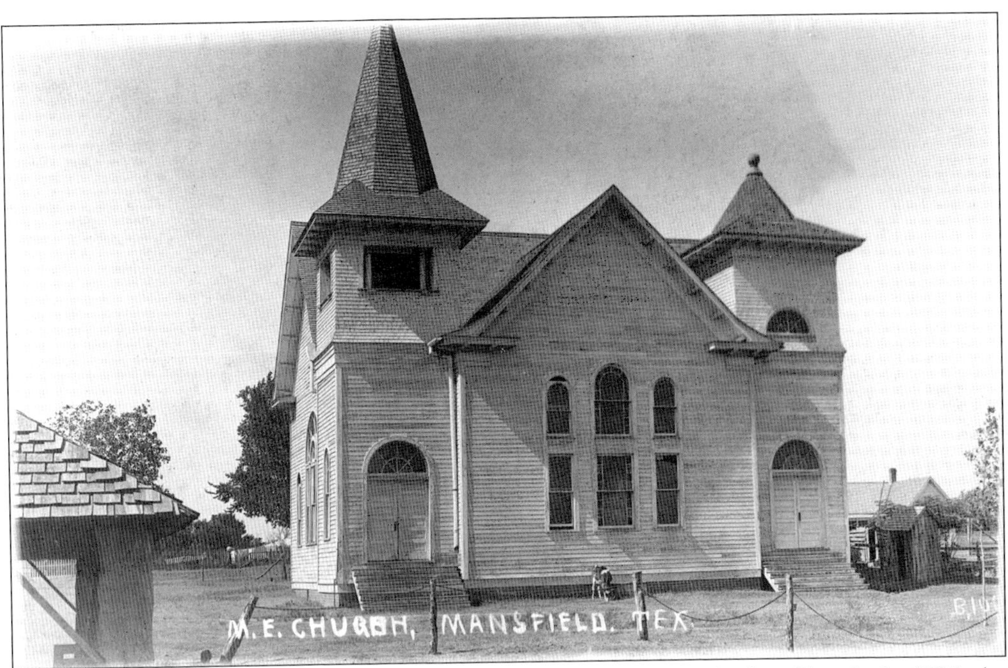

Mansfield Methodist Church began in 1872 as Wyatt's Chapel Methodist Church. In 1885, the church merged with another and was renamed. In 1891, a new one-room building was constructed. However, the building was damaged by a storm in 1903, and a larger structure was constructed and used until a fire destroyed it in 1942. Clara Nifong, a parishioner, entered the burning building and single-handedly carried out the pulpit filled with Methodist hymnals.

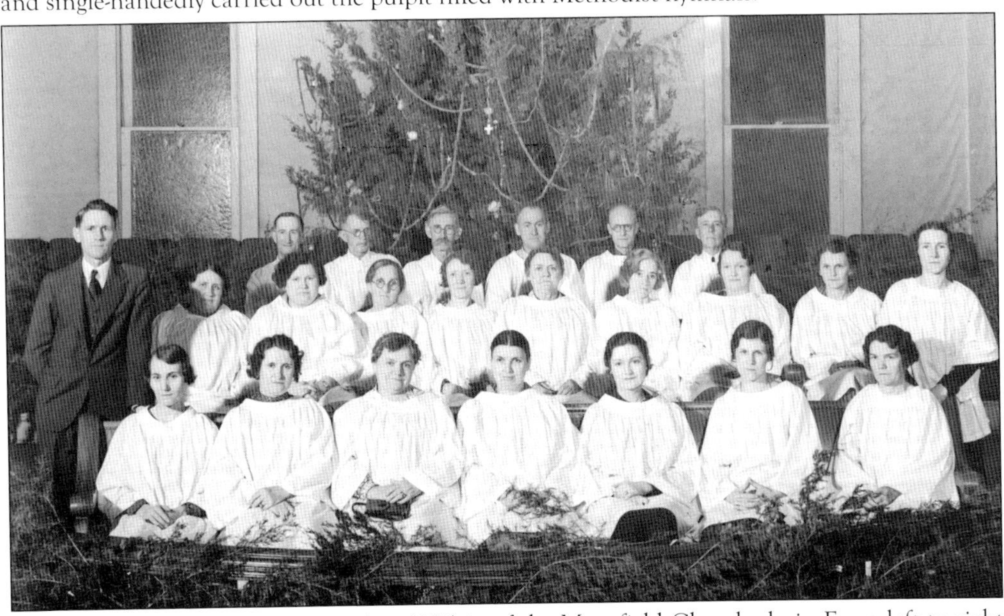

This photograph, taken in December 1935, is of the Mansfield Church choir. From left to right are (first row) Mrs. Hennesay, Mrs. Walker, Mrs. Nifong, Mrs. Holland, Hannah Ann House, Mrs. Marney, and Mrs. Galloway; (second row) Mr. Marney, Mrs. Rosier, Mrs. Halbert, Mrs. Gilstrap, Mr. Gibson, Mrs. Collier, Cora Gallaway, Mrs. Galloway, Mrs. Baker, and Clara Malone; (third row) Albert Craig, Eddie Capps, P.C. Gilstrap, Roy Mitchell, E.A. Rosier, and George Hackler.

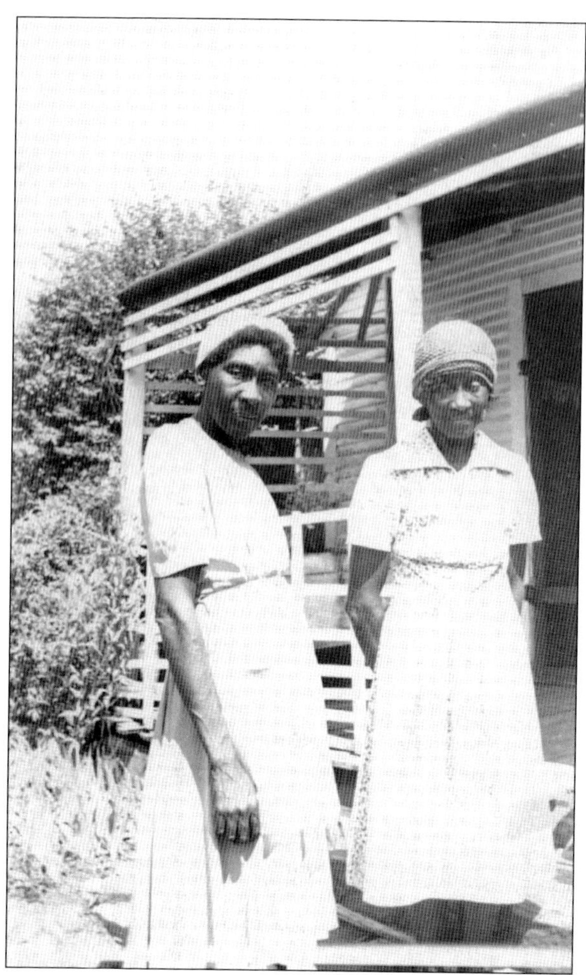

The two women pictured in this 1940s photograph, Lydia "Littie" Nolan Briscoe and Lucy "Poss" Nolan Bennett, were the daughters of Mansfield pioneers Ben and Sofy Nolan. Briscoe was known for her magnetic personality and for pitching in when others needed help. Bennett spent her free time making quilts for people throughout the community.

The Kerr House was built in 1899 for Elber and Edward Kerr at 210 West Oak. The contractor is unknown, but the double brick fireplace was built by a Kerr relative, Samuel W. Hook. Kerr was a pharmacist in downtown Mansfield until 1899 and then became a rural mail carrier.

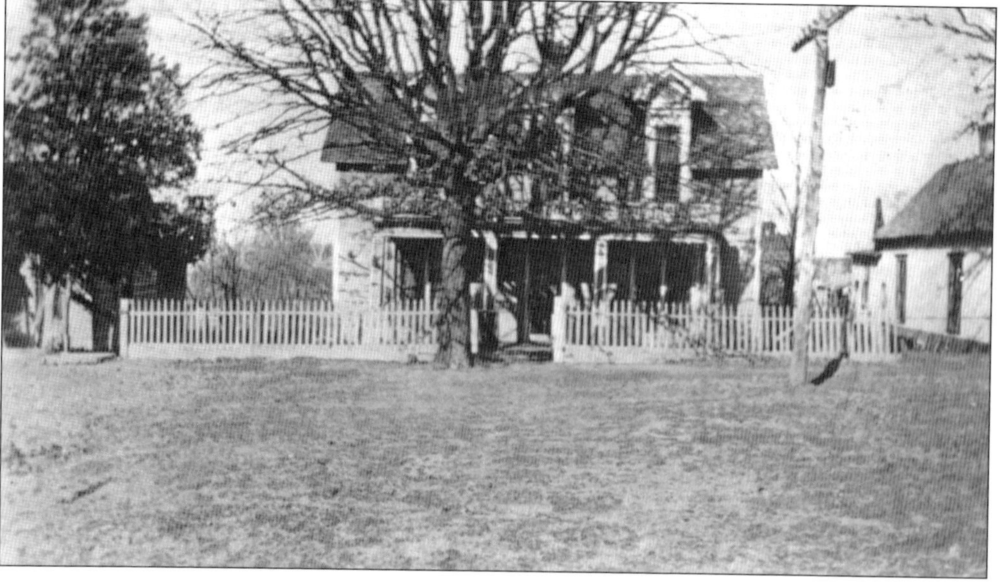

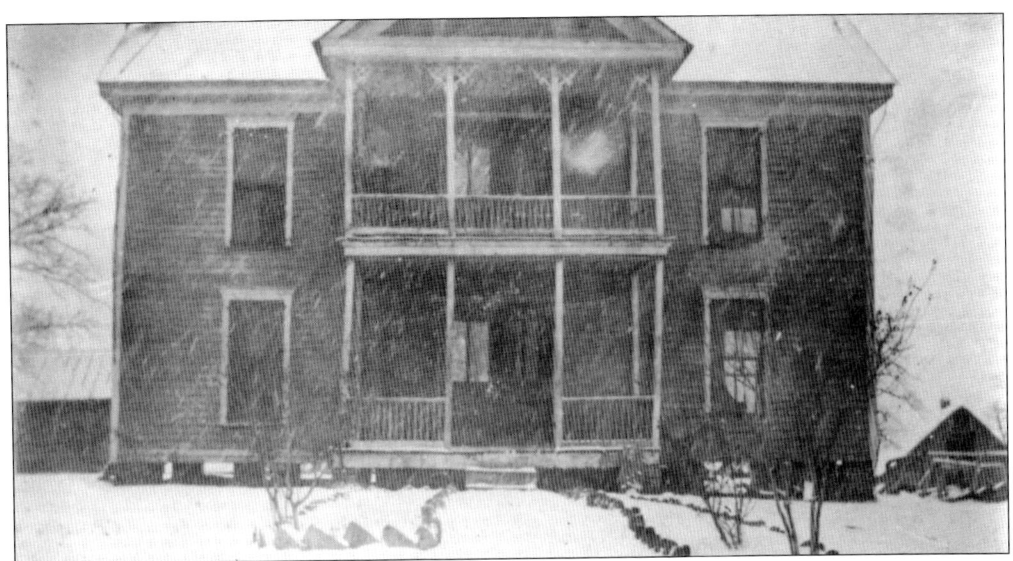

E.D.L. Tims built this home when he arrived in Mansfield in the 1870s. The two-story Victorian was built on Church Street, now known as Walnut Creek Drive. In 1919, J.C. and Bettie Talley bought the home and had it remodeled. H.P. Spears bought the home in 1931 and tore it down, building a new home with the materials from the original house.

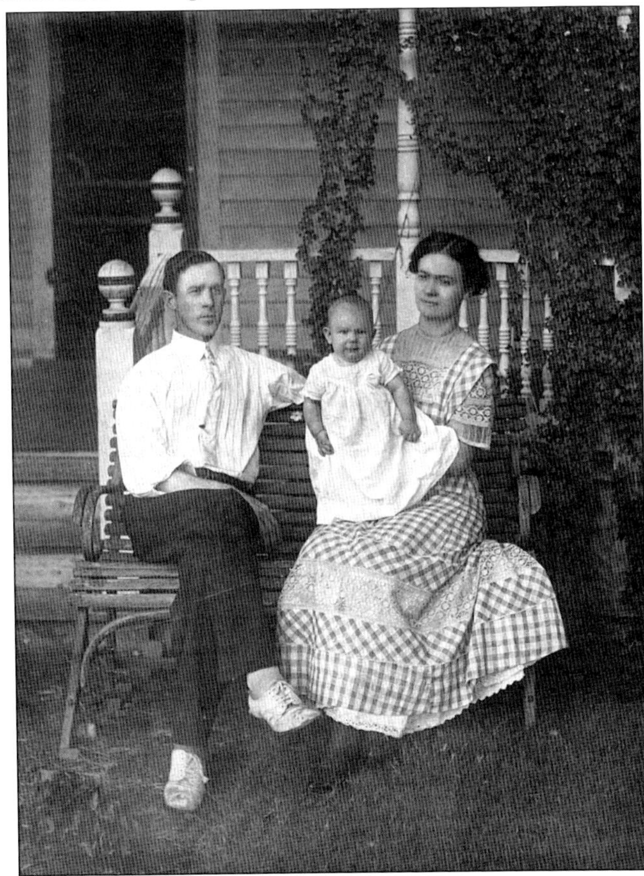

James Bratton "Jim" Chorn was one of seven children born to Ebenezer and Hannah Chorn. Jim's father was a farmer who eventually operated a freight business and pharmacy, the Board and Chorn Drug Store. Jim worked as a pharmacist for 50 years and operated his father's business. He also served as the mayor of Mansfield from 1913 to 1915. In the photograph, Jim poses with his wife, Annie, and their son Etheredge.

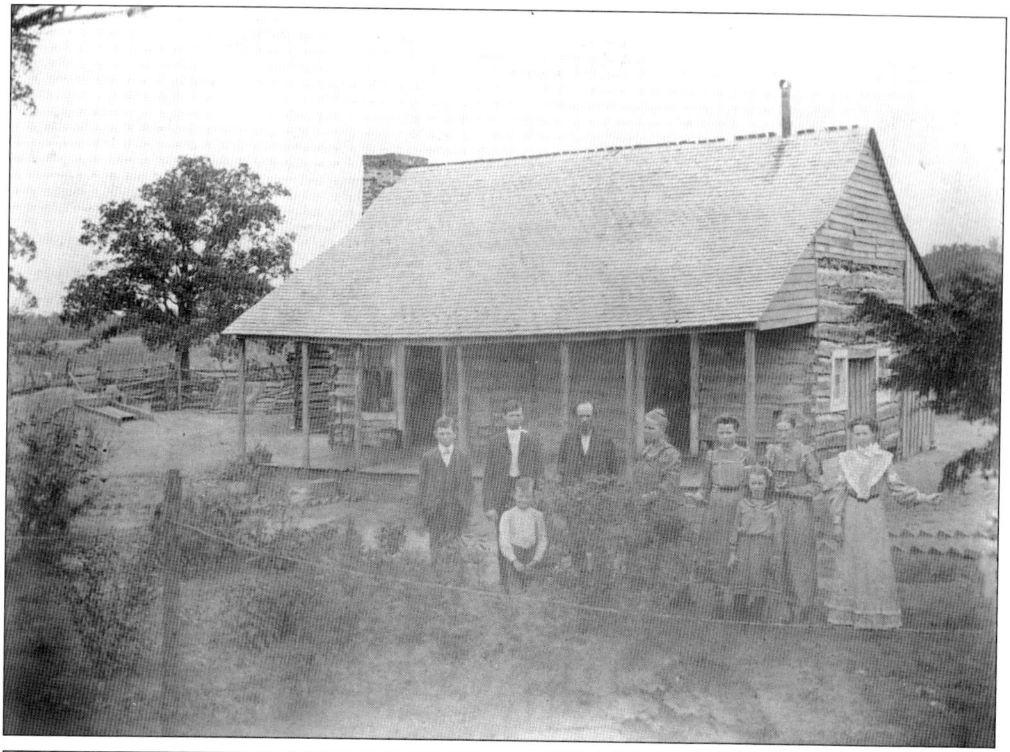

The Gibson family settled in the Mansfield area in the 1850s. Four brothers moved to the area with their wives, along with four other families. One of the brothers, Garrett Gibson, built this cabin around 1854. Pictured are Benjamin, one of Garrett's sons, with his family. From left to right are Albert, Benjamin, Bernard, Melinda, Sally, and Effie. The others are not identified.

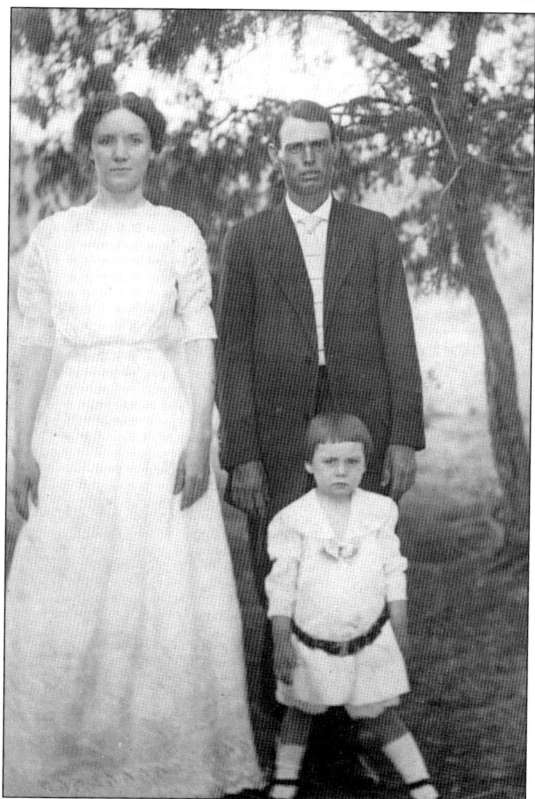

The Gibson family made an impact on the early development of Mansfield. Benjamin Gibson operated a hotel and served as justice of the peace. Another of Garrett Gibson's sons, McNary, opened one of the first community stores in Mansfield. Members of the Gibson family have remained in Mansfield for generations. This 1914 photograph shows Albert Gibson with his wife, Ethel Collier Gibson, and his son Ira.

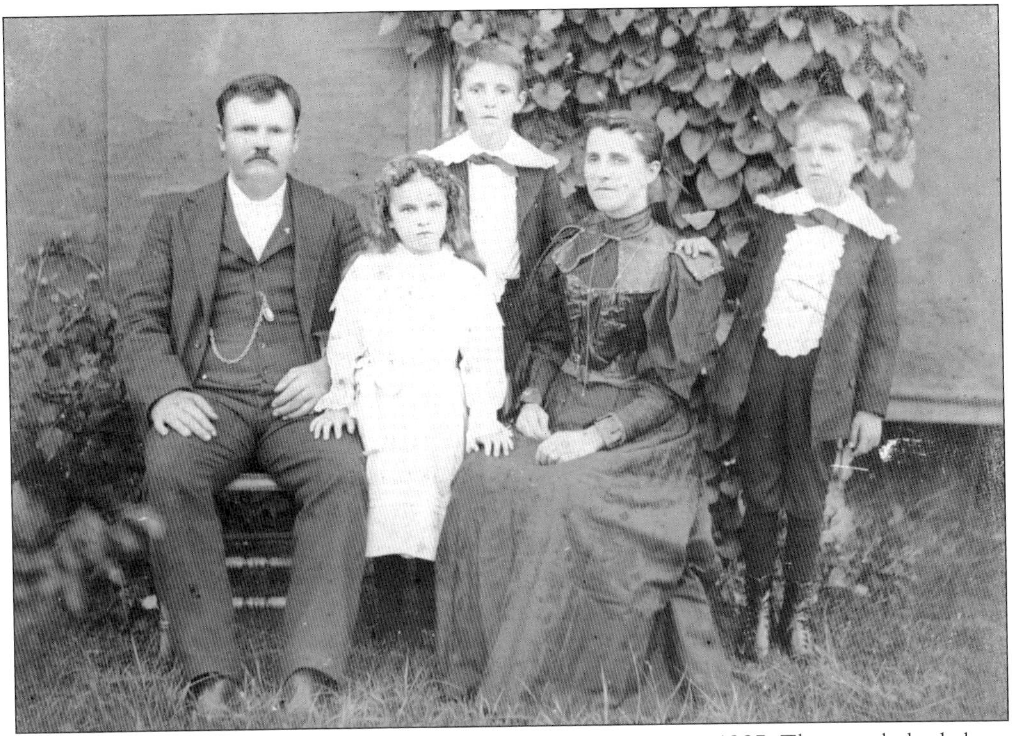

Jacob Martin Back, a Mansfield native, married Alida Muncy in 1887. The couple had three children. Back spent his life farming, stock trading, acquiring land, and giving assistance to those less fortunate. The family members pictured here are, from left to right, Jacob Back, Nancy Lucinda Back, Claudius Verna Back, Alida Muncy Back, and Colston Addison Back.

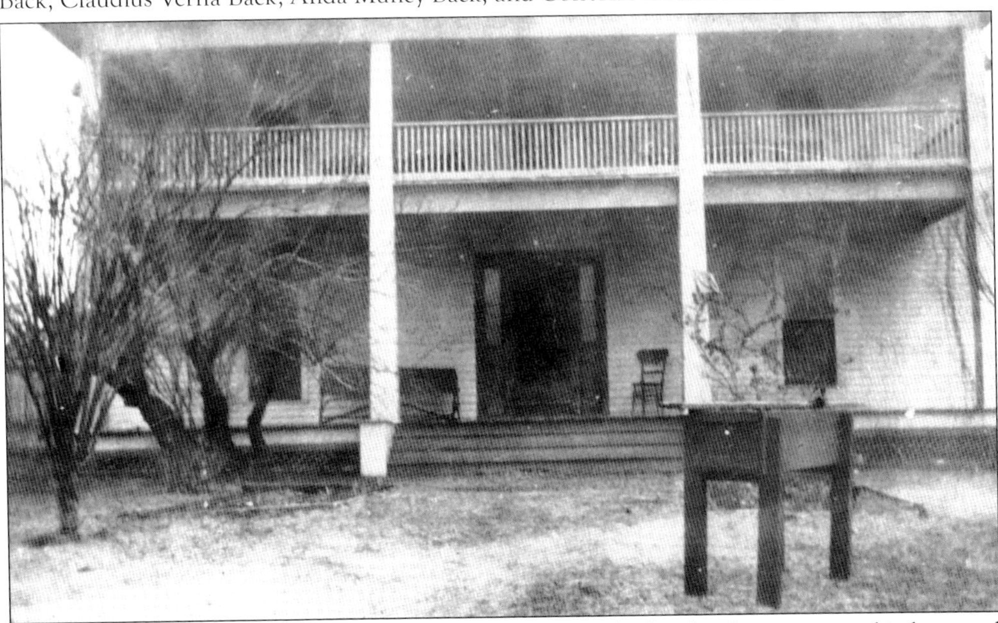

The Jacob M. Back house was built in 1894 and originally had only a large room, a kitchen, and the porch. The house was enlarged around 1900 and again in 1910. The house was located near the railroad depot to facilitate the shipping of livestock to Fort Worth. The house still stands today.

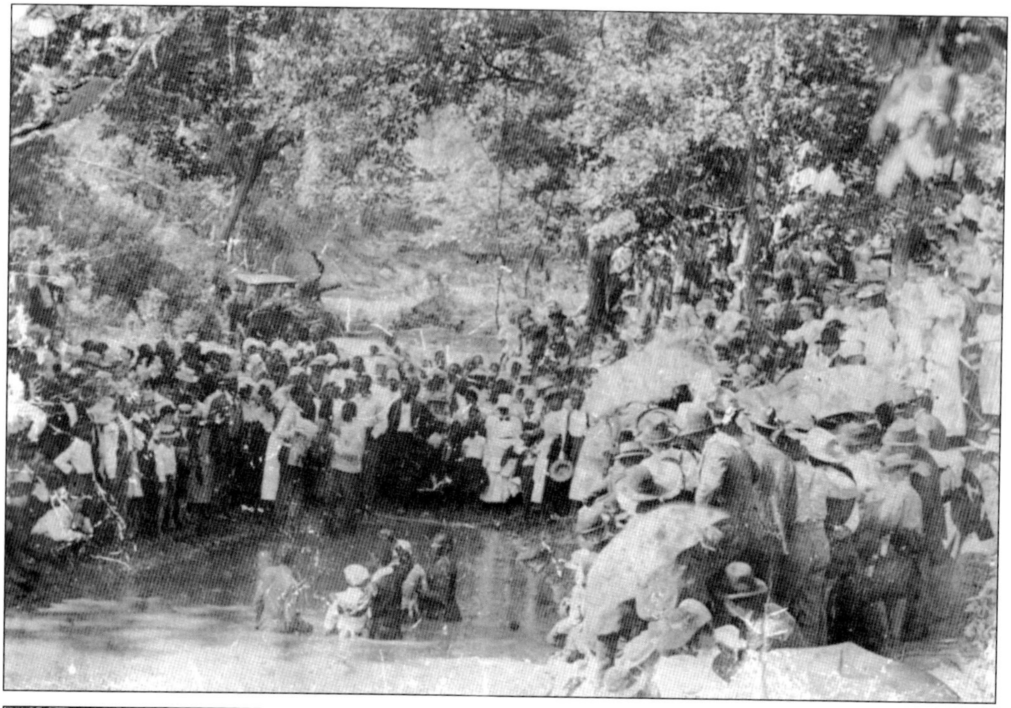

This baptism of African Americans took place in 1902. The event was held at Rock Creek, where a depression or dip in the road once existed that fed into the Walnut Creek area near what is today Moody Road. Candidates for baptism are wearing white, as are some of the congregation, to mark the occasion.

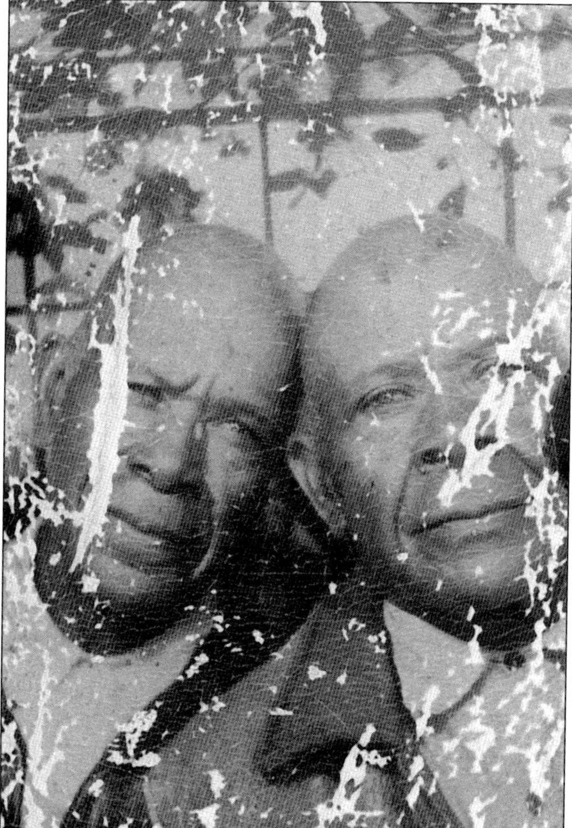

Thomas and Willie Jones were twins who each owned homes on East Dallas Street. Sons of Julius and Matilda Brown Jones, their widowed mother lived in a small home between the two men. Willie Jones married Maggie Davis and was the father of longtime Mansfield educator Thelma Jones. His brother married Harriette Davis and had a son, S.B. Jones, who worked for the railroad.

A.J. Dukes served in the Civil War, and it is said that, in 1865, at the war's end, he walked from Shreveport, Louisiana, back home to Mansfield, Texas. He first worked for wages and board until he could buy land. Pictured here is his family from 1894, and they are, from left to right, Leonides Dukes, Maggie A. Hopson Dukes, Mattie Lena Dukes, and A.J. Dukes.

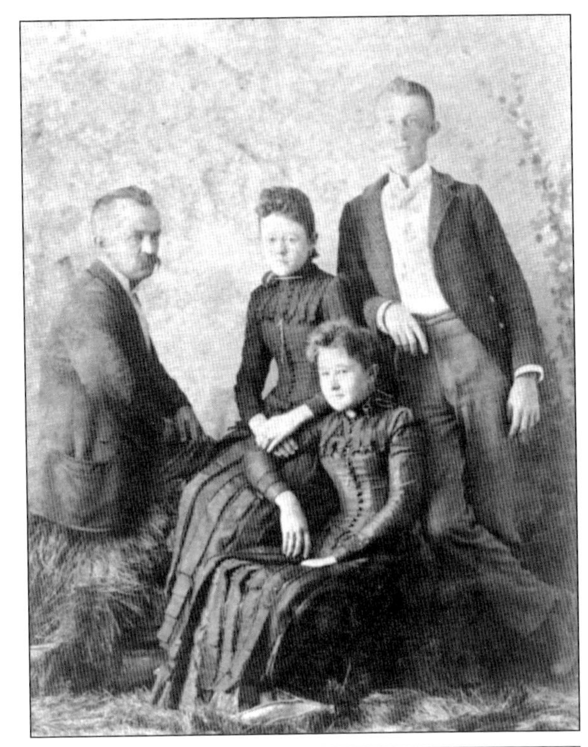

The Dukeses' house was built on South Main Street and shows a double-gable Victorian home with square columns. The double-gable style was vastly different than other houses of that time. This photograph shows the home with the family. It is believed that the Dukes family owned Mansfield's first bathtub. It was too large to fit in the kitchen, so a bathhouse was built next to the house.

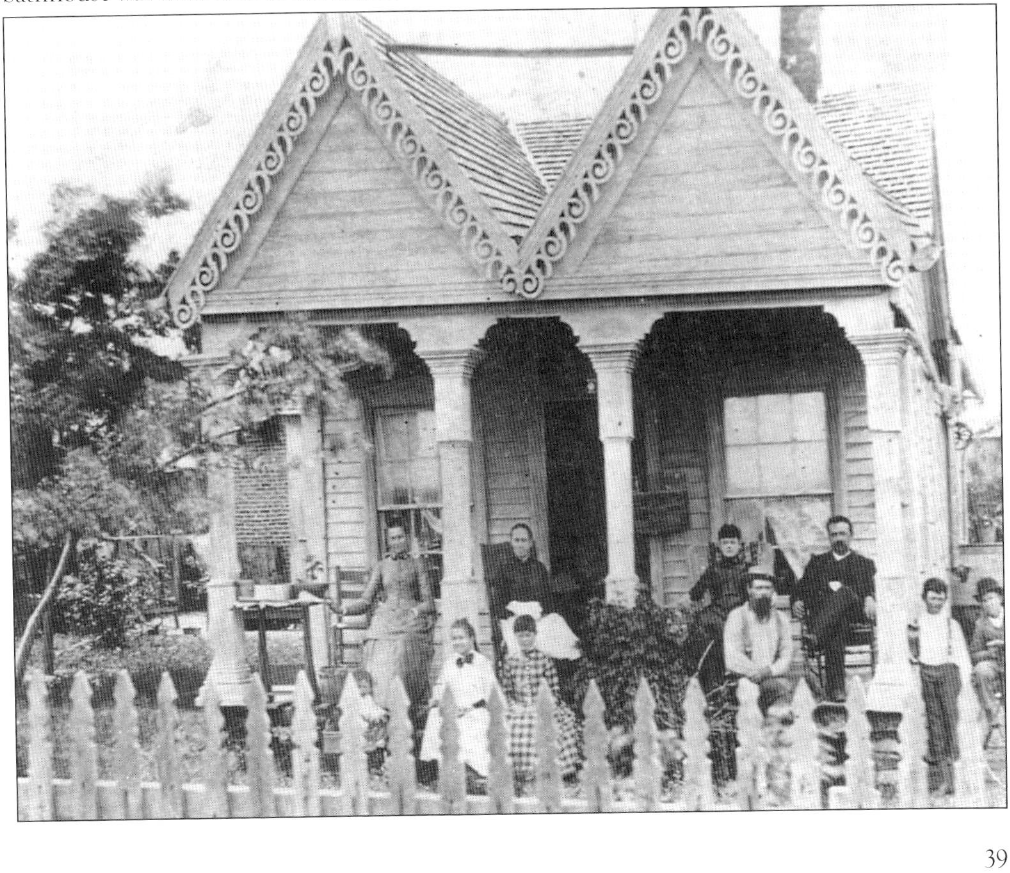

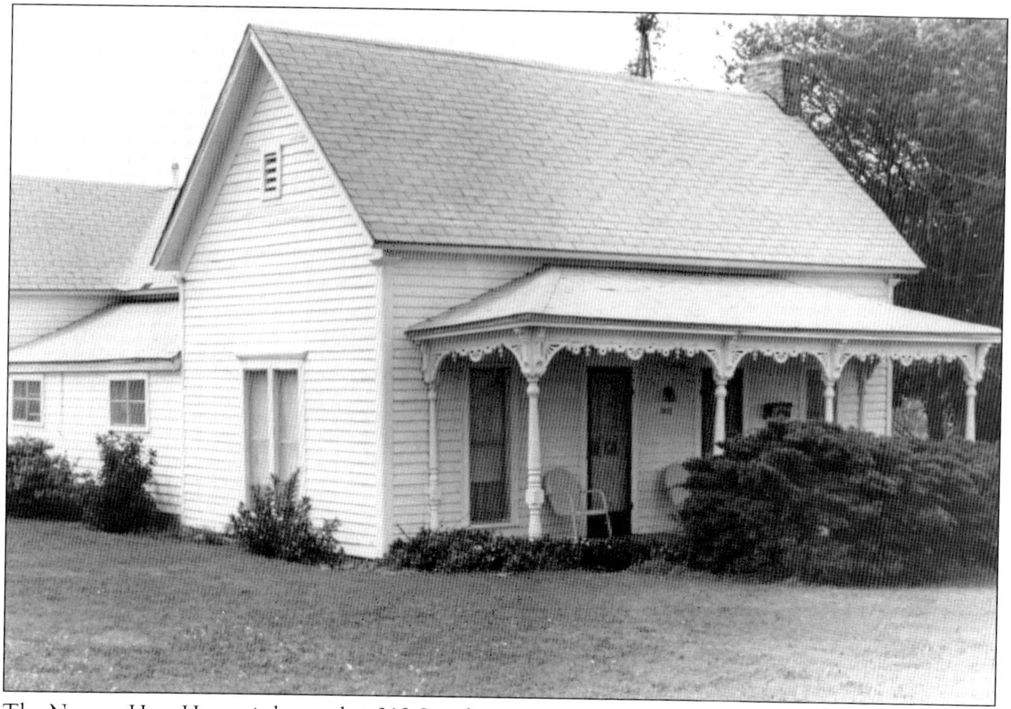

The Nugent-Hart House is located at 312 South Waxahachie Street. Joseph Nugent built the house between 1892 and 1893. After several other owners, the Jonathan Hart family purchased the house in 1920. The house has seen many modifications and additions and still sees life as the parsonage for St. Jude Catholic Church.

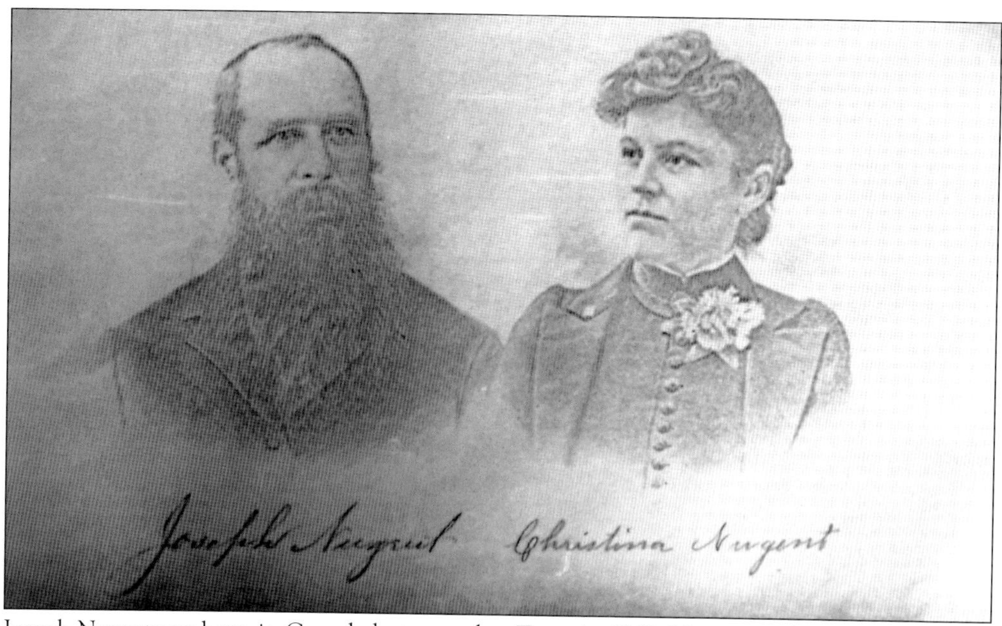

Joseph Nugent was born in Canada but moved to Texas in 1851. He operated a private school in Mansfield in the 1850s, then taught at the Mansfield Male and Female College. In 1891, he was elected as the city's second mayor. Nugent also married his wife, Christina Cowan, in 1891. The couple is pictured here.

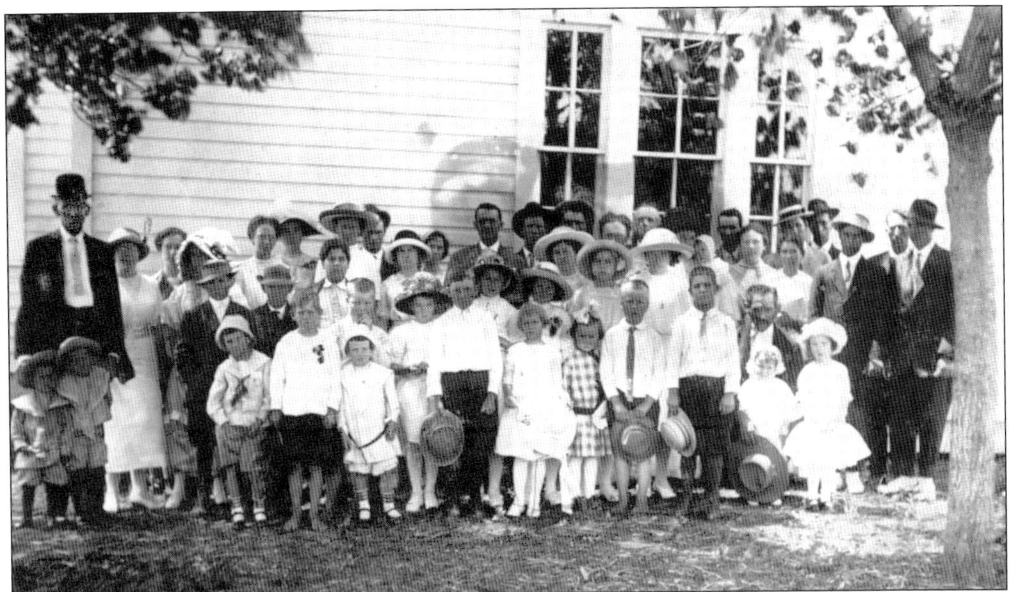

Britton Methodist Church was located in Britton, Texas, a community originally located about four miles east of Mansfield. The town has now been annexed into Mansfield. The church was founded in 1880, and the congregation met in the Britton schoolhouse until W.G. McGee donated land for the building to be constructed in 1905. This is a photograph of the 1908 Britton Methodist Church Sunday school class.

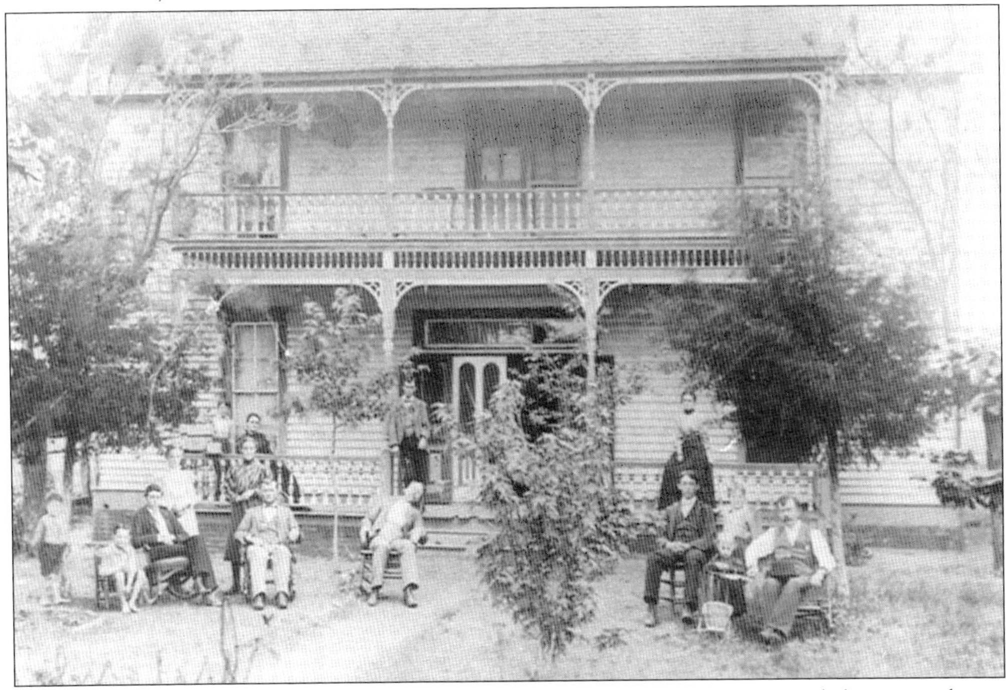

This home at 309 East Broad Street was built by Abner Pyles in 1886 around the original one-room brick house constructed in 1880. He and his wife, Martha "Mattie" Berry, had 10 children. After Abner Pyles's death in 1897, Mattie Pyles operated a boardinghouse until the family moved to California in 1909. John and Jessie Hubbard purchased the house in 1932.

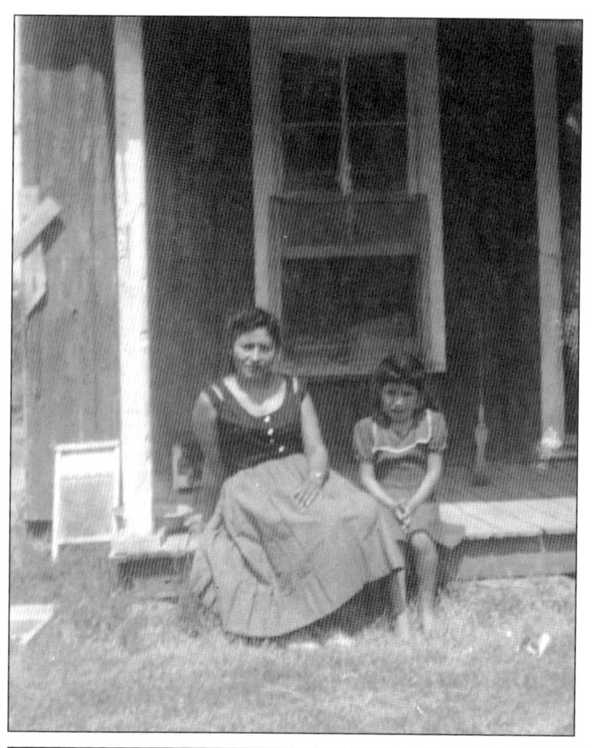

Guadalupe "Lupe" Longoria Sr. and Maria Mercedes Juarez were both born in South Texas. After they married, Longoria Sr. worked for William "Wink" Patterson on his farm. When Patterson decided to move back to Mansfield to care for his ailing father, he encouraged the Longorias to move there by providing them with work and a house to live in. After the move, they settled into life in Mansfield and raised a family of four children: Guadalupe Jr., Eva, Jane, and Joe. Lupe and Maria lived in Mansfield for the rest of their lives, and several descendants continue to make the area their home. Pictured at left is Mercedes Longoria with her daughter Jane. The photograph below is of the Longoria family. From left to right are (first row) Guadalupe Sr. and Maria Mercedes; (second row) Guadalupe Jr., Jane, Eva, and Joe. (Jane Longoria Rizo.)

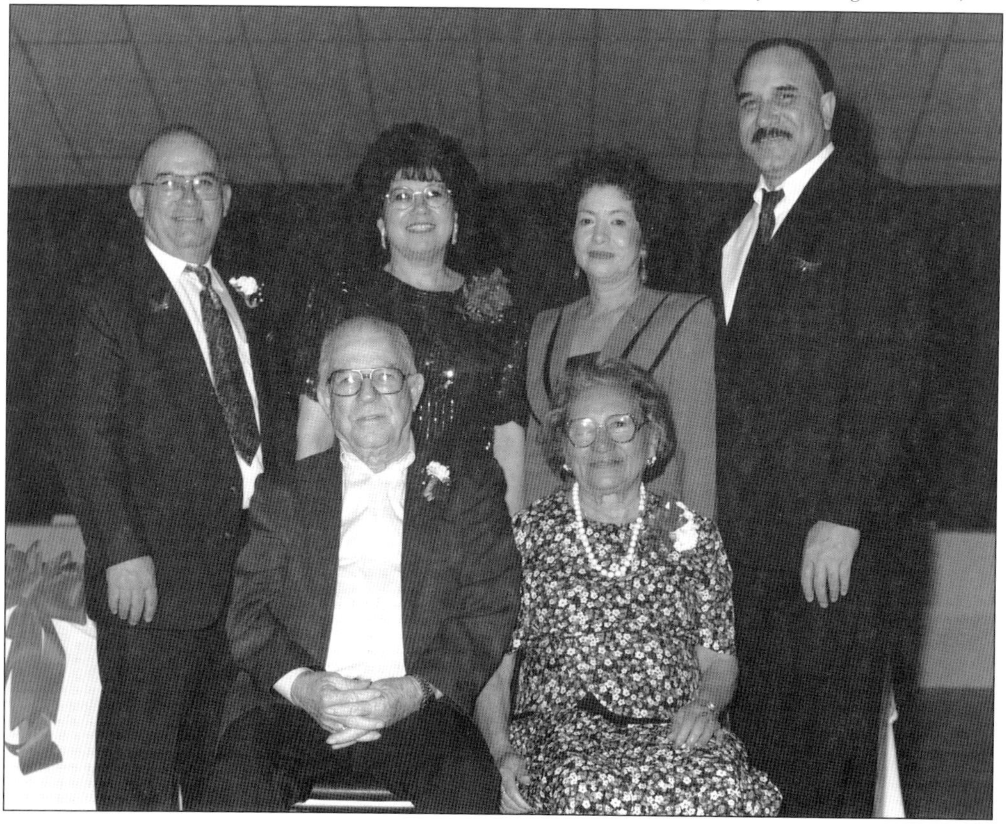

Three

Education

Education has always played an important part in the history of the Mansfield community. The first official record of a school in the Mansfield area was in 1854, and it was designated as Tarrant County District 20. The school was known as Nugent School. It was named after Joseph Nugent, who was a teacher there and later went on to become Mansfield's first mayor. There were also numerous private schools held in people's homes.

In 1870, Dr. John Collier established Mansfield Male and Female College, where one could begin in the primary grade and stay to complete a bachelor's degree. The college closed in 1887, and education moved back into citizens' private homes.

In 1901, citizens of Mansfield organized the Mansfield Academy Association. A new brick building was constructed and served the academy until it closed in 1909.

Mansfield Independent School District (MISD) was organized in 1909. Classes were conducted in the academy buildings and local churches until they were outgrown. In 1924, an election was held to approve funds for a new brick building, which is standing today. A 1940 Works Progress Administration project added the Rock Gym to the campus. It is still standing and being used today.

West of town, MISD had a school that served Black students with very few amenities. Black high school students were sent to I.M. Terrell High School in Fort Worth. MISD delayed integration due to opposition, resistance, and noncompliance with federal law. The school district successfully integrated in 1965. MISD has continued to grow as the community has grown. As of 2025, it comprises 49 school campuses.

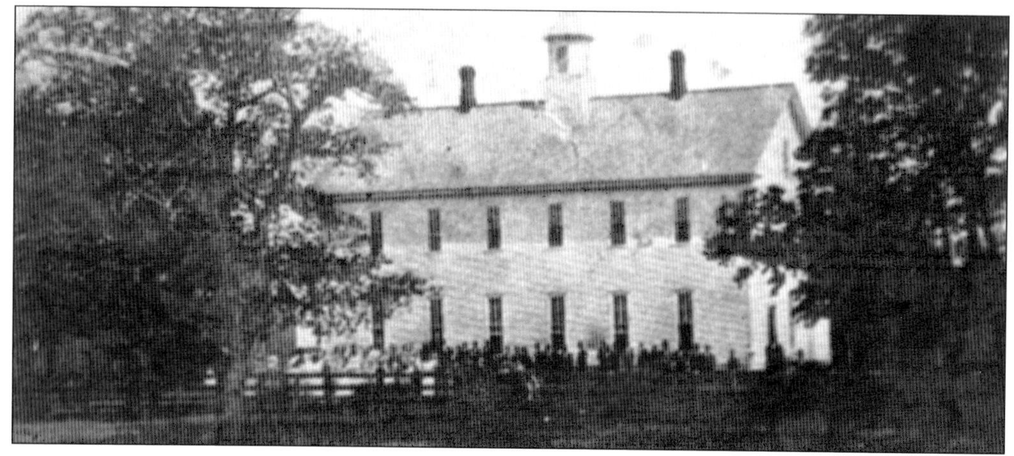

The Mansfield Male and Female College was the first major school in Mansfield and was founded in 1870 by John C. Collier, a Presbyterian minister. The land for the college was given by Julian Feild, one of Mansfield's founders. Collier built a home on the west side of the school campus (pictured below). Rooms on the second floor were used to house female students who boarded at the college and female teachers. In 1878, the *Fort Worth Democrat* newspaper rated the college "first place among institutions of learning in the state." Before closing in 1887, the school produced many local lawyers and congressmen.

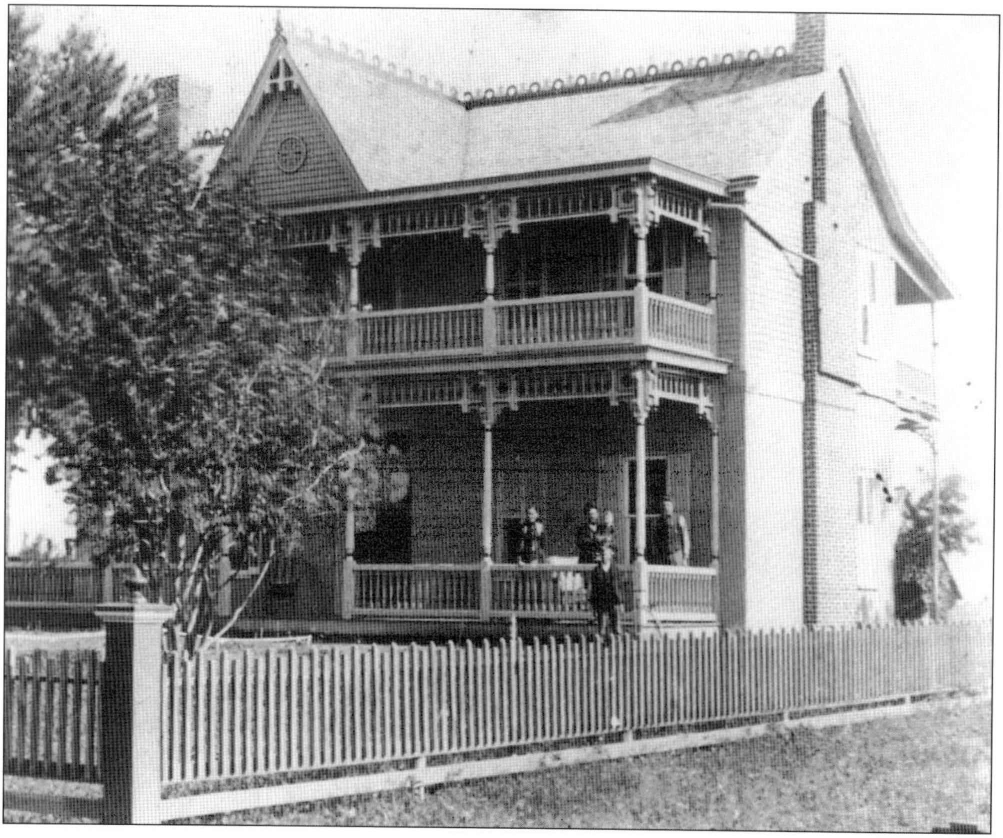

John C. Collier was born in 1832. He attended Cumberland College in the 1850s. Records show he became a licensed Cumberland Presbyterian minister in 1854. He came to Texas in 1856, where he married Mary Ellen Fowler. They had nine children. After serving in the Confederate army as a scout and chaplain, he returned to Johnson County and started Oakland College in Grandview, Texas. Because there was a strong demand for a school and he was known as an excellent teacher, Collier was recruited by Mansfield residents in 1869. He started Mansfield Male and Female College. In 1887, the college closed, and Collier moved to Waxahachie. These photographs are of John C. and Mary Ellen Collier.

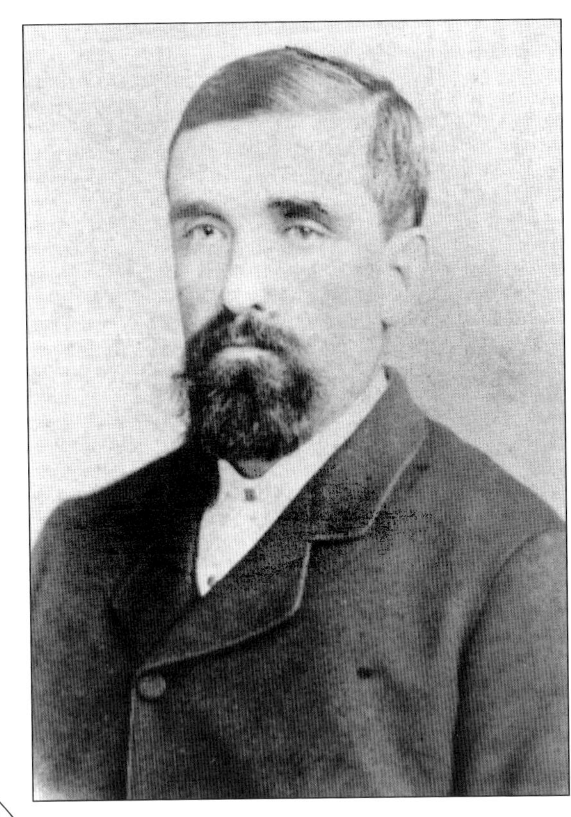

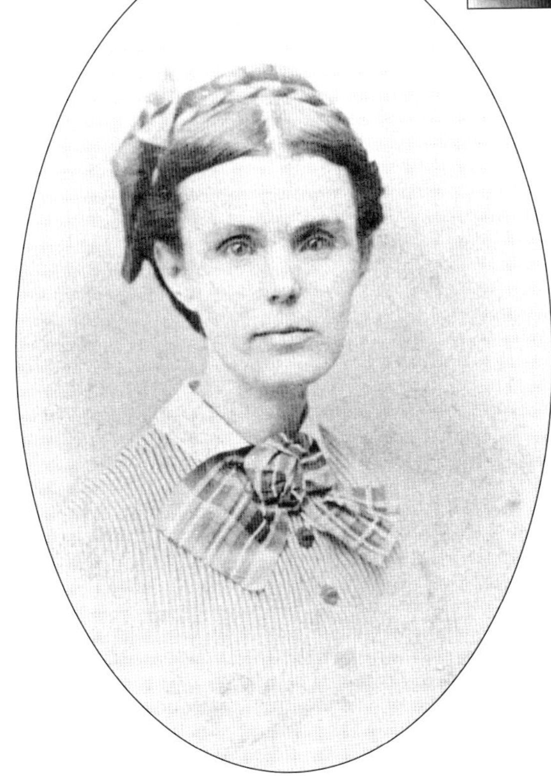

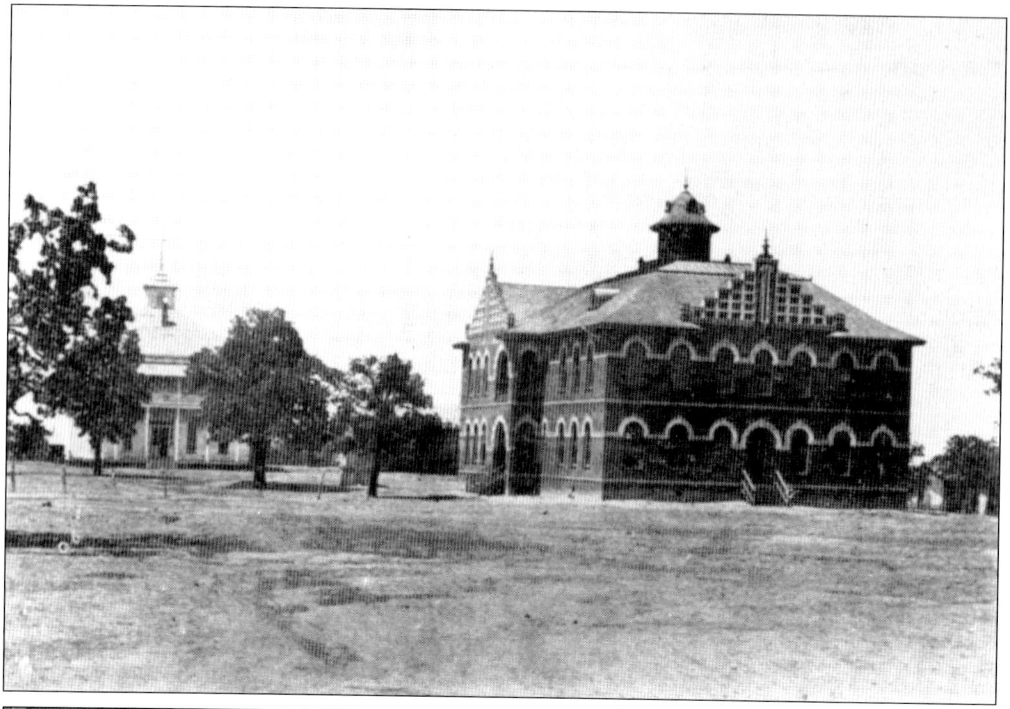

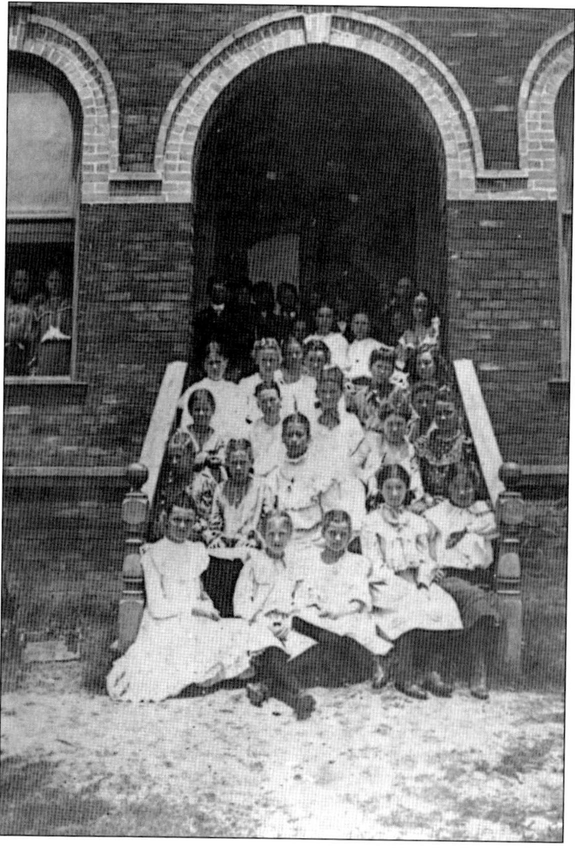

The Mansfield Academy was organized in 1901 and covered primary through high school. A new two-story, red pressed-brick structure trimmed with white bricks was erected and used as the main building. Two other brick buildings were used for intermediate and lower grades. Pupils could pursue regular or irregular courses and had the option to study in the different departments, with the advice and assistance of the faculty. In high school, studies included English, modern languages, ancient languages, history and civics, natural and physical sciences, philosophy, elocution and oratory, music, and business. The academy always closed for the year in May with a colorful week of performances—drills, plays, orations, and piano recitals—attended by families who came in from their farms. The academy closed for good in the summer of 1909 when the MISD was organized. At left, students sit on the steps of the Mansfield Academy building.

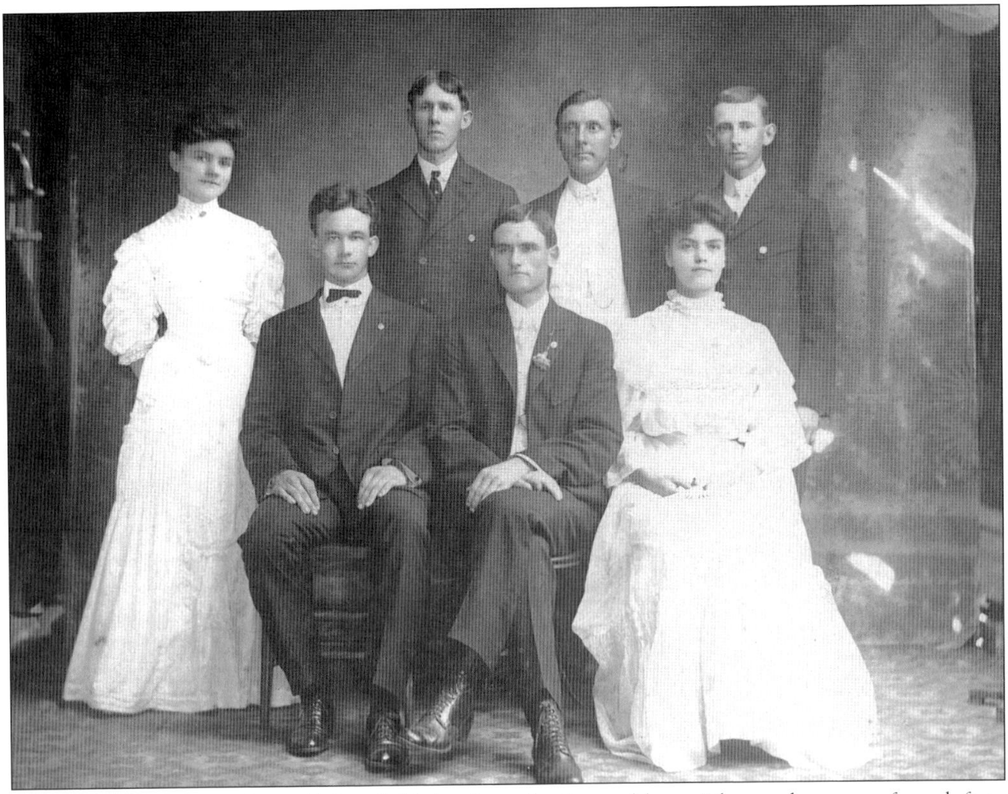

The 1906 graduating class of Mansfield Academy is pictured here. The students are, from left to right, (first row) unidentified, Louis Reed, and Nellie Williams; (second row) "Tad" Ramsey, Jim Chorn, unidentified, and Billy Harrison. The Mansfield Academy operated as a boarding and day school for elementary through high school students from 1901 to 1909.

This photograph, taken in 1921, shows the Mansfield High School boys' basketball team. The team stands on the basketball court at the Mansfield School when it was still held in the Mansfield Academy facility. The team was coached by Ralph Walker, who is standing in the middle of the second row.

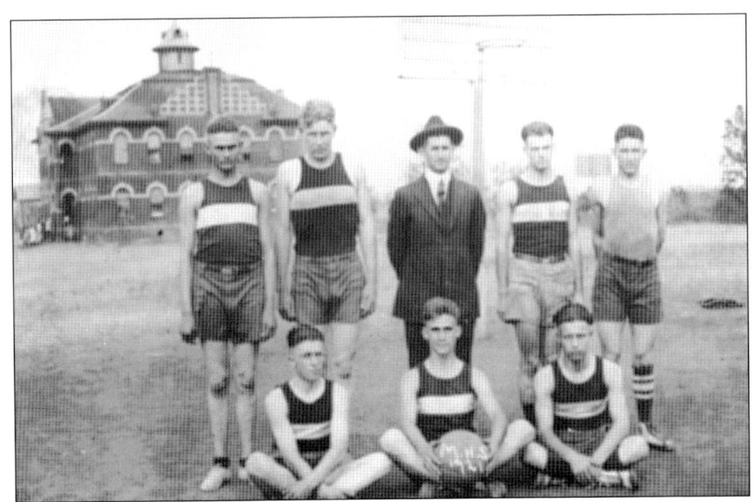

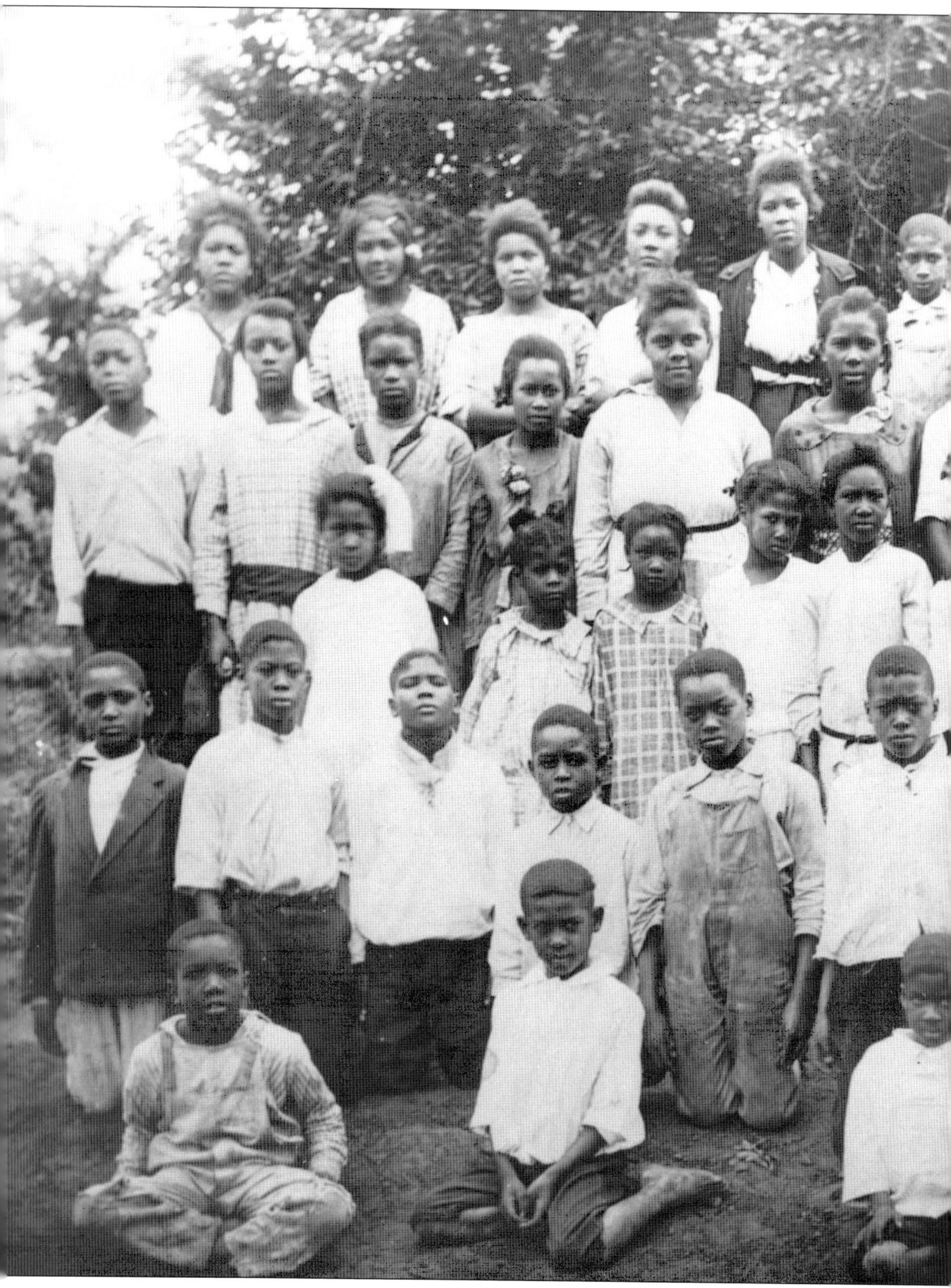

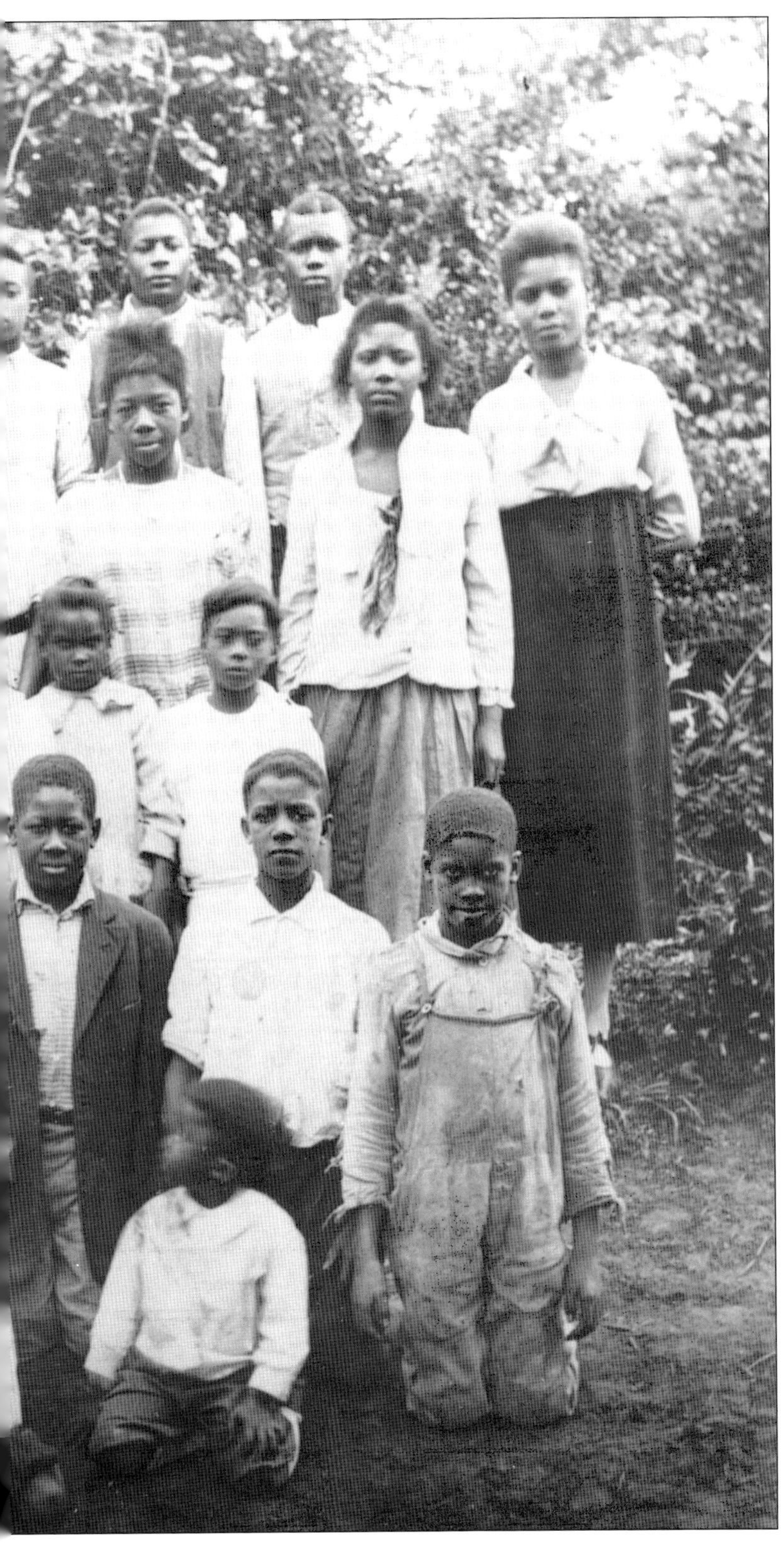

Mansfield's one-room "colored" school was operating as early as 1879 with an enrollment of 33 students. In 1929, it had become a two-room school. By 1950, the school consisted of two long, barracks-style buildings with no electricity, running water, or plumbing. In spite of these dire circumstances, the school produced several teachers who later greatly contributed to the Mansfield School District and now have schools named in their honor. The teacher in this photograph is Thelma Jones (pictured far right). She grew up in Mansfield but left to study teaching at Bishop College. She went on to get a master's degree in education at the University of Colorado. Jones returned to Mansfield to teach and later served as principal of the Mansfield Colored School. She worked at the school for 49 years, touching the lives of generations of students.

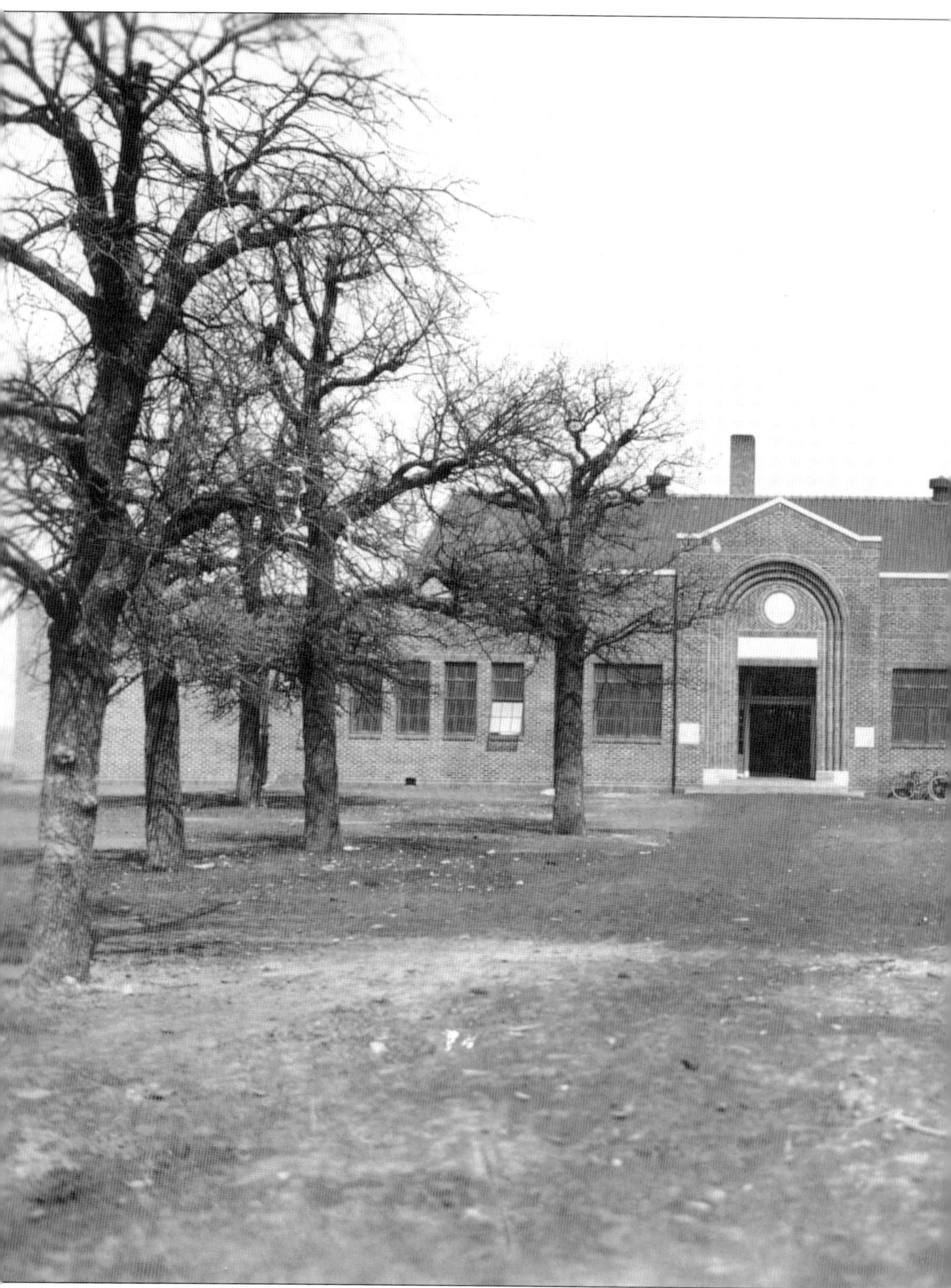

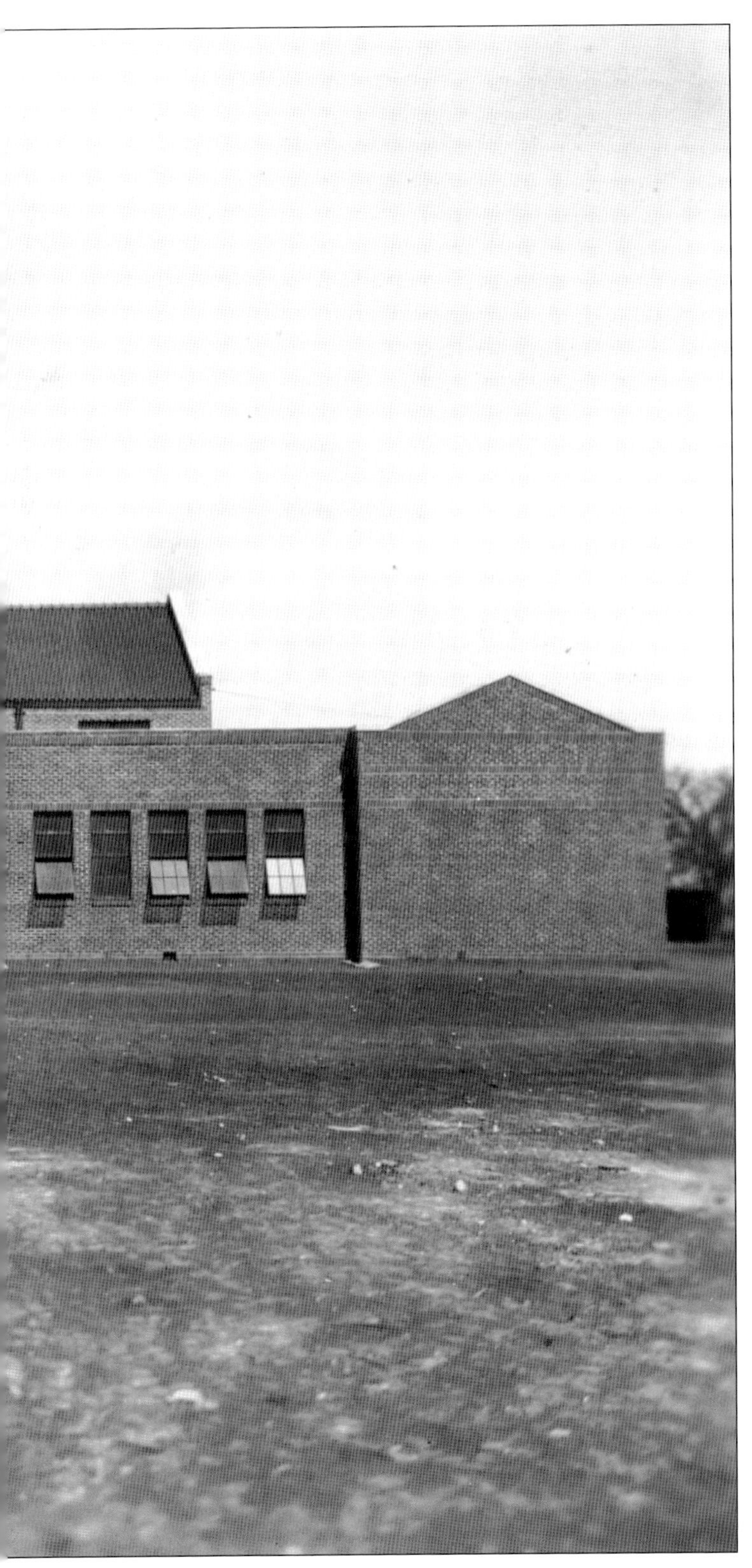

In 1909, the first board of trustees was selected and charged with bringing public schools into existence. These trustees negotiated with those of the Mansfield Academy for its buildings, and so the Mansfield Independent School District was established. Funding for maintenance, teachers, and supplies was sporadic, occasionally relying on donations from the community. By 1924, the district had outgrown the academy buildings, and some classes were held in various churches. An election was held for construction and equipment purchases, and the first public school was built by the board. This school housed all White students from first grade through eleventh grade until 1953. In 1940, the Rock Gym was built. The 1940 enrollment included 190 students in high school, 140 in grade school, and 40 in the "colored" school.

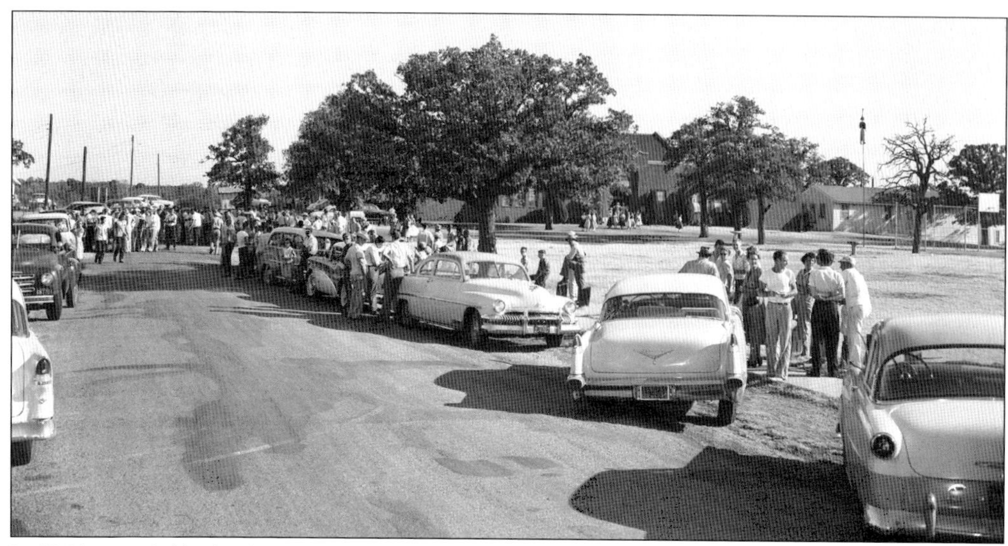

In 1956, Mansfield schools were strictly segregated. Facilities for young Black students were underfunded, and high school students were bused to I.M. Terrell High School in Fort Worth. Before the start of the 1956–1957 school year, in compliance with a federal desegregation order, Mansfield ISD approved a plan to admit Black students to Mansfield High School. What followed became known as "the Crisis at Mansfield." On the day students were required to report to the high school to register for school, crowds of segregationists guarded the school and patrolled the streets, threatening to use force to prevent Black children from registering. Above, a group blocks the high school. Below, from left to right, students Gracie Smith, Hattie Neal, Floyd Moody, John Hicks, and Charles Moody wait beside a school bus, away from the crowd, to see if they will be allowed to register. (Both, *Fort Worth Star-Telegram* Collection, Special Collections, the University of Texas at Arlington Libraries.)

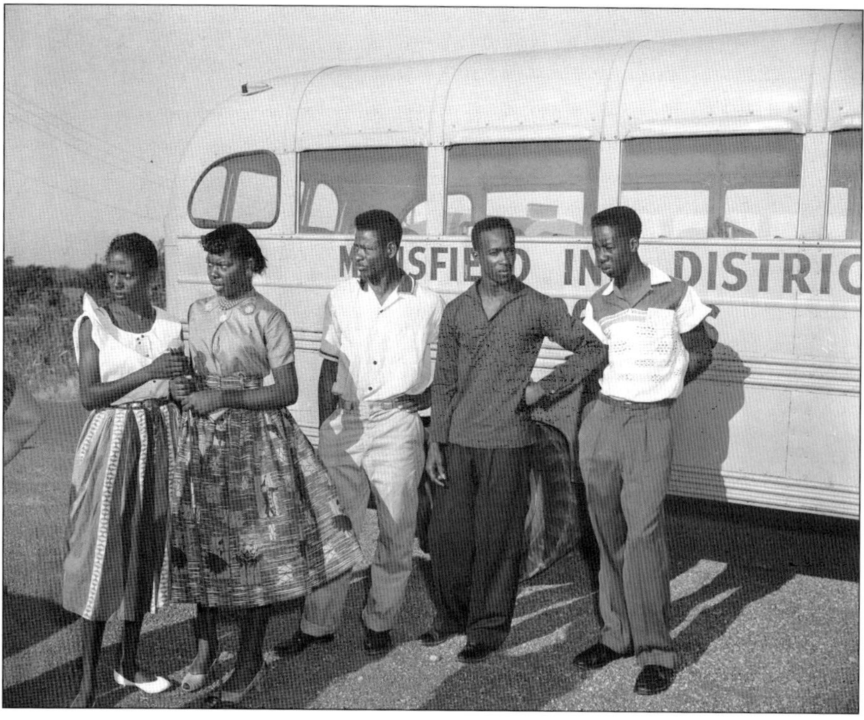

Outside the school, the mob hung an African American effigy at the top of the school's flagpole and set it on fire. Attached to one pant leg was a sign that read, "This would be a terrible way to die." On the other leg, a racist epithet warned Black students to stay away. A second effigy was hung over the front entrance of the school building. (*Fort Worth Star-Telegram* Collection, Special Collections, the University of Texas at Arlington Libraries.)

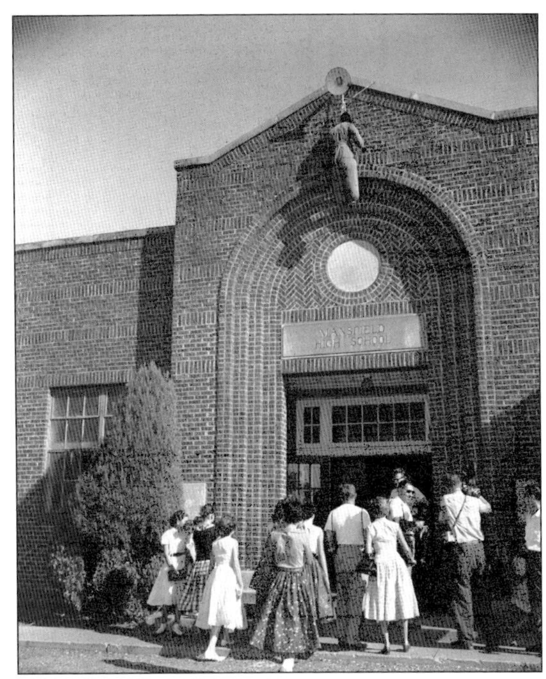

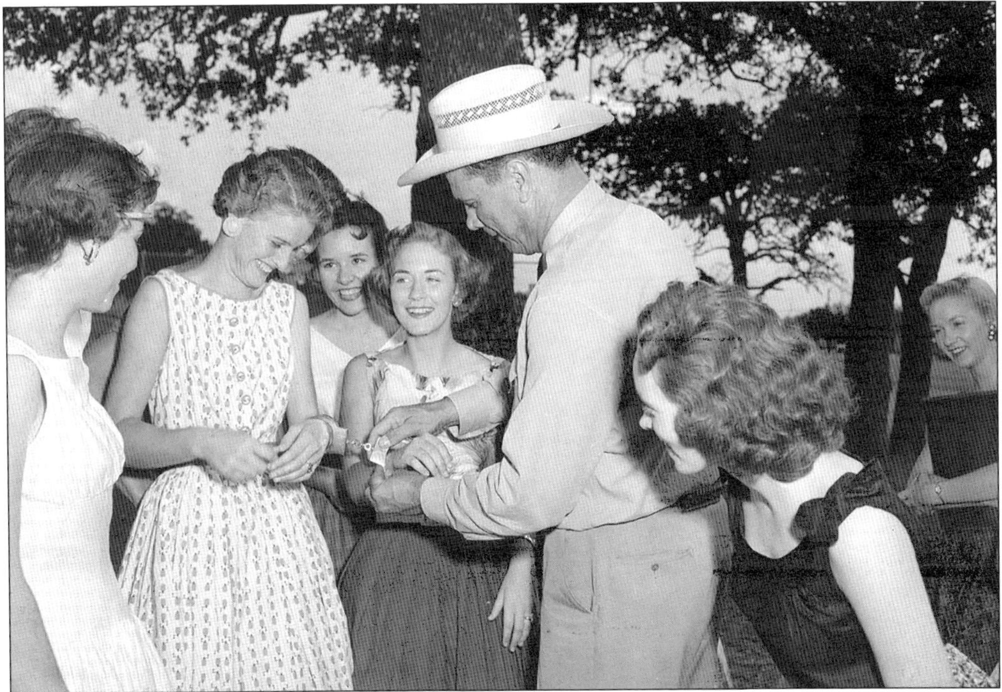

In response to the unrest on the first day of registration, Texas governor Allan Shivers sent six Texas Rangers to Mansfield with instructions to "maintain law and order" and transfer any students White or Black whose attendance or attempts to attend Mansfield High School would be reasonably calculated to incite violence. No Black students were able to register for Mansfield High School. Here, a Ranger entertains the crowd. (*Fort Worth Star-Telegram* Collection, Special Collections, the University of Texas at Arlington Libraries.)

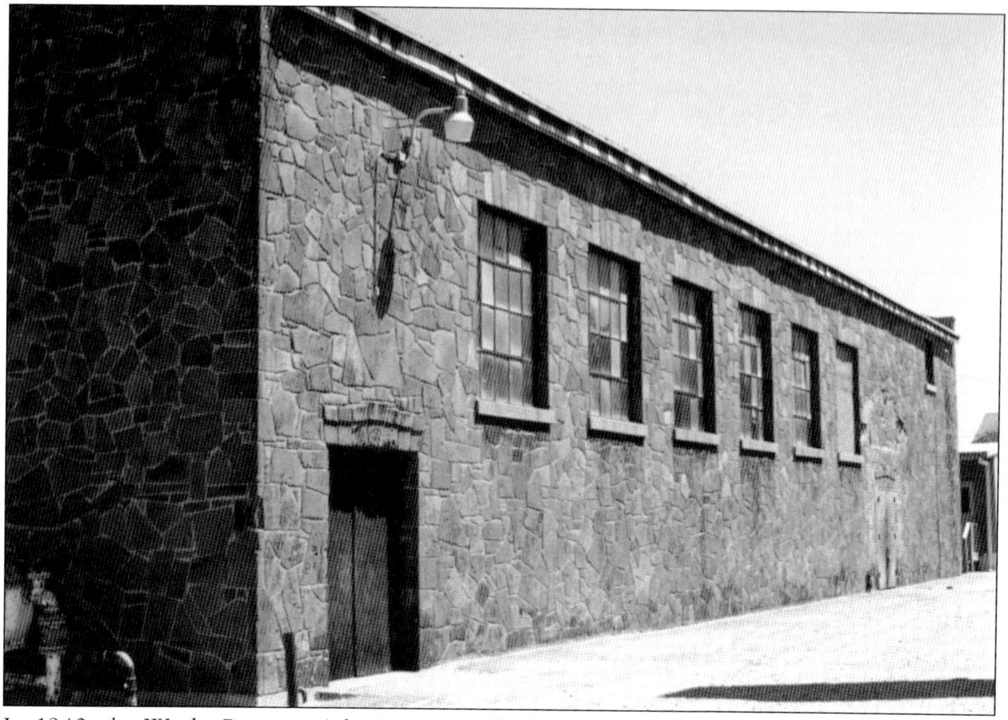

In 1940, the Works Progress Administration built a gymnasium for the Mansfield ISD that became known as the Rock Gym. The project employed 40 men, many of them from Mansfield. The building is made of stone from nearby Bisbee, Texas. The only machinery used on the project was a portable concrete mixer and the trucks used for hauling the stone. A lunchroom was built directly over the gym. The roof was constructed of 28-gauge tin. While it was durable, there was an unforeseen problem. In winter, ice formed inside the roof.

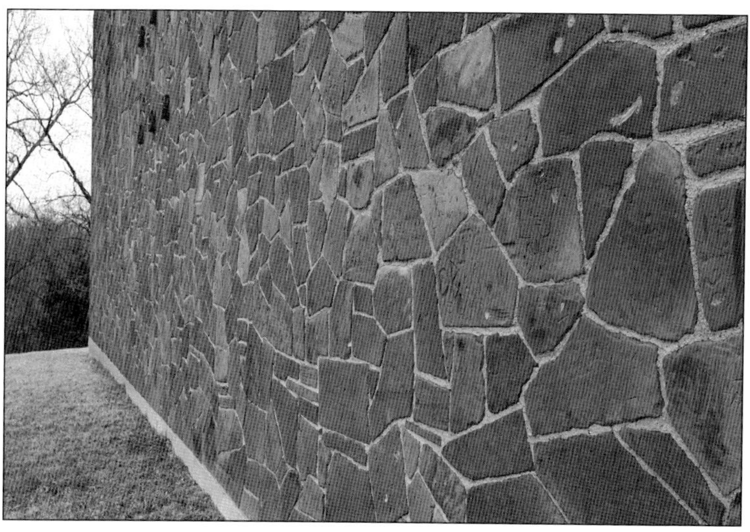

The building has served the city and the school as a recreational center for over 60 years. The "Old Rock Gym" stands as a memorial to the spirit of Mansfield. For many years, it was tradition for students to carve their names into the stone. The names remain as a reminder of a bygone era. (Bill Thomas.)

Seen here is a picture of the 1929 Mansfield High School Orchestra. Classical and popular music would have been played at its concerts. At that time, music expressed itself as happy and carefree. From left to right are Hardy Allman, Andy Galloway, Joe Brantley, Homer Stone, Sue Grow, Fritz Hostead, J.B. Killian, Clada Molone, and Ira Gibson.

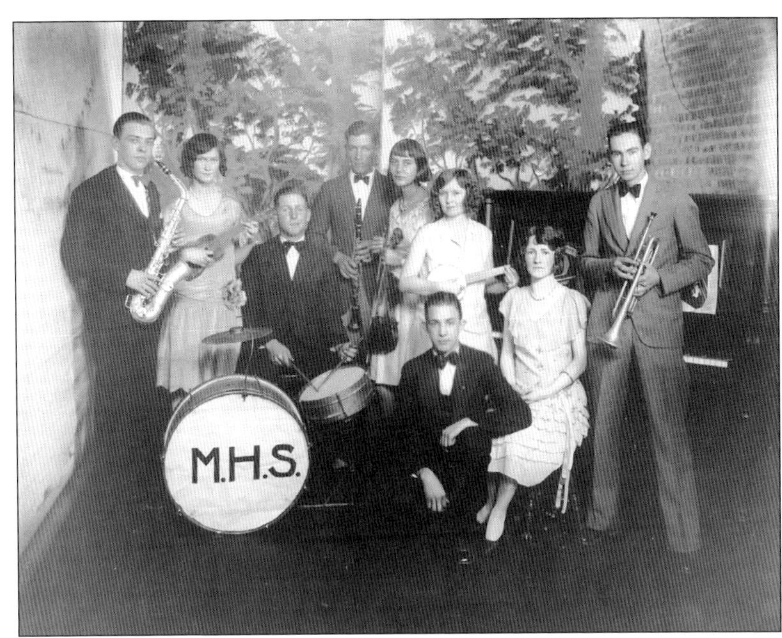

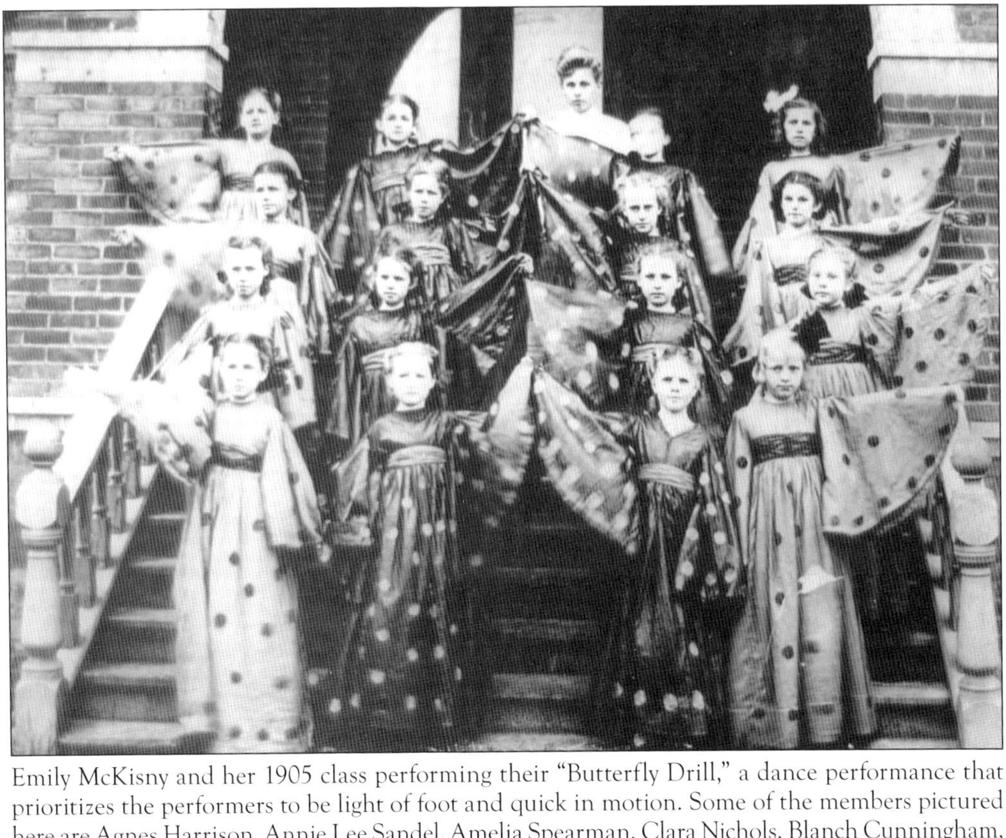

Emily McKisny and her 1905 class performing their "Butterfly Drill," a dance performance that prioritizes the performers to be light of foot and quick in motion. Some of the members pictured here are Agnes Harrison, Annie Lee Sandel, Amelia Spearman, Clara Nichols, Blanch Cunningham, Eula Marrs, Effie Tipps, Lillian Maclin, Kate McKnight, Miriam Yeates, Marie Erwin, May Allmon, Myrtle Fowler, Nell Harrison, and Ruth ?.

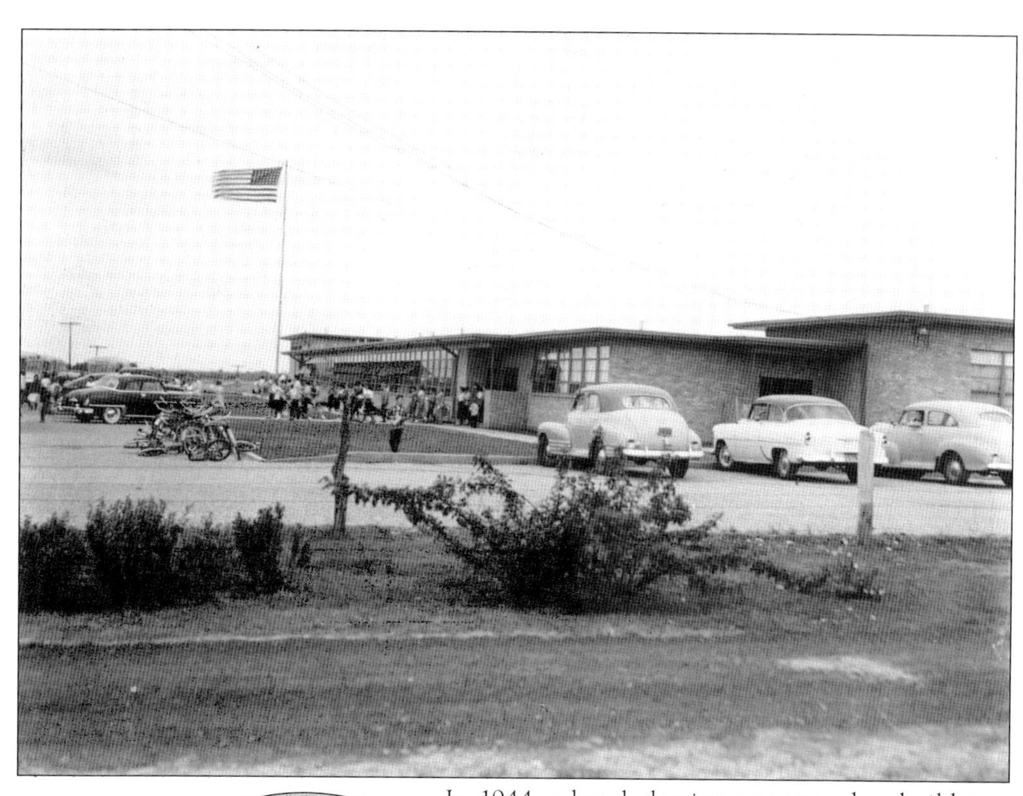

In 1944, a bond election was passed to build two elementary schools: Erma Nash, for the White students, and Willie Brown, for the Black students. The Erma Nash buildings were completed in 1953. Erma Nash Elementary School opened with 440 students in grades one through eight. There were 15 members on the staff.

The school was named for Erma Nash, affectionately known as "Miss Erma" to all. She grew up in Lillian, Texas, and attended college in Denton. She began teaching in the Mansfield school system in 1926. By the time her teaching career ended with her retirement in 1963, she had taught three generations of students.

In September 1972, a group of 22 girls joined the Mansfield High School band on the football field to perform as a precision dance team. They were called the "Dixie Dolls," a name selected to coordinate with the school fight song, "Dixie." A coincidence was their sponsor's name, teacher Dixie Dibley. The end of that half-time was filled with satisfaction and exhaustion from smiles and high kicks. (Carol Cook Cooper.)

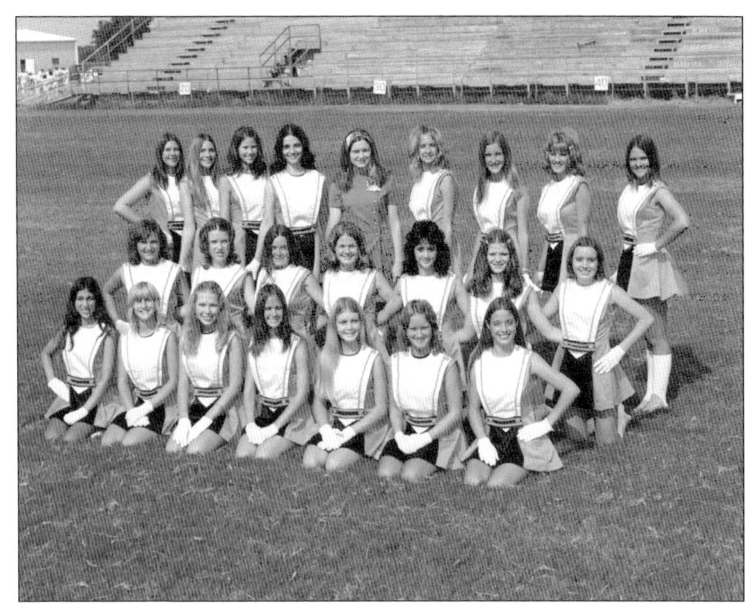

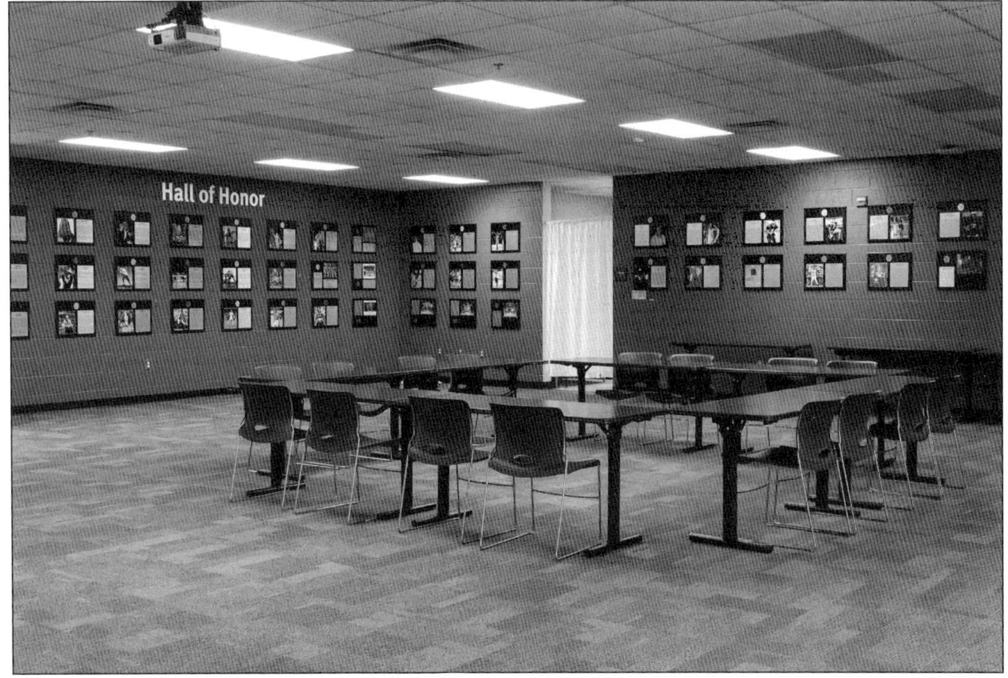

The Mansfield Athletic Hall of Honor, located in the Community Room in the Vernon Newsom Stadium and part of the Mansfield Independent School District, recognizes the efforts and contributions of former student-athletes, teams, coaches, athletic administrators, and distinguished volunteers who have brought honor and excellence to the MISD. A Hall of Honor Rewards Reception, which formally recognizes inductees, is held annually in the fall since its inception in 2013. (Bill Thomas.)

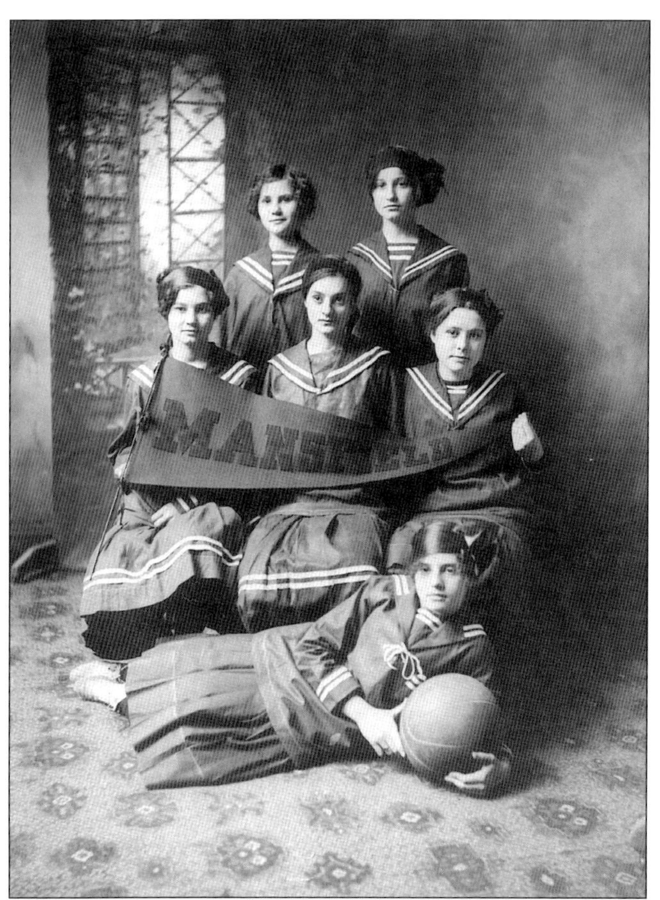

Clothed in uniforms quite different from today's basketball attire, the Mansfield High School girls' basketball team in 1913 was comprised of, from left to right, (first row) Mattie Carroll, captain; (second row) Blanch Cunningham, Esta Shaw, and Mattie Smith; (third row) May Hilmon and Dorothy McKnight. Over the years, the Mansfield girls' basketball teams have gone on to win multiple state championships.

From the inception of the Mansfield Independent School District in 1909, girls were included in the school's sports program. With good coaching, the early years saw the girls' teams win several championships. This team in 1921 was coached by Una Walker Spears (far left). On the team were Mae Watson (third from left) and Eunetta Ball Perry (far right).

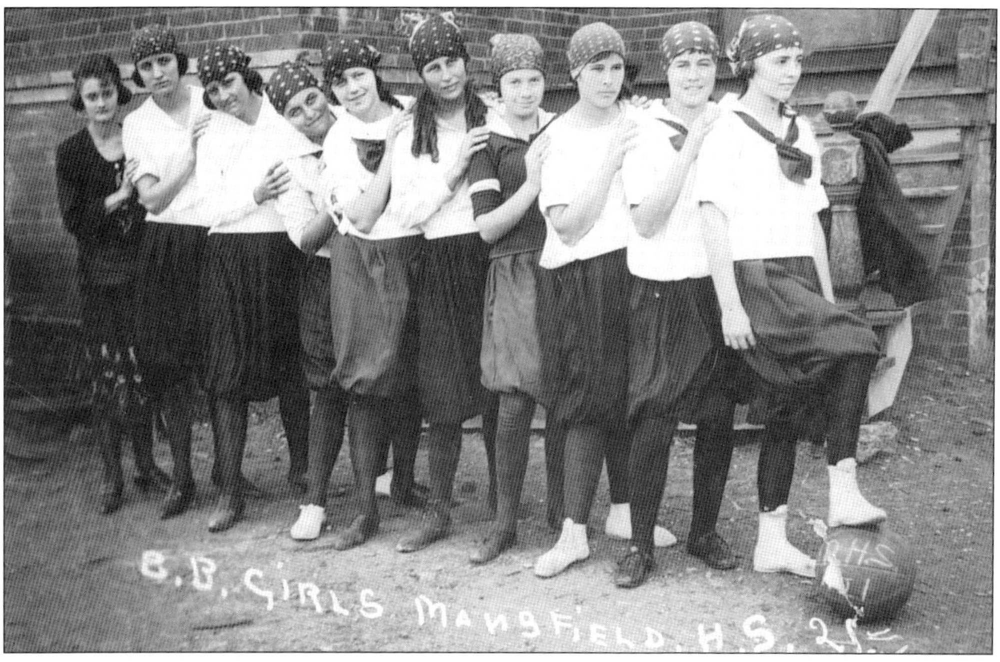

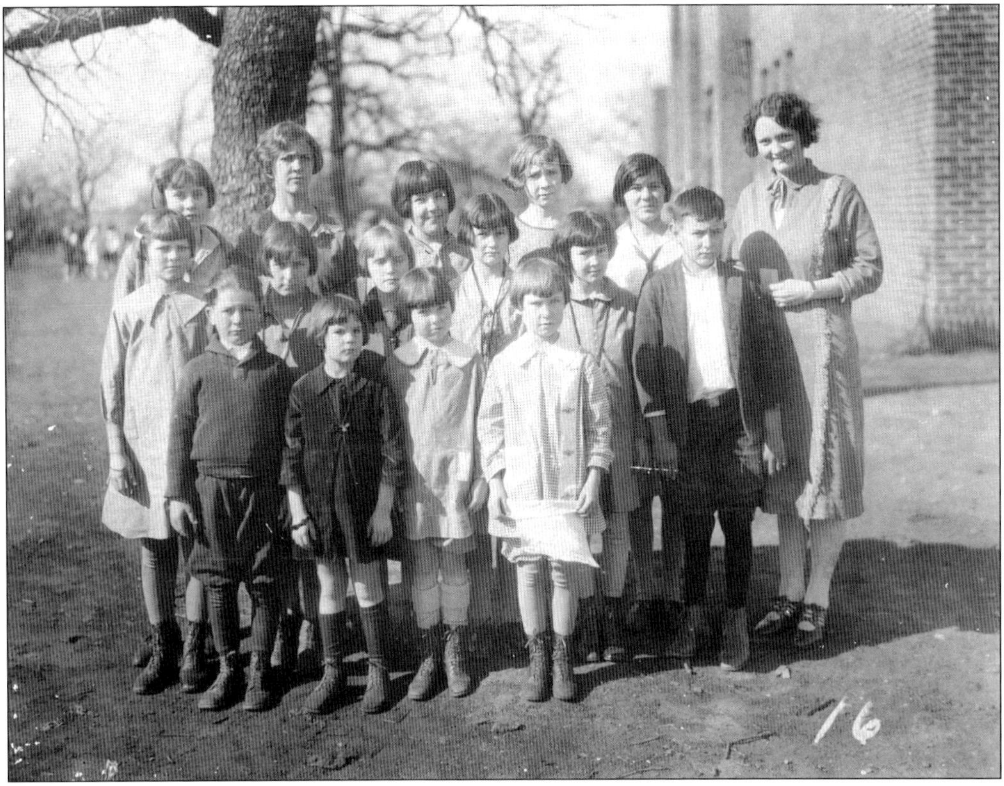

Pictured in this image is the 1924 expression class, which encouraged creative self-expression through art, drama, and writing. The class of schoolchildren was taught by Grace Galloway. From left to right are (first row) Troy Sells, Dorothy Jane Lamb, Louise Foote, and Henriette Bacon; (second row) Frances Sells, Lillian Hart, Hortense Hogg, Mayme Ruth Killian, and C.J. Prater; (third row) Bernice Ray, Lois Ellis, Vivian Hackler, Walterine Ellis, Ira Mae Wheeler, and Galloway.

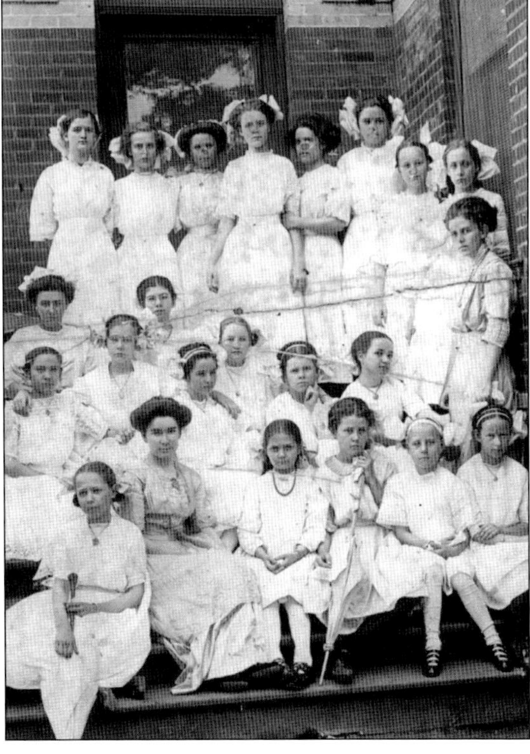

Seen here is the 1910–1911 high school music class. From left to right are (first row) Bernice Board, Allie House, ? Owens, Lola Rawdon, Mary Smith, and ? "Tip" Witherspoon; (second row) Eula Marrs, Annie Sandel, Patsy Carroll, Kate McKnight, Tom Smith, and Faye Johns; (third row) ? Bell and unidentified; (fourth row) Miriam Yeates, Agnes Harrison, Effie Tipps, Elenor Harrison, Virginia "Jennie" Lamb, Martha Smith, Dorothy McKnight, Minnie Bowman, and Glenna Florence.

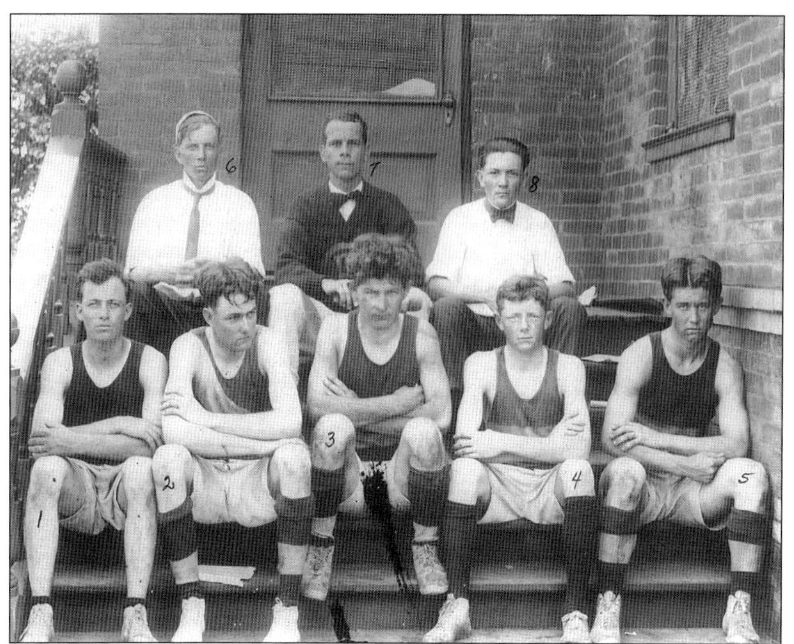

The high school boys' basketball team of Mansfield is pictured with their coach, Hal S. Lattimore, in 1914. The five players and their coaches are, from left to right, (first row) Julian Nichols, Marcellus Griffith, Clyde Holland, Neely McCaleb, and J.W. "Spud" Murphy; (second row) Lattimore, Verne Rumph, and an unidentified assistant coach.

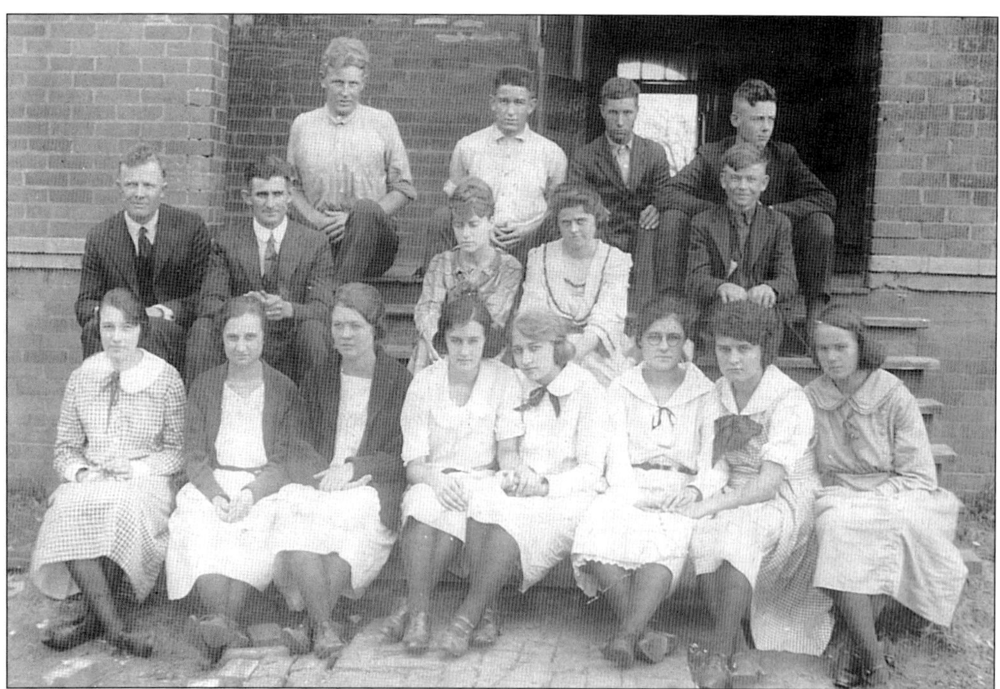

The graduating class of 1922 from Mansfield High School and principal P.E. Wentworth are shown above. The individuals are, from left to right, (first row) Madge Harrison, Ora Roe, Rose Stone, Inez Edgemon, Minie Lou Richardson, Flora McKennon, Marie Bratton, and Ruby Dobbs; (second row) Wentworth, Ralph Walker (coach), two unidentified, and Henry Ward; (third Row) Elbert Myers, Virgil Stephens Murphy, ? Messerang, and John Graves.

The schools in Mansfield have a history of excellence in basketball, with the 1920 Mansfield High School basketball team winning the state championship. It was made up of, from left to right, (first row) Marie Stewart, Cleo Hammett, and Ida Edgemond; (second row) Minnie McCaleb, Bonnie Kemp, Lucy Dunn, Abbie Dalton, Jewel Ellard, Verna Galloway, Marie McElvaney, and Irene Trimble.

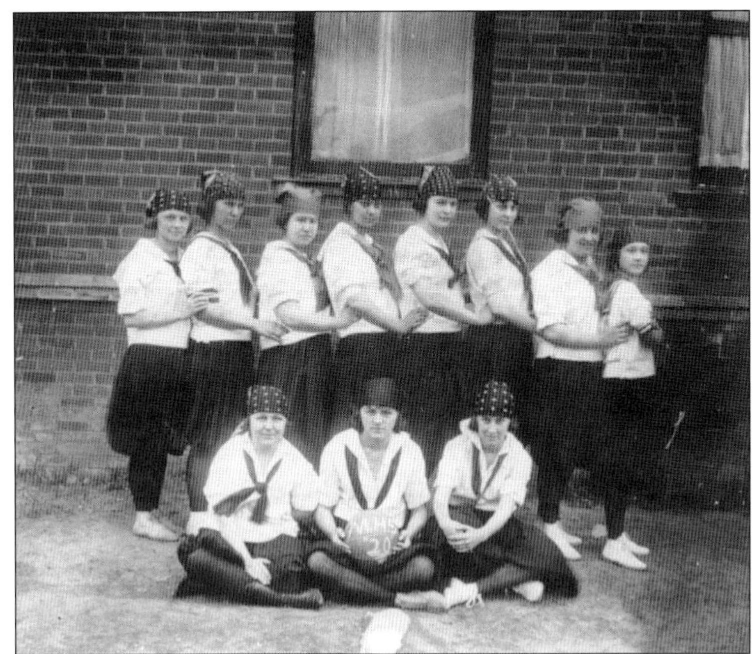

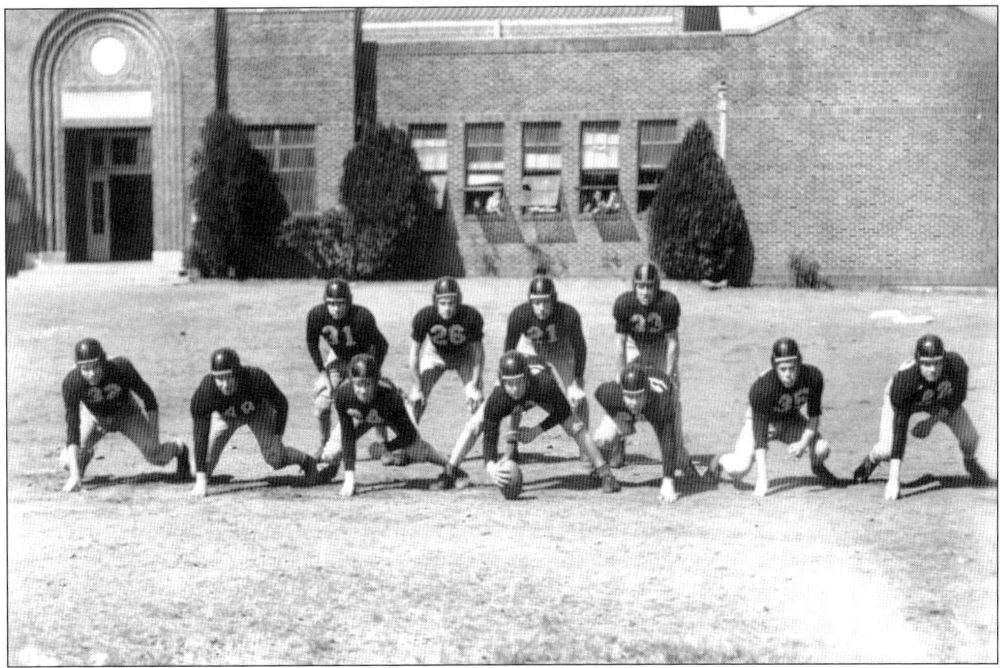

Pictured are some of the football players from Mansfield High School's team in 1948. From left to right are (first row) Gene Selman (defensive end), Winford Brown (right tackle), Emmitt Williams (right guard), Burl Watson (center), Vernon Helmick (left guard), Harper Mitchell (left tackle), and E.W. Smith (defensive end); (second row) running backs Johnnie Metcalf, Wayne Seeton, James Coble, and Royce Womble.

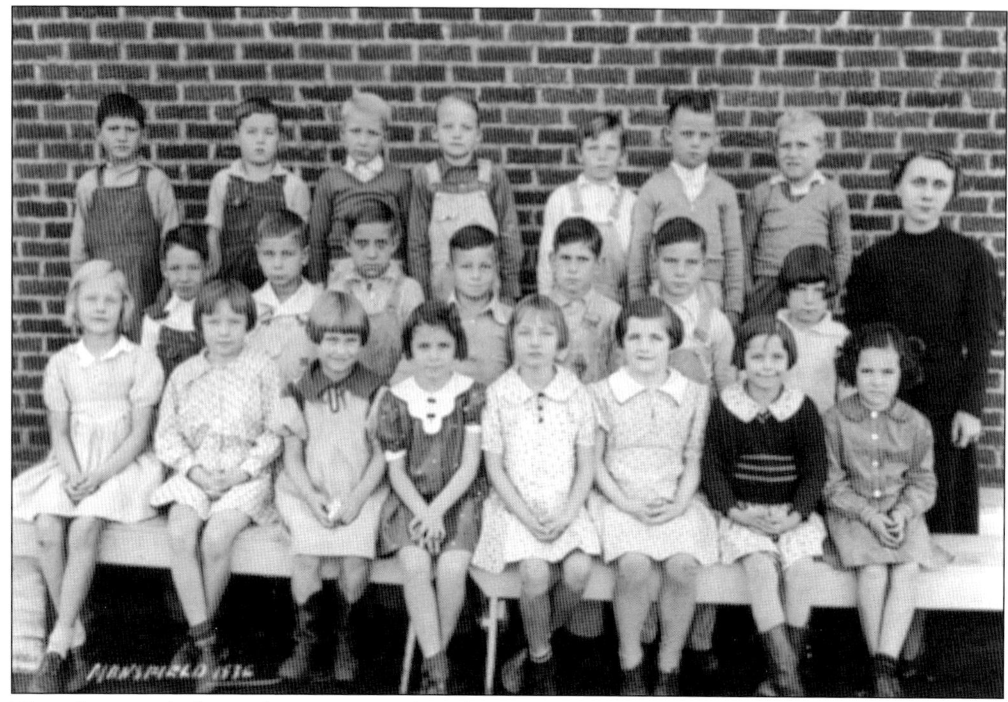

This photograph shows the 1936 second-grade class of Mansfield. From left to right are (first row) Jane Mayfield, Marilynn Ward, Geraldine Garretson, Mildred Mandelstamm, Margaret Keene, Doris Vincent, Mabel Farquhar, and Ellen Oliver; (second row) Weldon Cantrell, Robert Wilson, Jimmie Pyles, Herbert Bell, Varley Redmon, Curtis Minor, and Betty Redmon; (third row) Kenneth Morris, Billie Whisenant, Clyde Hairston, Gene Hogan, Ralph Roberts, Billie Casstevens, Joe Coble, and Roberta Tipps (teacher).

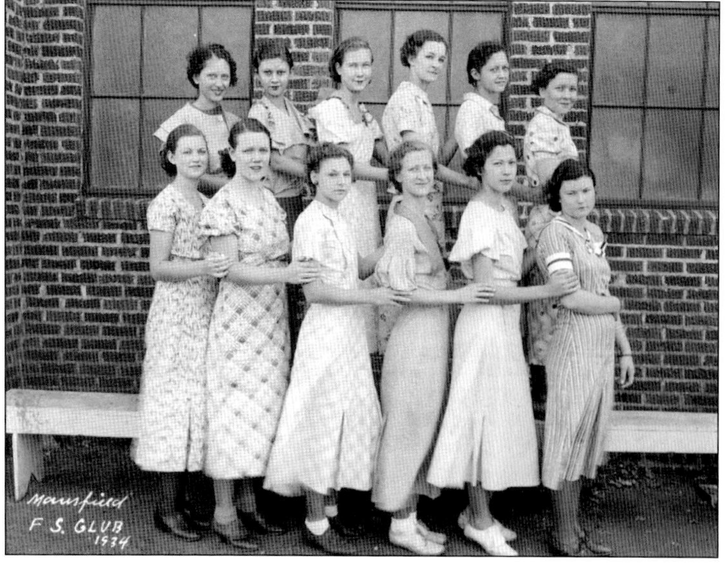

Pictured here is the 1934 Female Society Club of Mansfield. The members are, from left to right, (first row) Mary Virginia Thomas Linn, Margaret Galloway, Maurice Craig Ellard, Evelyn Ellis, Sis Patterson, and Elsie "Sprinkle" Sells; (second row) Ruby Lee Green Robason, Dorothy Myrle Galloway, Harrietta Bacon, Jo Anna (Watson) Britton, Hazel Weaver, and Edna Murle Ward Thomas.

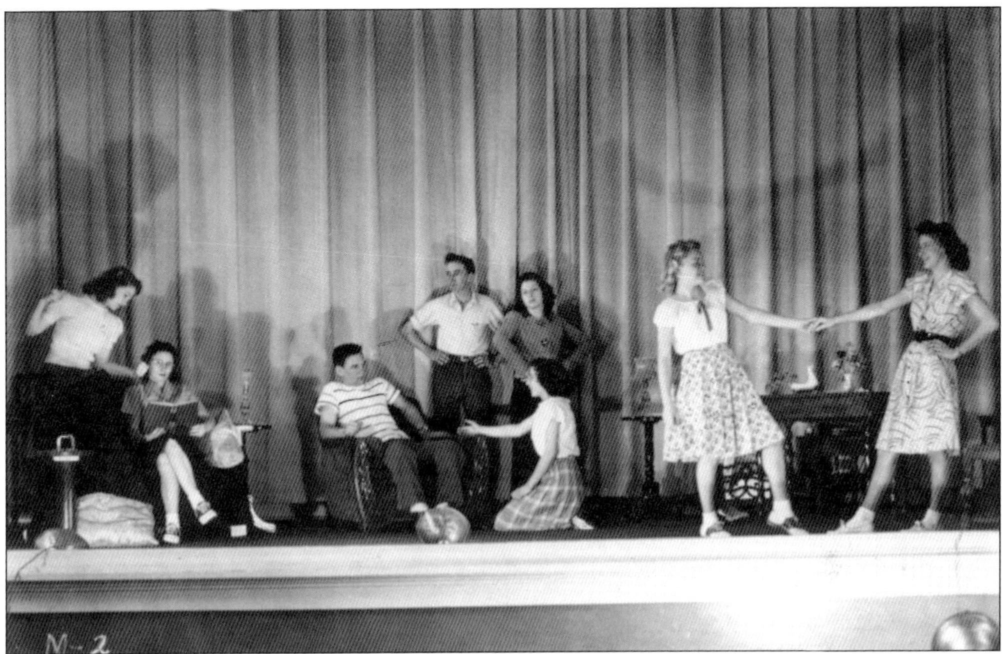

The 1948 junior class from Mansfield High School works on their unknown class play to entertain all grades from first to eleventh. From left to right are Dorothy Faye Galloway, Louise Crocker, James Coble, Billy Dale Roberts, James Olen Tipps, Dutchie Grant, Vada Nelson, and Freed Mae Reeves. This production was held at the original high school, built in 1924 on East Broad Street.

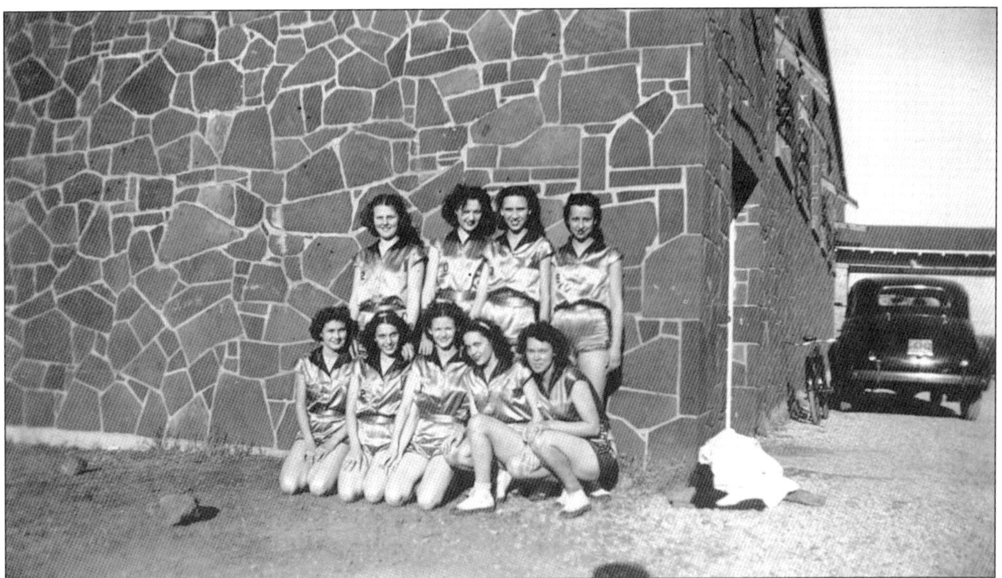

The 1945 Mansfield High School girls' basketball team members are, from left to right, (first row) Lora Lee Tips, Paulajene Ray, Maxine Rawdon, Pauline Ray Nichols, and Betty Jean West; (second row) Betty Lou Parker, Beth Brown, Edna Turner, and Helen Barrett. The team is pictured in front of the Rock Gym behind Mansfield High School.

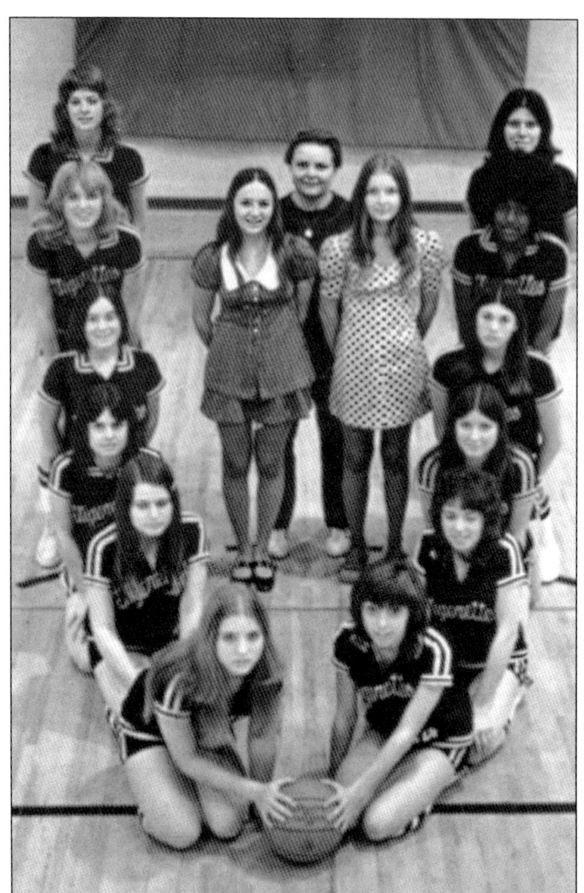

This photograph features the 1972–1973 Mansfield High School Tigerettes basketball team. The district championship team members are Suzy Moore, Kim McMahon, Linda Parker, Debbie Durant, Pam Dycus, Kathryn Perry, Cheryl Perry, Debbie Odom, Terrye Selman, Claudia Wiggam, Paula Jones, and Davida Hopkins. Pictured in the center are coach Mary Jo Sheppard and managers Belinda Perry and Cindy Wilson.

Pictured is the 1950 football team from Mansfield High School, the Mansfield Tigers, practicing before their next game. Pictured are, from left to right, (first row) Clayton Jordan, D.L. Watson, Leon Rawdon, John Paul Watson, Jim Noles, Donald Kepple, and Bobby Jordan; (second row) Glynn Farris; (third row) Ernest Allcock, Luis Harrison, and Tommy Galloway.

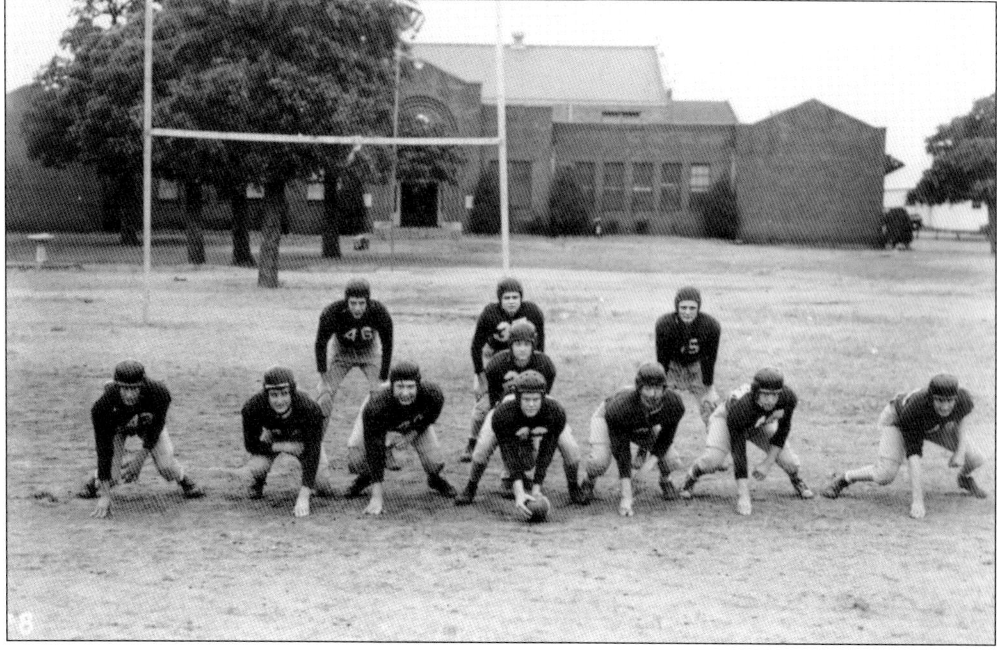

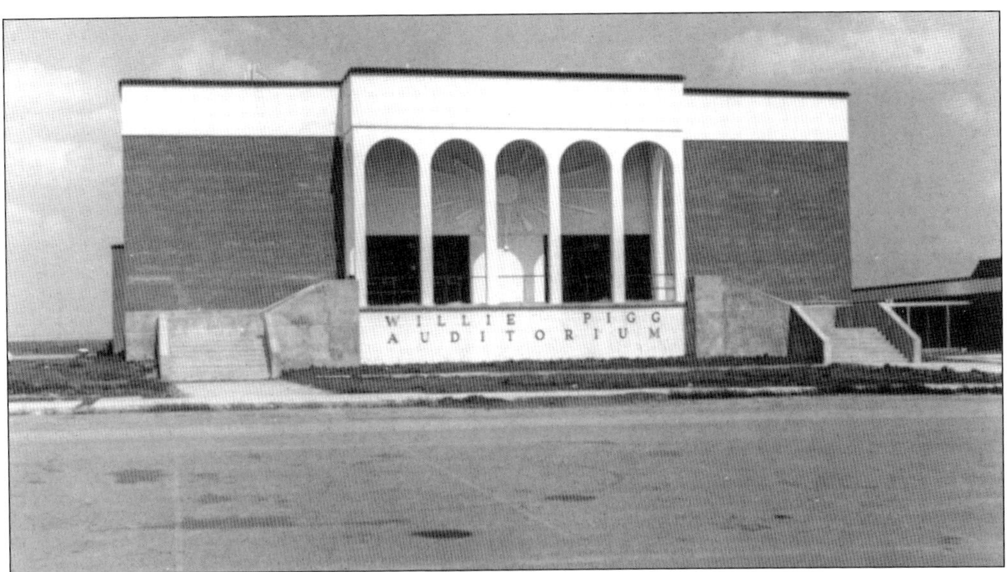

Willie Pigg Auditorium was named after Willie Pigg, a teacher, coach, principal, and superintendent for Mansfield Independent School District from 1947 to 1979. The auditorium, along with J.L. Boren Elementary School, opened in 1978 and was ahead of its time, being the first school buildings in the state to be entirely powered by solar energy. The technology was still too new and had to be removed after a few years.

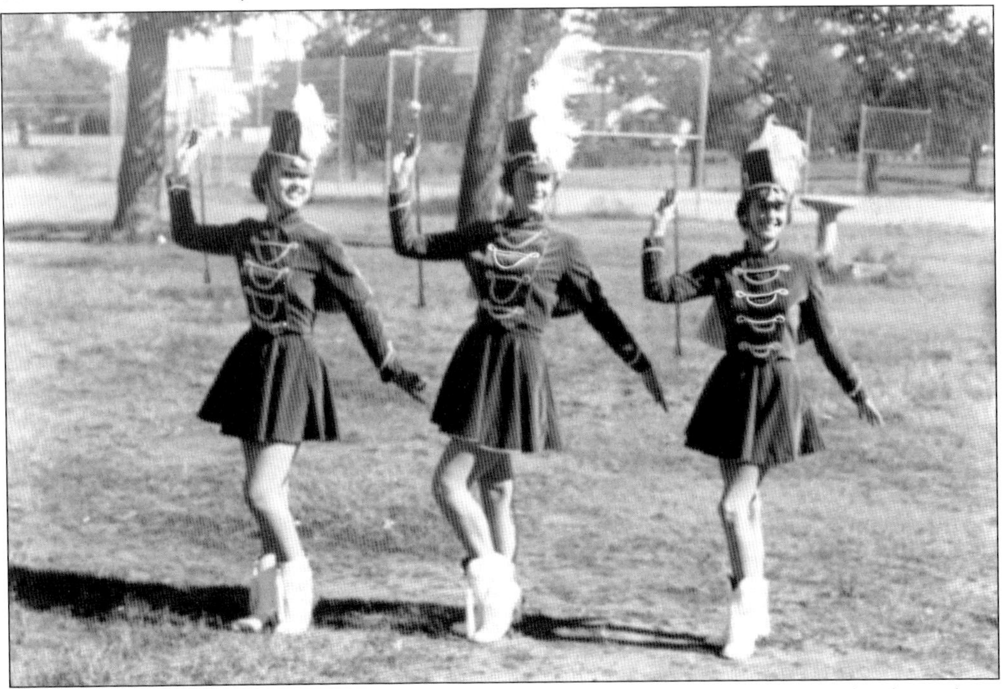

With no band for years, the Mansfield Independent School District organized a school marching band in 1956. Originally, the band members wore no uniforms until they were able to purchase used uniforms from another school. Audrey Galloway altered the uniforms for each member. A few years later, majorettes were added to the band. Featured in a 1960 photograph are, from left to right, Mary Beth Hailey, Karen Kelly, and Jayne Jones.

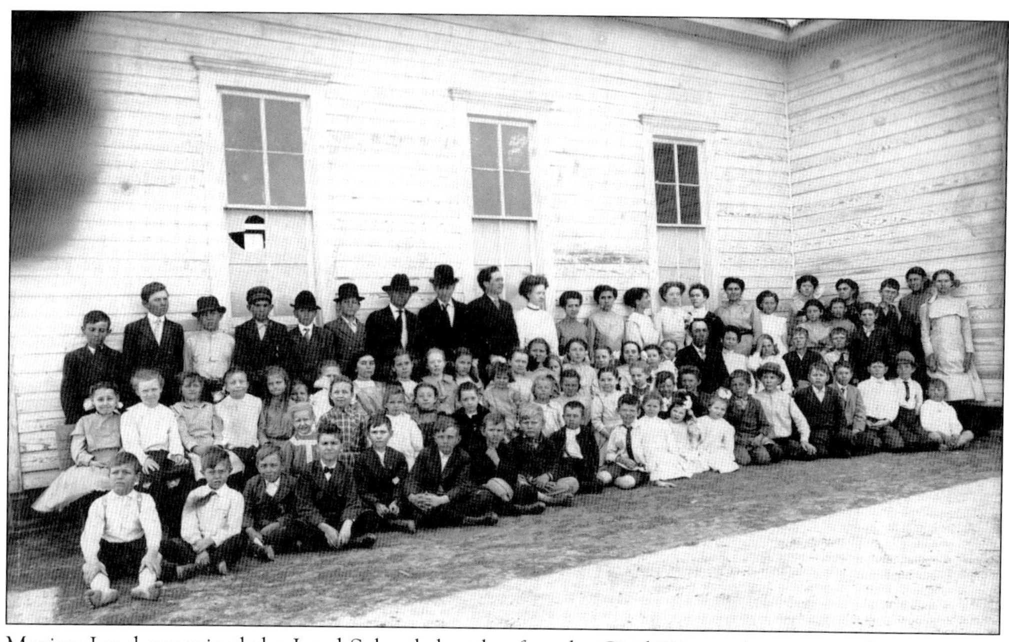

Marion Loyd organized the Loyd School shortly after the Civil War and encouraged everyone to learn to read and write. Adults who were not too busy and young children were encouraged to attend, and in the early 1900s, Loyd's school merged with the nearby Webb school to accommodate more students. The students seen here are from after the two schools merged in 1910.

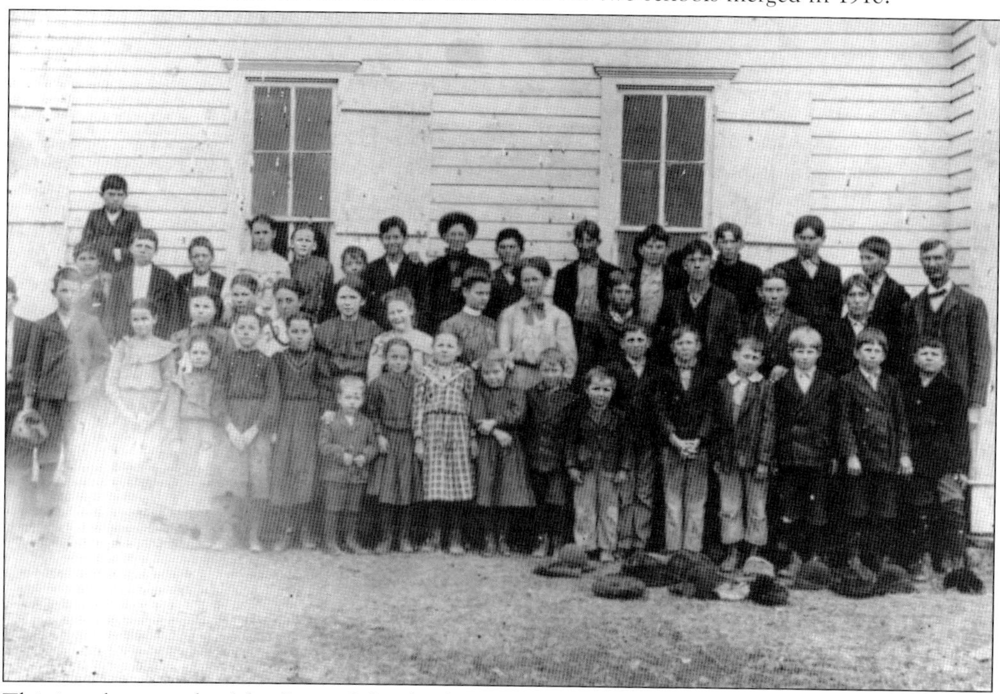

This is a photograph of the Gertie School. The school was operating as early as 1885. It was located on Mansfield-Cedar Hill Road, about a mile from the Friendship Baptist Church. The land for the school was donated by Martin Ballweg. The first building was wooden and was torn down around 1918, when it was replaced by a brick structure. The school closed in the 1940s.

Four

Businesses

Since Mansfield's inception, businesses have played a crucial role in developing the town as an incentive to settle in the area. The importance of local businesses began with the town's cofounders, as Ralph Man and Julian Feild established Mansfield around their three-story, steam-powered mill. With a successful mill established in the area, pioneers settled nearby to use the mill to grind their crops. In addition to the mill, Man and Feild also opened a general store, and Henrietta Feild ran a hotel out of the Feilds' family home. Though more than 150 years have passed since those earliest days, local businesses continue to play a vital role in shaping the community.

In 1890, with a population of around 400, a blacksmith, carpenter, and cooper were necessary in an era where the primary method of travel was horse and wagon. A variety of stores, doctors' offices, and pharmacies opened in downtown and saw to the well-being of local citizens. The main industry that supported the town continued to be the many mills and gins in the area. For decades after these early days, the population of Mansfield remained small. However, as time progressed, the businesses in operation shifted because of the new industrial and technological developments. Department stores replaced general stores, and auto shops replaced livery stables. Small restaurants became gathering places for the community, and manufacturing plants became the city's biggest employers. Longtime residents look back at the businesses that supported the small town of Mansfield in the mid-20th century as tent poles of the community. They consider these businesses to be vital to establishing Mansfield's sense of identity. Though Mansfield's population has exploded from 400 settlers to the current 80,000 residents, businesses continue to be established in Mansfield to support the local community as it grows.

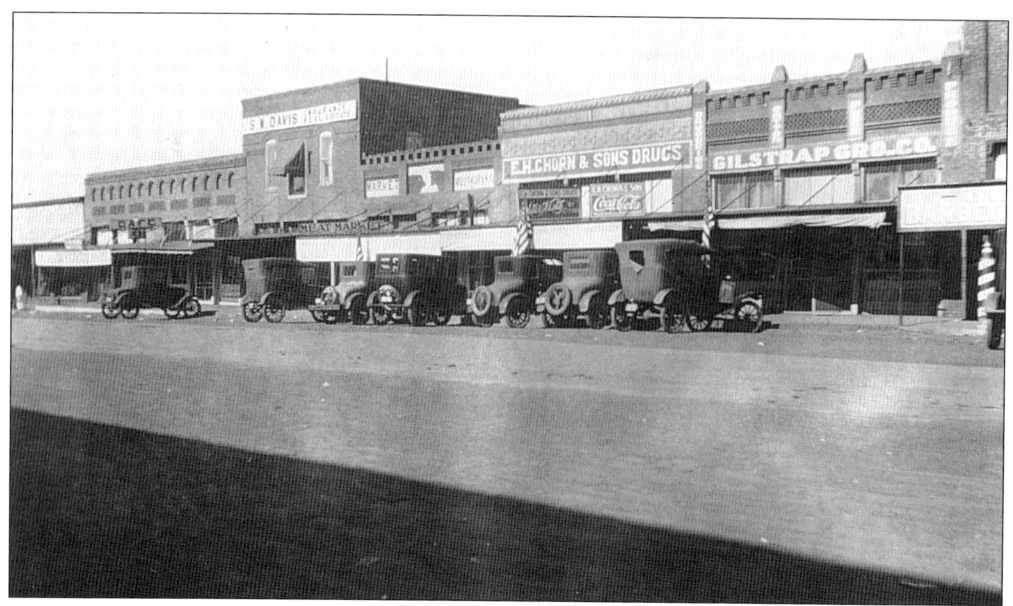

This photograph of downtown Mansfield, taken in 1927, shows the east side of Water Street. Some of the businesses visible in the photograph are Gilstrap Grocery, Chorn and Sons Drugstore, and S.W. Davis Insurance and Real Estate. On the far right of the photograph is the post office. In 1958, the street was officially renamed Main Street.

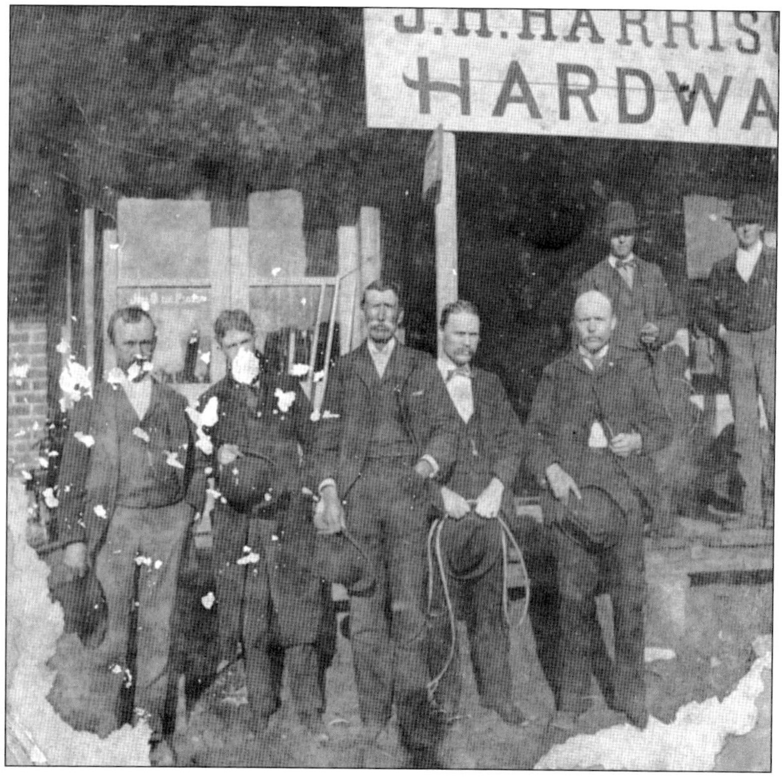

Located at 115 Water Street, J.H. Harrison Hardware opened in the former Dukes and Poe Hardware store. The building was erected in 1890 by Dennis Mahoney and was deeded to Harrison in 1919. Pictured here in front of the shop around 1909 are, from left to right, J.H. Harrison, Joseph Edwards, T.B. Huitt, A.J. Bravin, and I.M. Elliott.

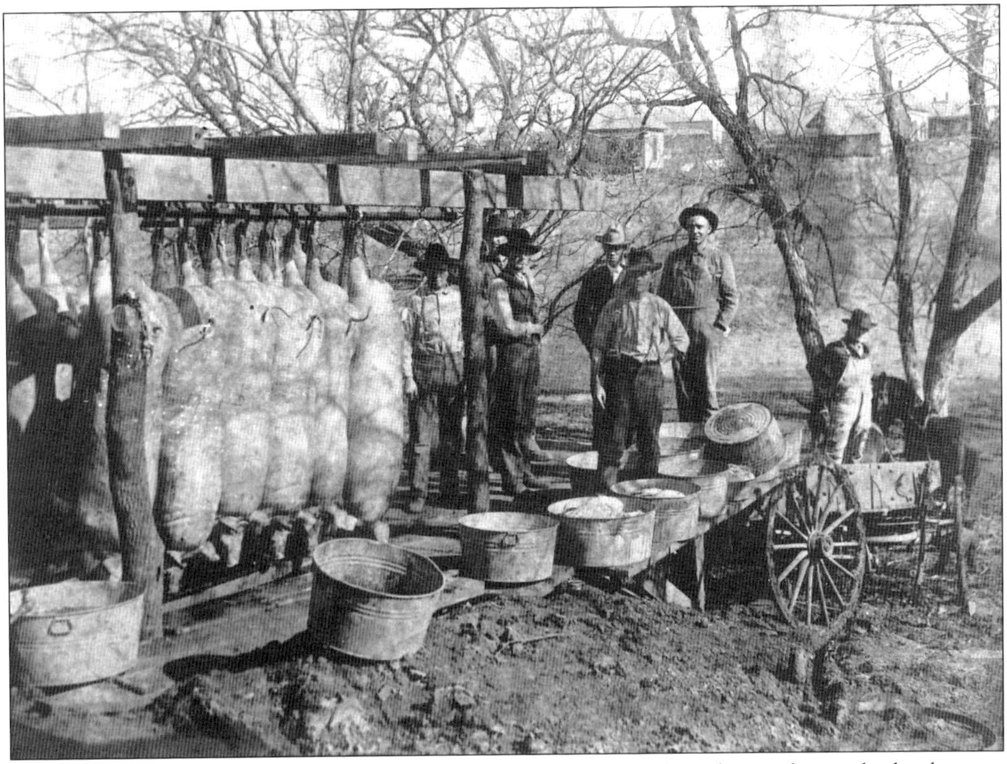

Just off Oak Street on a branch of Walnut Creek, Charlie Nichols and Joe Edgmon had a thriving business of dressing hogs for the public. One busy day, they prepared 90 fat swine for their customers. They employed seven or eight extra helpers during the busy season. The workers and visitors seen in this c. 1916 photograph are, from left to right, "Shorty" Berryman, two unidentified people, Charlie Nichols, Khi Balch, Jay Grow, and Joe Edgmon.

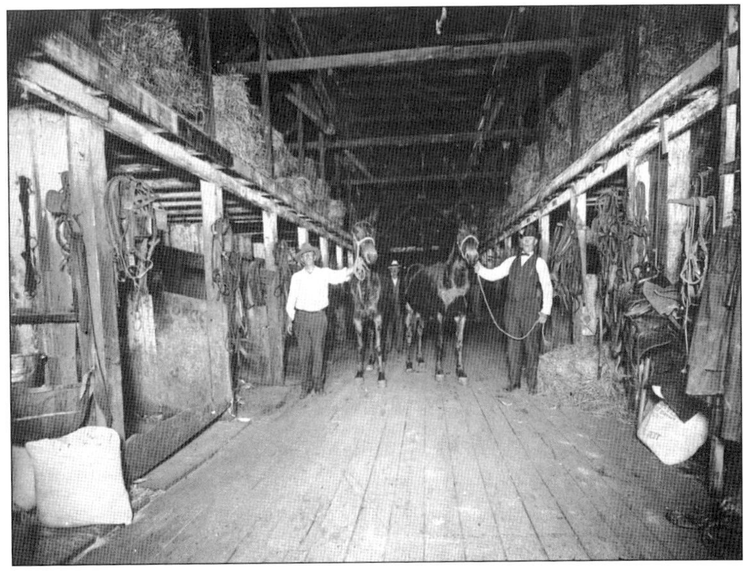

In the early 1900s, the livery stable was located at the corner of Water and Oak Streets. Ed Galloway is in the derby hat, and "Uncle Billy" Pyles's oldest son is in the white shirt. The going rate to hire a horse and buggy was $2.50 a day. It was demolished around 1920, and G.A. Henderson erected a tin building on the site that was used as an automobile repair garage.

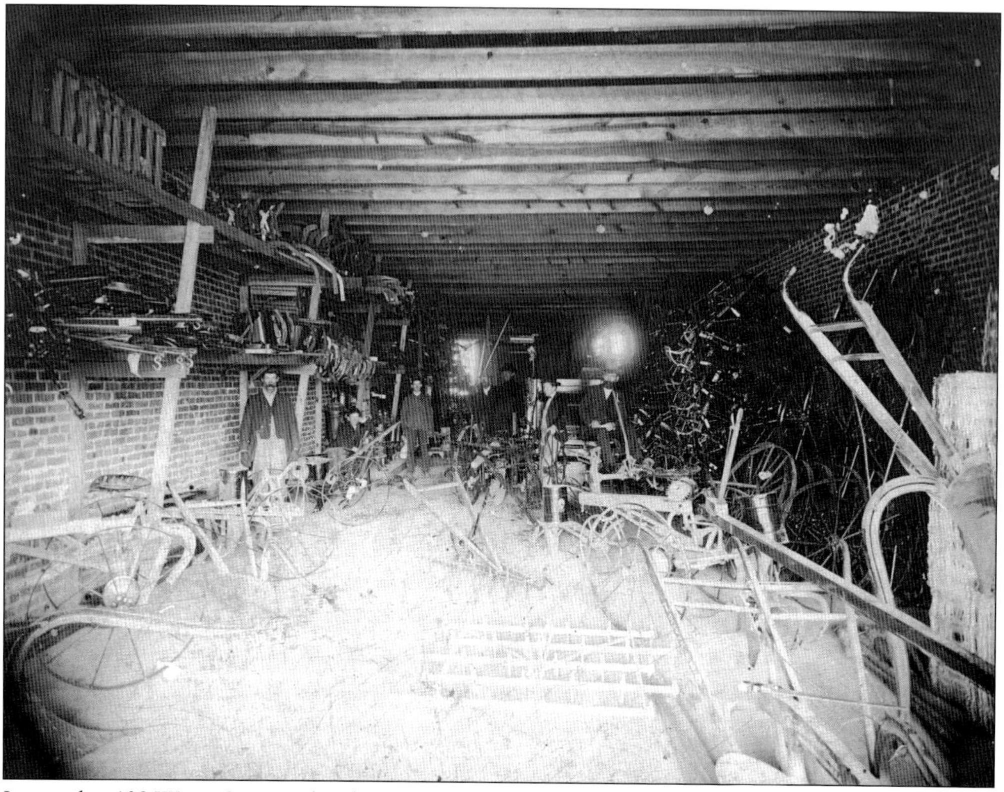

Located at 103 Water Street, a hardware store operated by Charles McLane and Benjamin Ramsey opened when the building was completed in 1900. Around 1906, the business was purchased by Jacob Back and James Bradford and adopted the name Back and Bradford Hardware. The store operated from that time until Bradford died in the 1960s. This image is the interior of Back and Bradford Hardware.

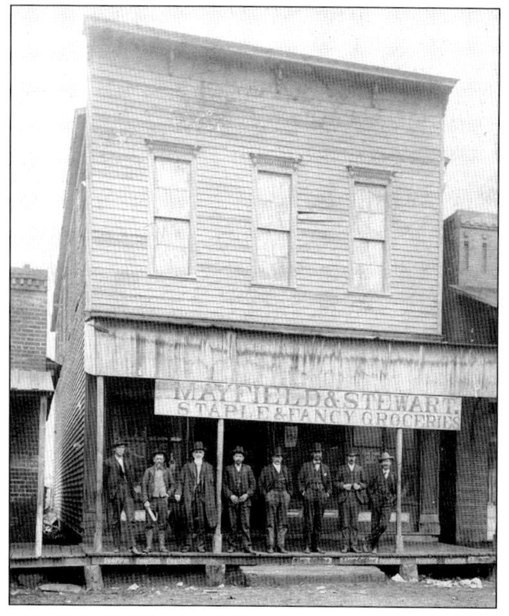

Thomas Mayfield and David Stewart opened the Mayfield and Stewart Staple and Fancy Groceries store in 1895. The store was located on Main Street north of the Masonic lodge. Mayfield transferred ownership to Stewart in 1906. It closed in 1910 after Stewart left Mansfield. Staple groceries were honey, sugar, molasses, flour, potatoes, cereal, and seasonal fruits and vegetables. Fancy groceries consisted of cheese, pineapples, bananas, spices, and special baked goods.

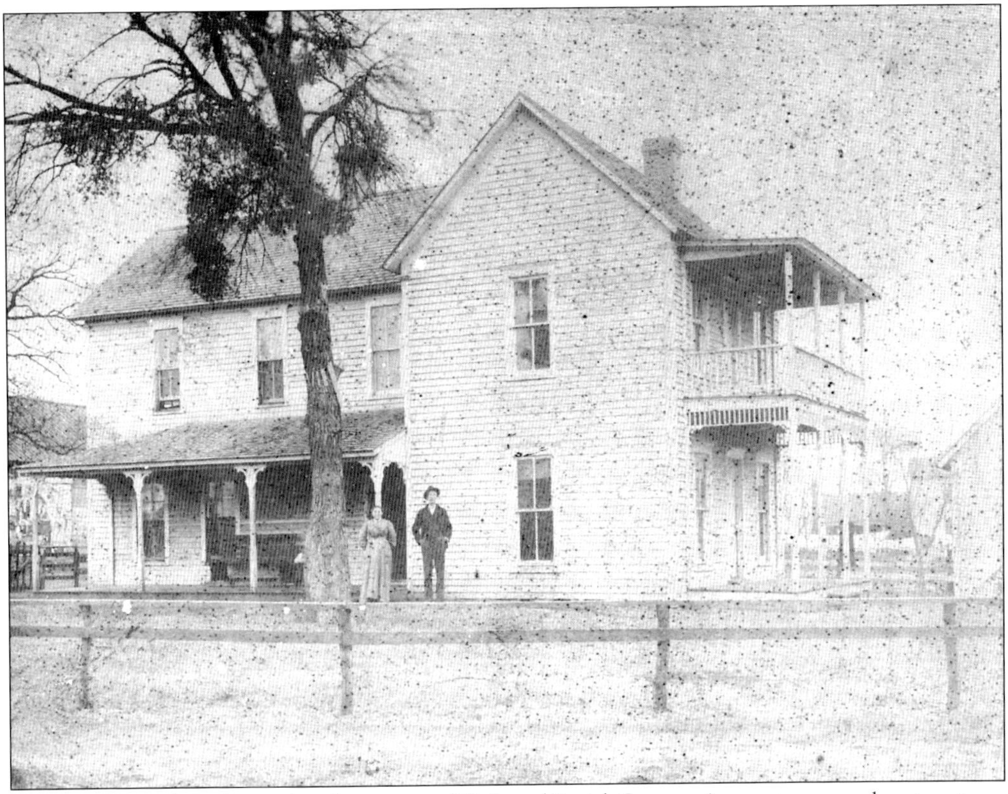

The Hotel Royal was located at the corner of Oak and Smith Streets. A two-story wooden structure, the hotel was enlarged in the early 1900s. The hotel was owned by William Philip Royal, who also served as mayor of Mansfield in 1915–1916. Though the date that the hotel opened is unknown, the hotel was remembered as being considered an older building in town in 1905.

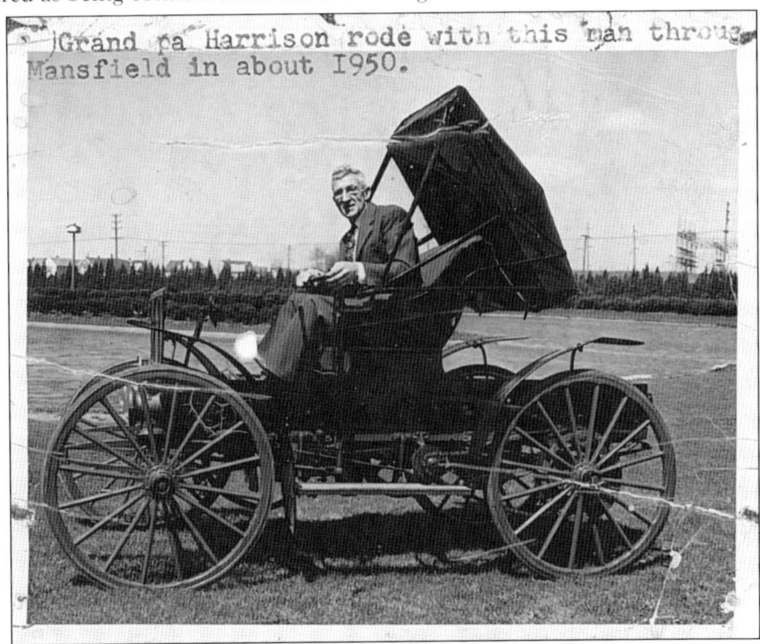

This Sears Roebuck motor buggy was owned by "Grand pa" Harrison, who drove it in Mansfield around 1950. Its previous owner had owned it for 30 years. The motor had been reconditioned once, and it had worn out at least six sets of tires (36-inch wheels covered in solid rubber). At a maximum speed of 30 miles per hour, its five-gallon gas tank could get 15 miles per gallon.

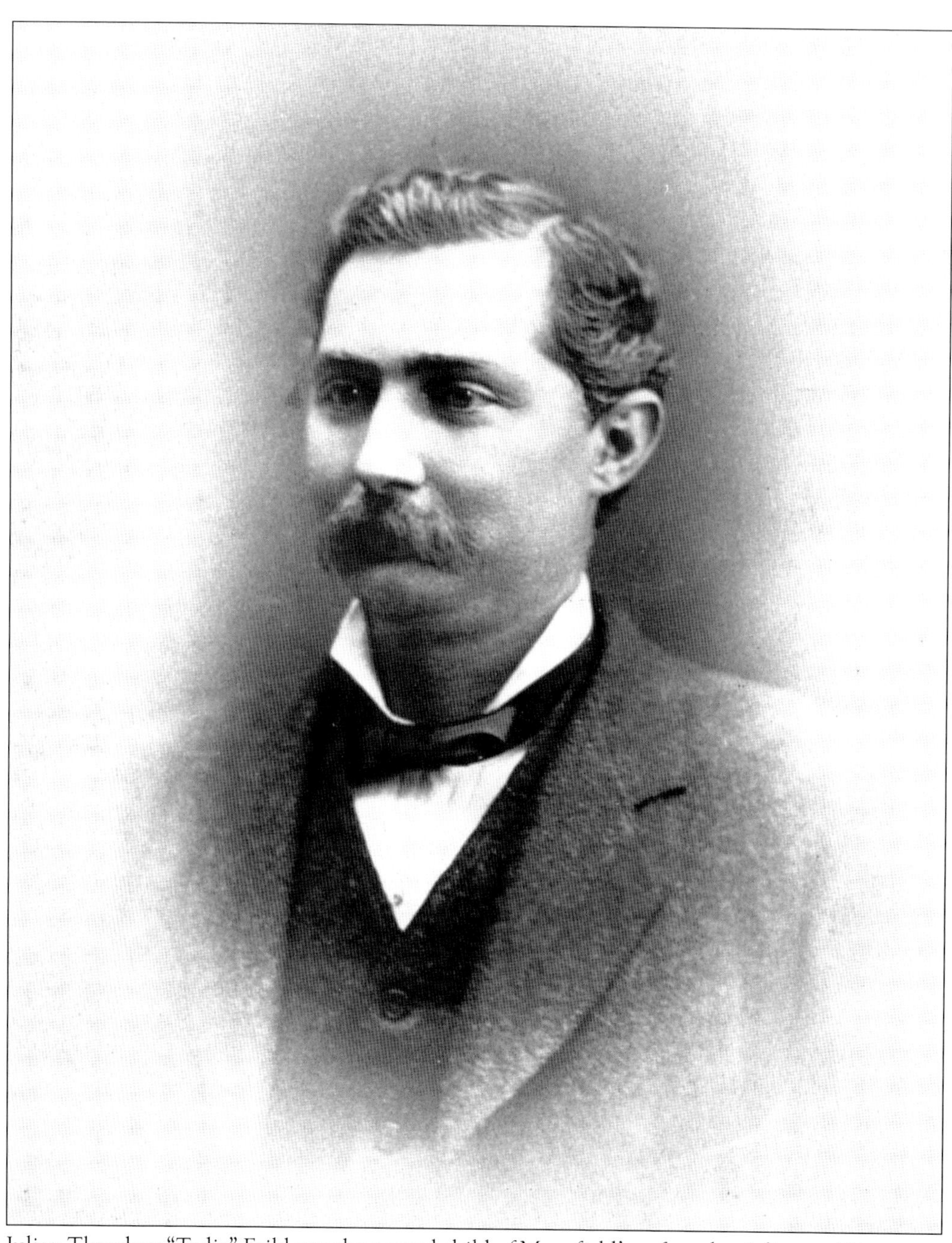

Julian Theodore "Tedie" Feild was the second child of Mansfield's cofounder, Julian and Henrietta Boisseau Feild. As a child, he and his family lived inside the Fort Worth stockade, where he studied under John Peter Smith. After his time in the Confederate army, he attended Louisville Medical College. He married Sarah Melinda Ferguson in Fort Worth, and the couple had four daughters. The family moved to Mansfield so that Dr. Feild could open a medical practice. In 1878, Dr. Feild performed a triple amputation—an arm at the shoulder and two legs below the knees. The patient made a full recovery. Feild was remembered for being a handsome man. He kept his energetic nature all his life, allowing him to appear and sound more youthful well into old age. He loved telling jokes, playing the fiddle, and dancing.

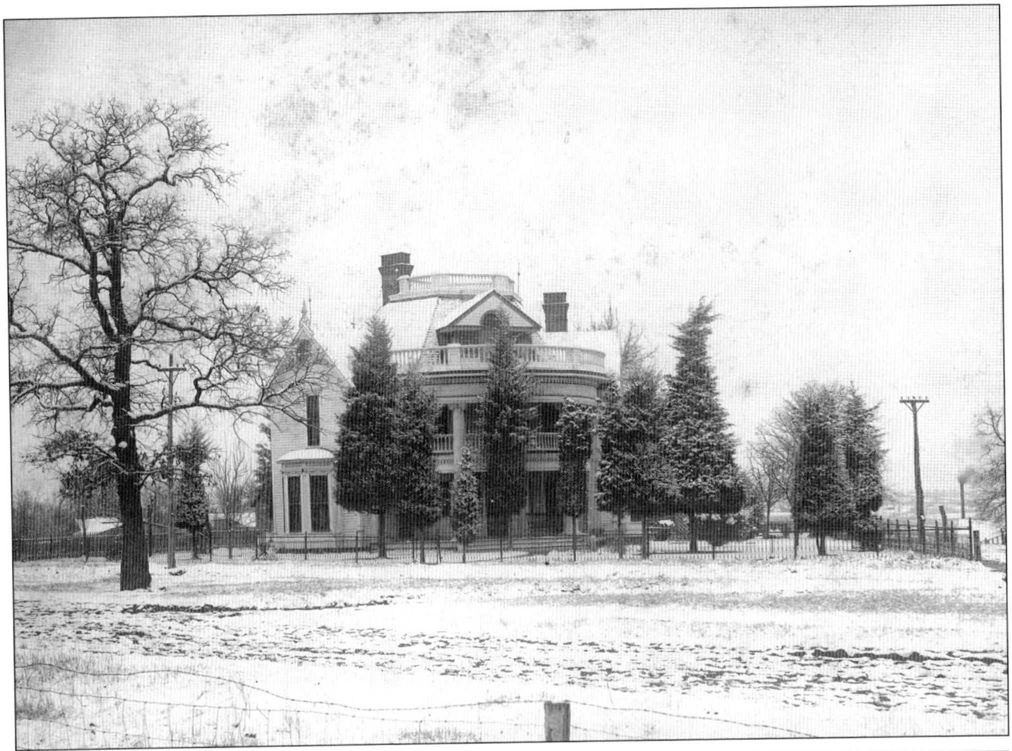

Dr. Julian T. and Sarah Feild built a home on Oak Street. The second owner was Dr. James T. Stephens, the third was Dr. William B. McKnight, and the fourth was A.J. Dukes. Dr. McKnight added the columns and porch after he bought the house. After its demolition in the 1920s, its lumber was used to build three smaller homes on the same site.

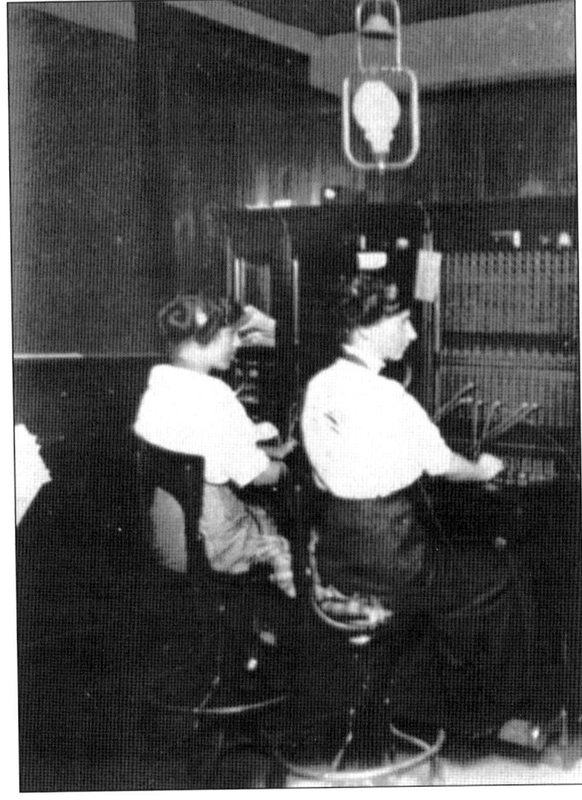

The telephone company was located on the upper floor of the McKnight Building at 102 East Broad Street. Pictured are Myrtle Thomas and Maggie West. Commercial telephones began in the mid-1880s. Back then, thumping a pencil against the phone let the party know you were calling. The transmitter for speaking also served for listening. On October 25, 1917, phones started buzzing at noon. Dial service work began in September 1949.

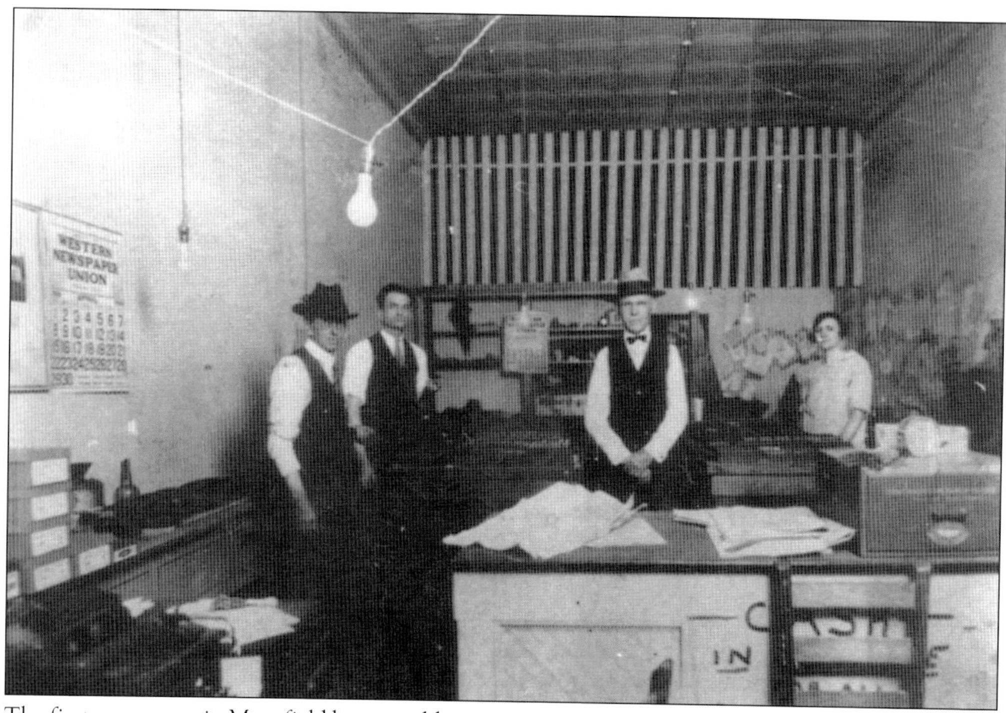

The first newspaper in Mansfield began publication in 1883. It was first called the *Mansfield Chronicle*, and it went by other names over the years, such as the *Tarrant County Banner*, the *Sun*, the *Mansfield Hawkeye*, the *Mansfield Mirror*, and the *Mansfield News*. No issues of these early papers survive; only scattered clippings have been found in family records. The newspaper was set by hand until 1940, when a linotype machine was purchased. In 1960, the *Mansfield News-Mirror* was formed by George Hawkes, and it was published until 2020, when operations ceased. Before its closure, Mansfield had the longest continually operating newspaper in Tarrant County.

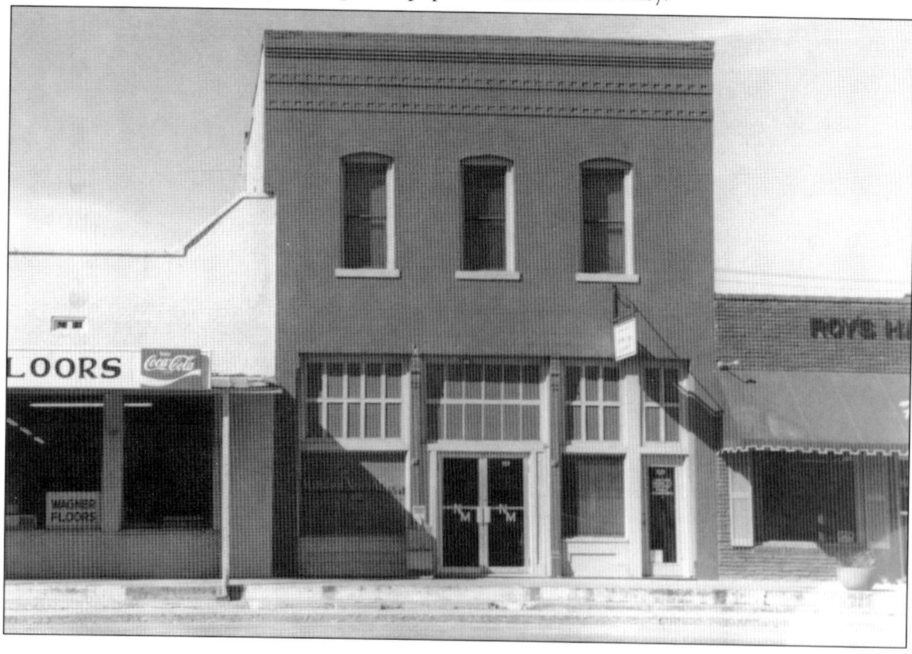

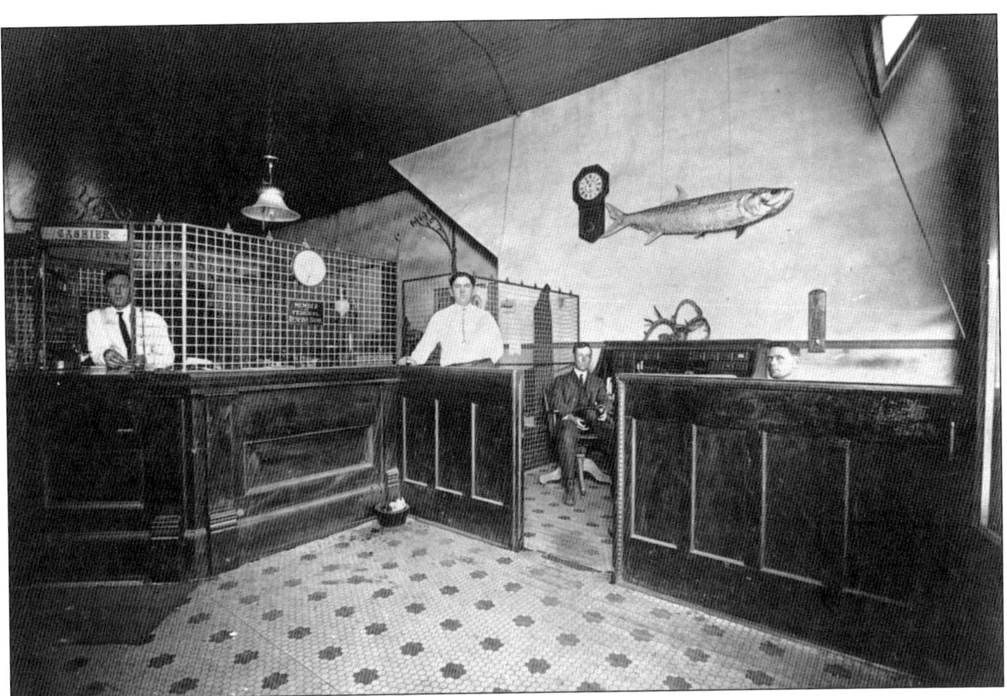

The First National Bank, located on Water Street (now Main Street), was built by Troy Hackler in 1904. Earl Holland, the bank president, stands to the right of the cashier, Frank Mayfield. George Hackler is seated to his right. The tarpon mounted on the wall was caught by Martha Dukes.

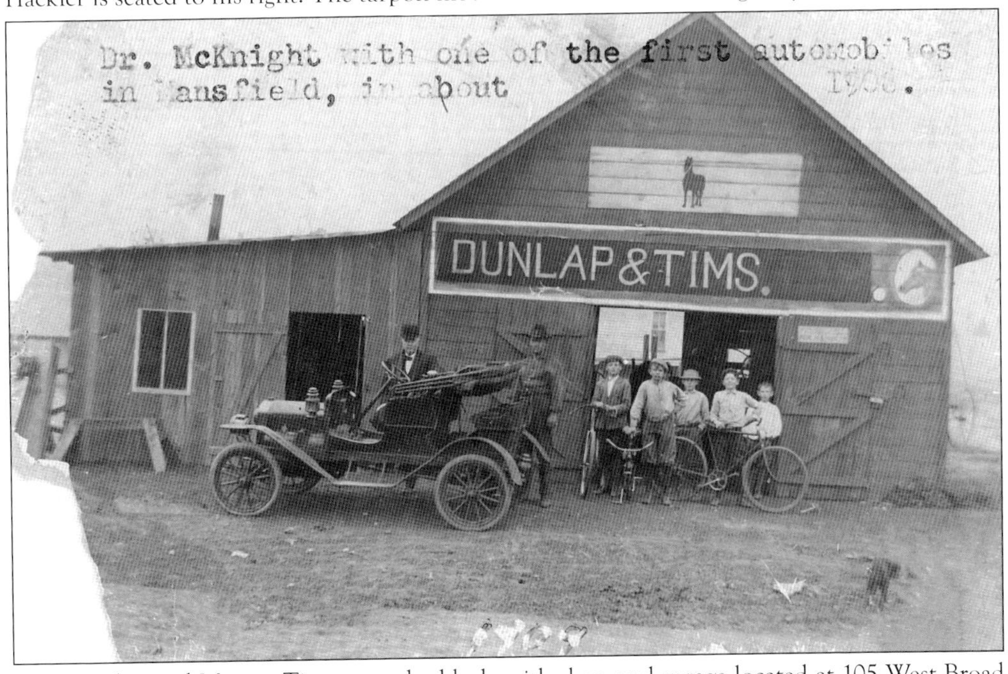

Rice Dunlap and Marcus Tims owned a blacksmith shop and garage located at 105 West Broad Street. This image shows Dr. W.B. McKnight, who had one of the first cars in Mansfield. Also pictured is Neily McCaleb and friends. The shop opened in 1860, and the building remained on West Broad Street until June 2015.

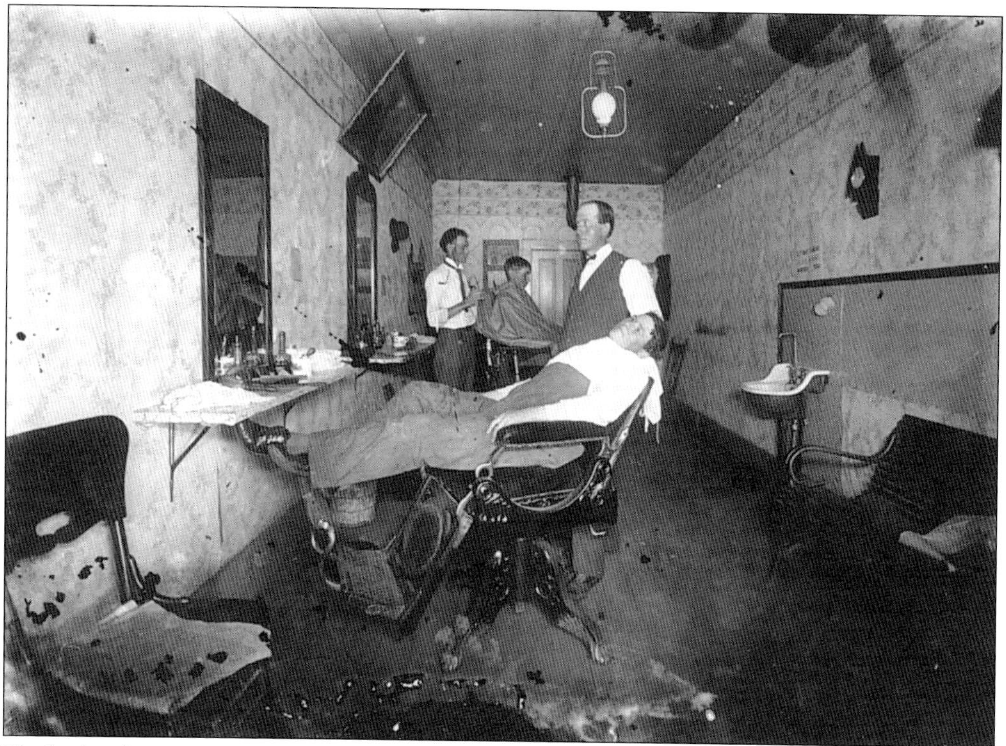

The barbershop at 127 North Main Street was owned by E.A. "Hatch" Rosier for 45 years. Pictured in the first chair is Rosier, with Herman Colp in the second chair and Coleman lamps in the background. The cardboard squares above the chairs were fastened together by a cord and spring, built to be pulled by cord to make the boards sway, which served as a fan and kept flies away.

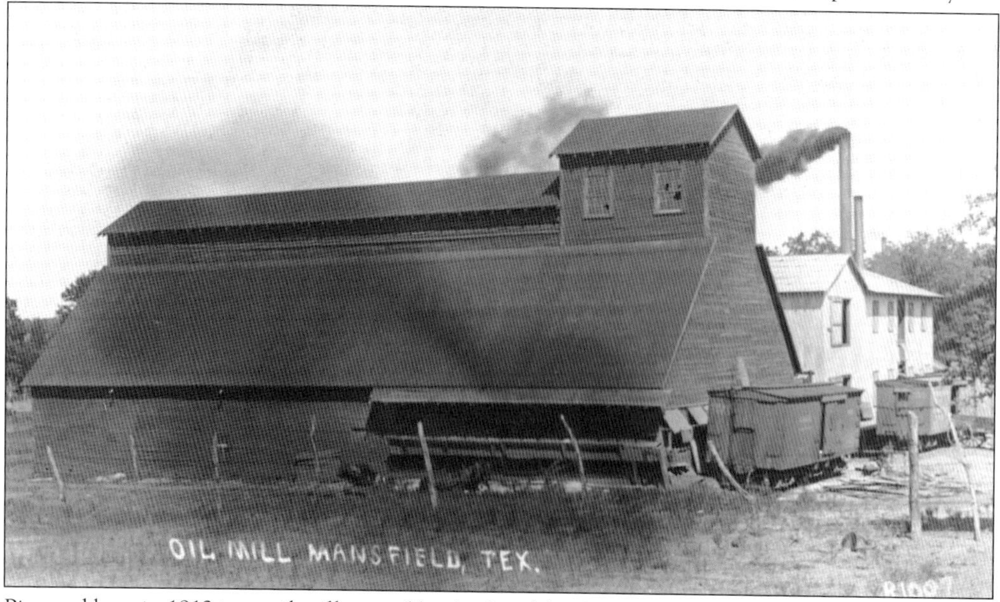

Pictured here in 1912 is an oil mill owned by the Southland Cotton Oil Company. The mill crushed cottonseed to create oil. Later, the mill expanded to make peanut oil as well. The mill was located west of Cardinal Road (now North Street) near one of the town's cotton gins.

William B. McKnight was born in Texas and spent most of his life there. His father, William D. McKnight, died early in the Civil War, and his mother, Mary Susan Wynne McKnight, moved her five sons and one daughter to Johnson Station, between Mansfield and Arlington. Dr. McKnight attended Mansfield Male and Female College and began his first practice in Springtown, Texas. He married Sallie Hodges, daughter of Mansfield's first doctor, and pursued postgraduate work at Bellevue Medical Hospital in New York. She called him home when a diphtheria epidemic broke out, and both cared for the sick until the danger passed. They had five children. Dr. McKnight was a founder of the Mansfield Academy, which took the place of the Mansfield Male and Female College. He contributed to his community until his death at 99 years old.

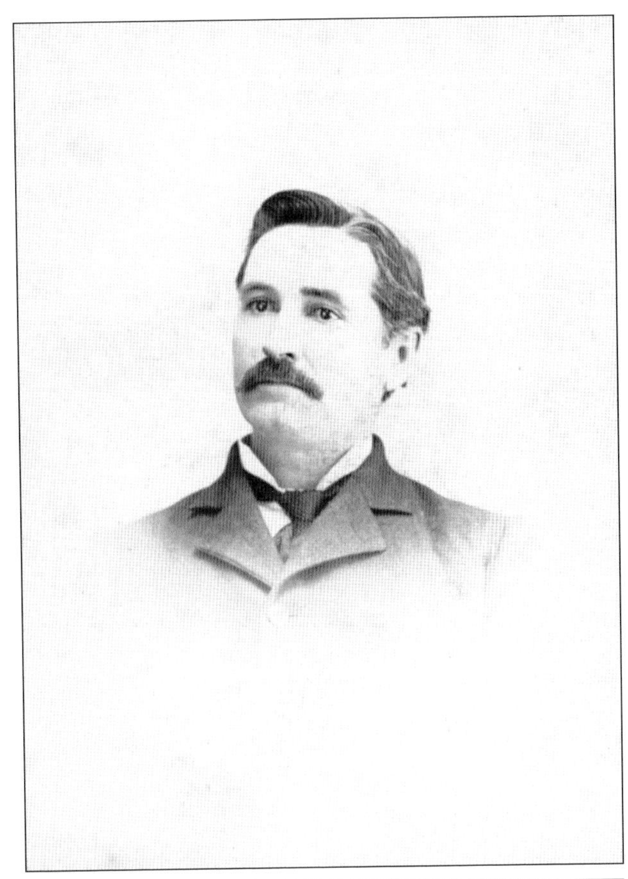

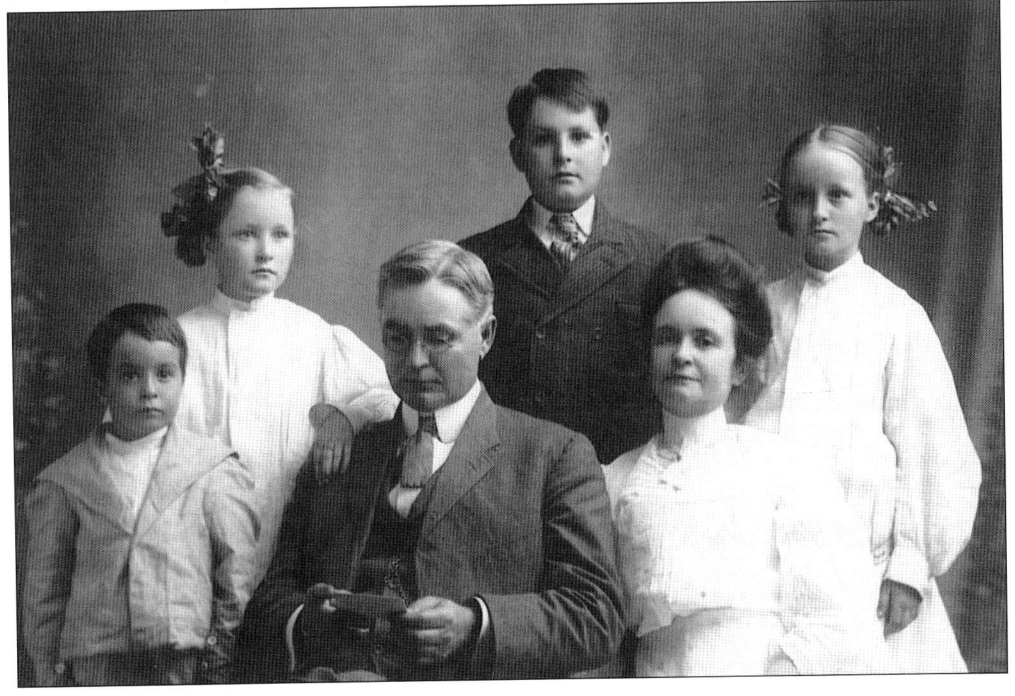

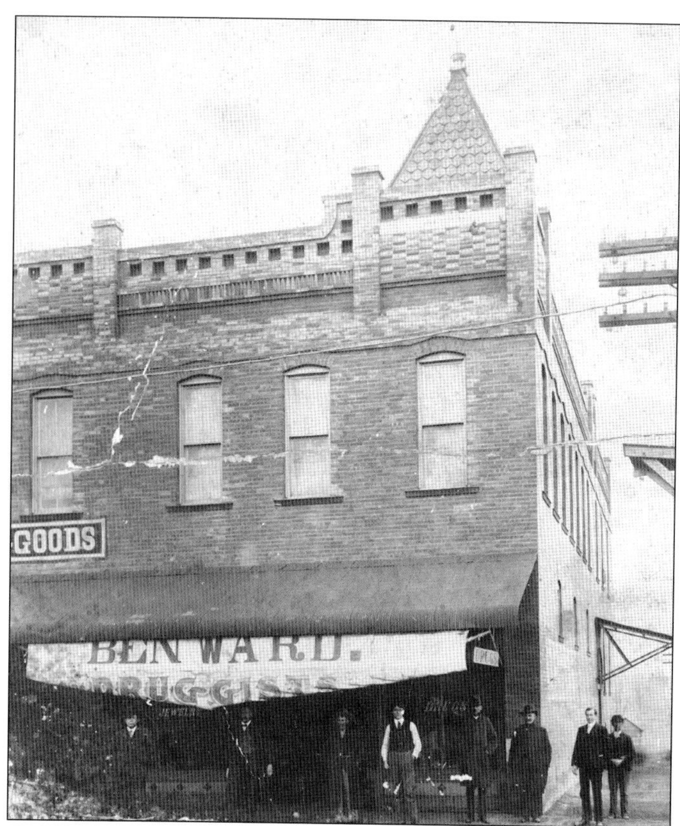

This building, owned by Dr. William B. McKnight, was constructed in 1895 at 102 North Main Street. In its earliest years, Dr. McKnight's office was located on the mezzanine level of the building. The first floor was the Ben Ward Drug Store. The top floor was the meeting hall for the Knights of Pythias, a fraternal organization.

The Bratton Furniture Company was owned by Andrew "Cap" Bratton. The business was located at 134 North Main Street in downtown Mansfield. In addition to selling furniture, Bratton made coffins and ran a funeral business in the back of his shop. This early-1900s photograph shows Bratton (right) standing in his store.

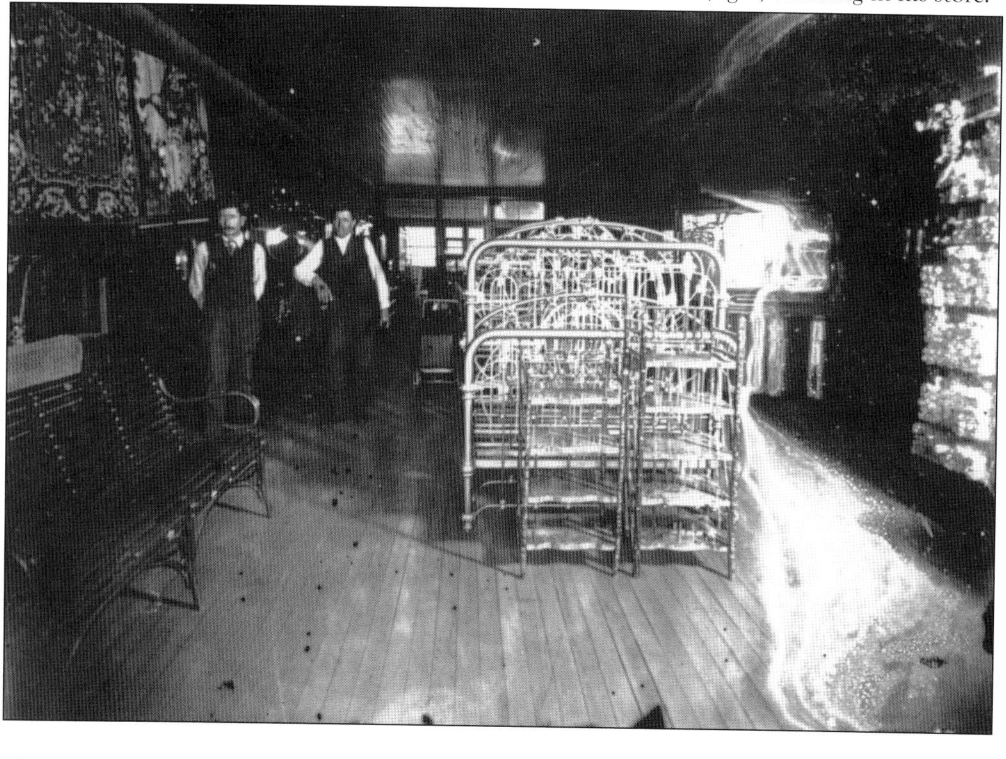

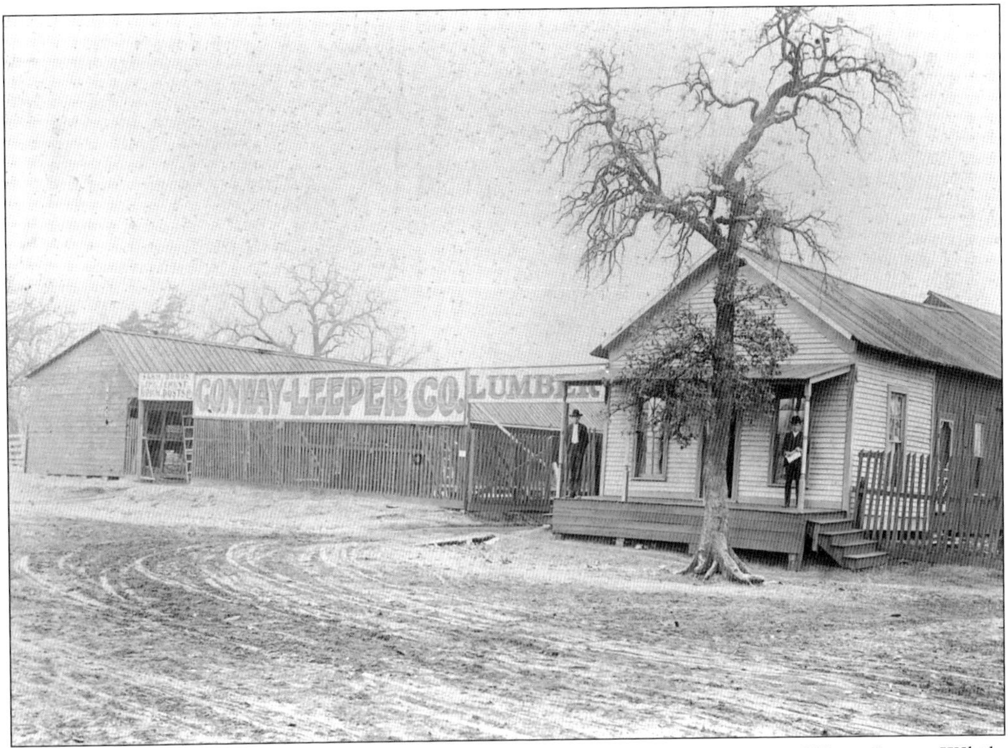

The Conway-Leeper Lumber Company was located on North Oak Street near Water Street. While it was owned primarily by a Mr. Conway and a Mr. Leeper, other individuals were part owners of the enterprise. Stockholders recalled that the lumberyard paid 10 percent to investors through most of the Great Depression. In 1934, the operation moved to Walnut Street to make way for the northern expansion of what is now North Main Street.

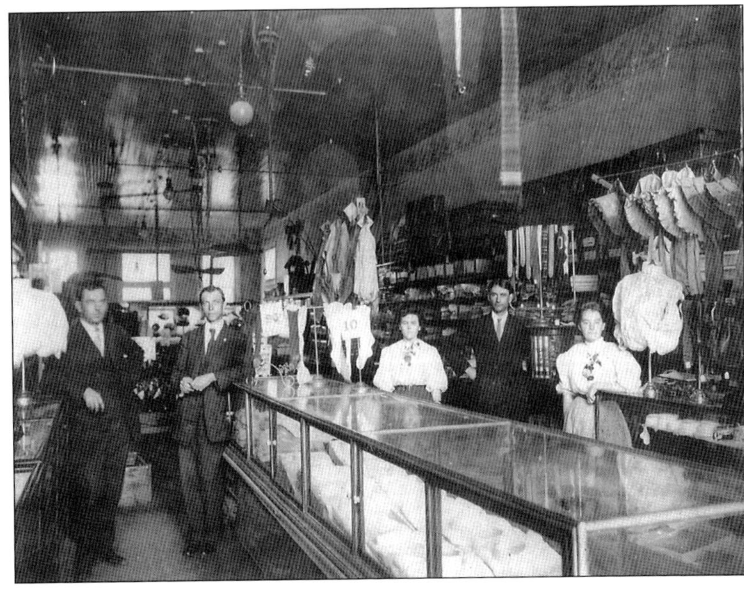

Monnig's Ready-to-Wear was located at 104 Water Street (now Main Street). The shop sold all kinds of clothing items. The ladies behind the counter are Edna Mae Erwin and Marie Erwin. One of the men is Paul Monnig, who owned the store. Monnig married Edna Mae in 1907. In 1911, they sold the store and moved to Fort Worth, where they opened new locations.

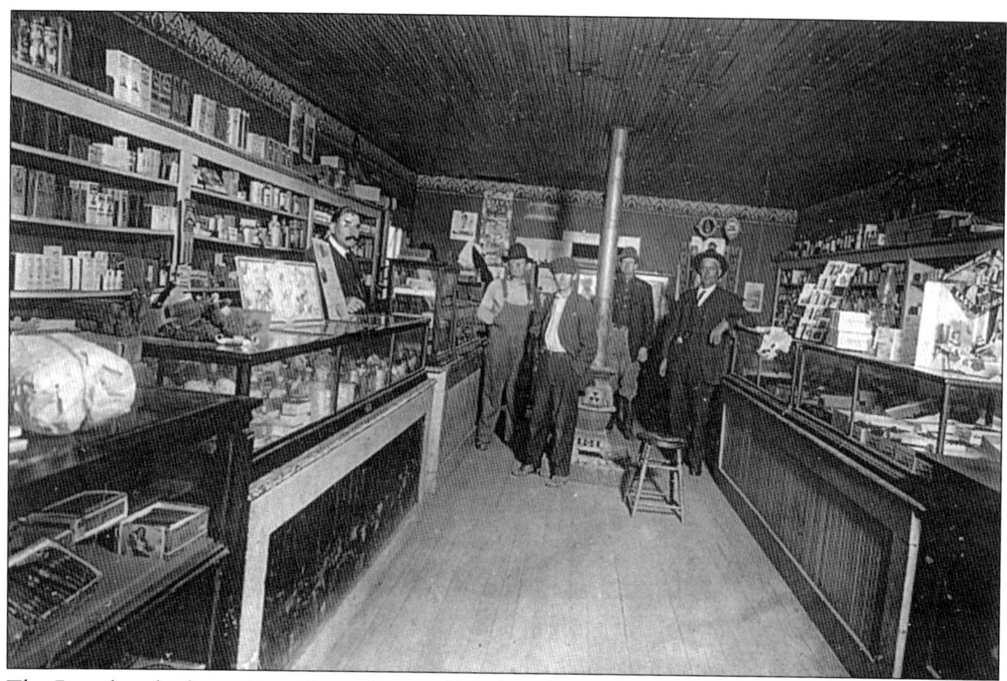

The Board and Chorn Drug Store, later called the Chorn and Mayfield Drug Store, was the hub of downtown activity in the 1920s and 1930s. Located at 126 North Main Street, the store had a popular soda fountain, and the building had a doctor's office behind the shop. The picture above was taken in 1898, when the shop was called the Board and Chorn Drug Store. The photograph below was taken in the Chorn and Mayfield Drug Store around 1946. Pictured are, from left to right, Mary Meeks, Arthur "Bulldog" Curry, Oscar Lynch, the proprietor James Chorn, and the unidentified Coca-Cola deliveryman.

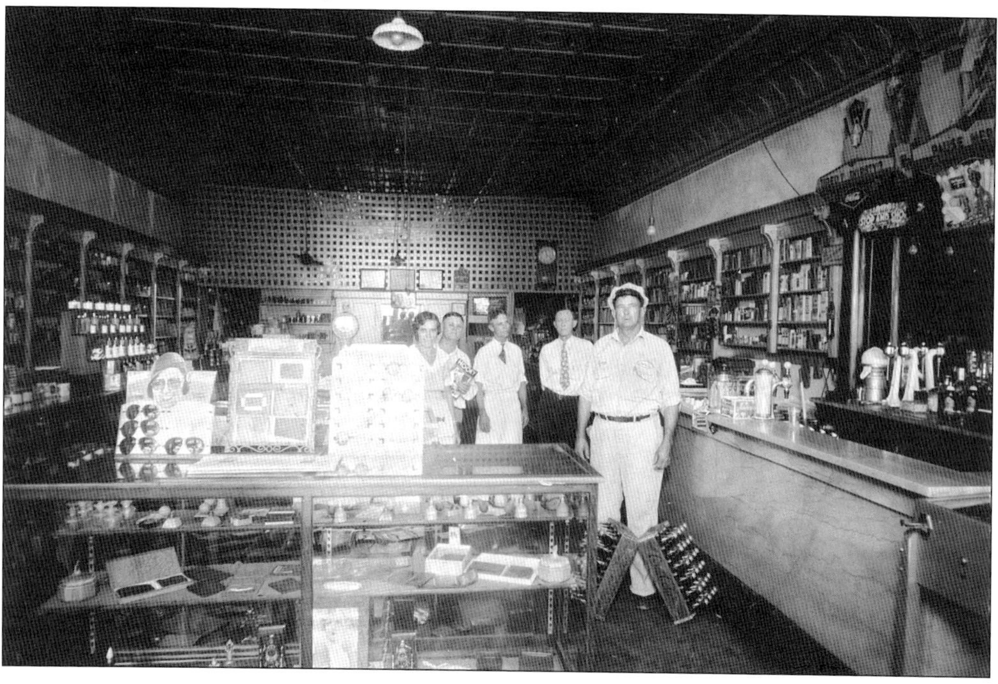

Dr. John Neal Thomas studied at Vanderbilt Medical College in Tennessee and at Tulane in New Orleans. He began his medical career in two eras, the horse and buggy days and the motorized period. He purchased his first automobile, a red, two-cylinder roadster, in 1910. It soon became one of the best-known cars in the area. Dr. Thomas is pictured here with his wife, Alice, and son, Dr. Raymond Thomas.

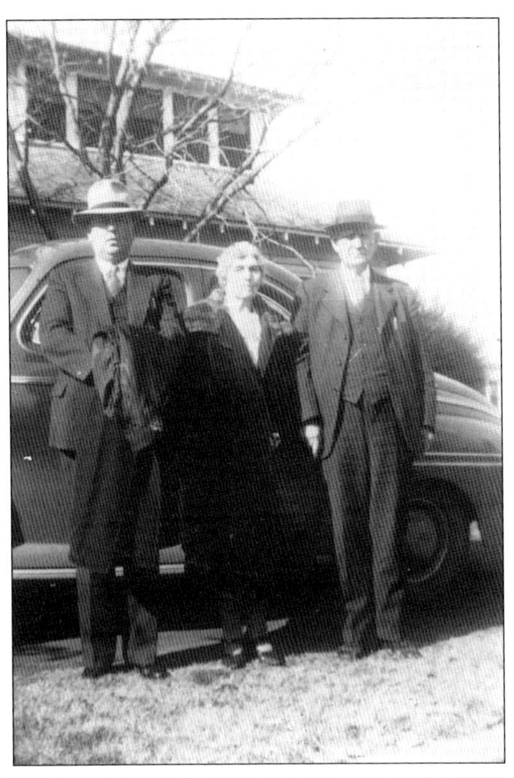

Dr. Raymond Thomas, the son of Dr. John Neal and Alice Thornton Thomas, was born in Mansfield. His education included Texas Christian University in Fort Worth and Baylor Medical College and Parkland Hospital, both in Dallas. Dr. Thomas joined his father's practice after completing his education and is remembered as a true country doctor. He supported Mansfield in other ways, too, serving on the school board, including a term as president.

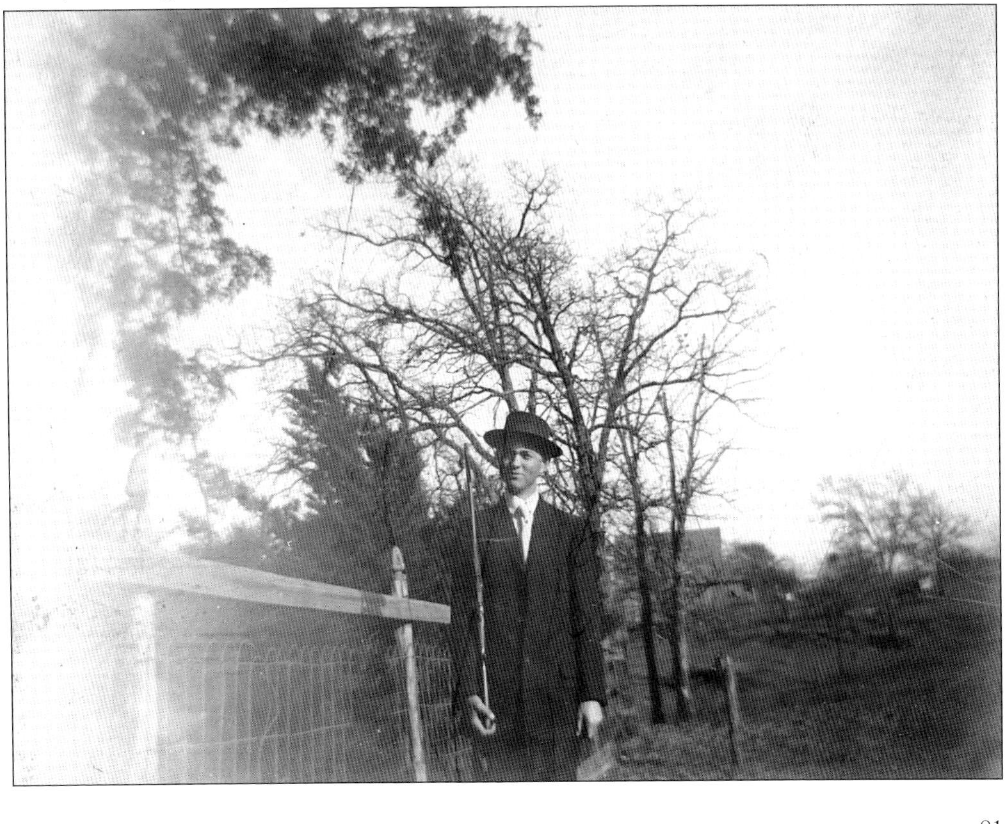

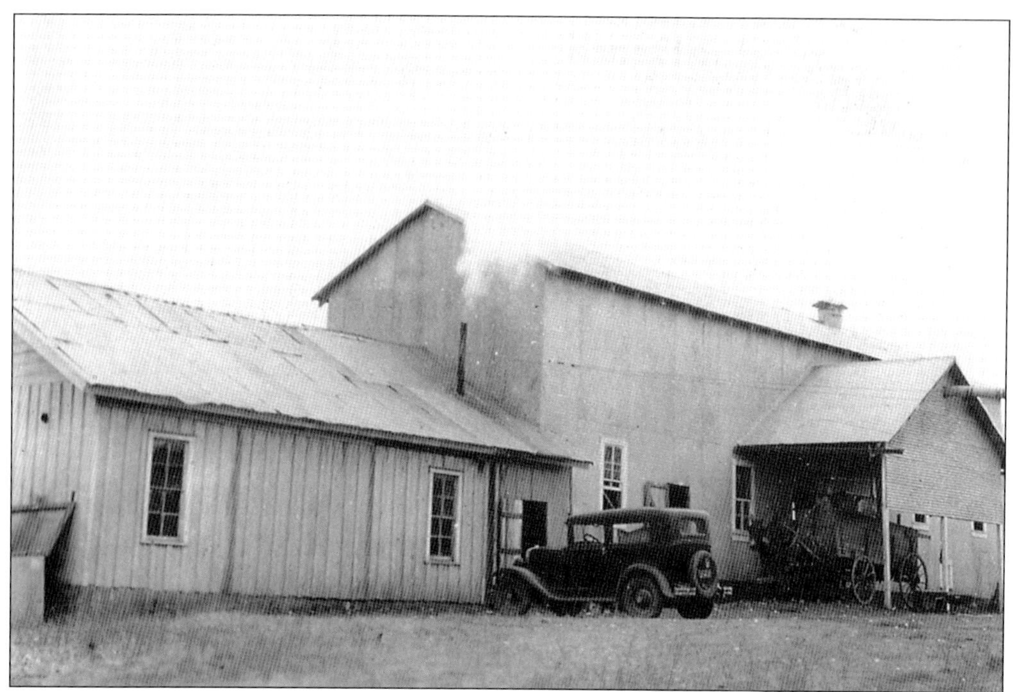

This cotton gin was located at the intersection of Dallas and Pond Streets. The picture shows a wagon parked in the entry where a large suction pipe was used to pull the cotton up from the wagon into the ginning cycle. One wagon load produced one finished bale, averaging 400 pounds. In peak season, the men would work 24 hours a day to turn out 30 to 40 bales daily.

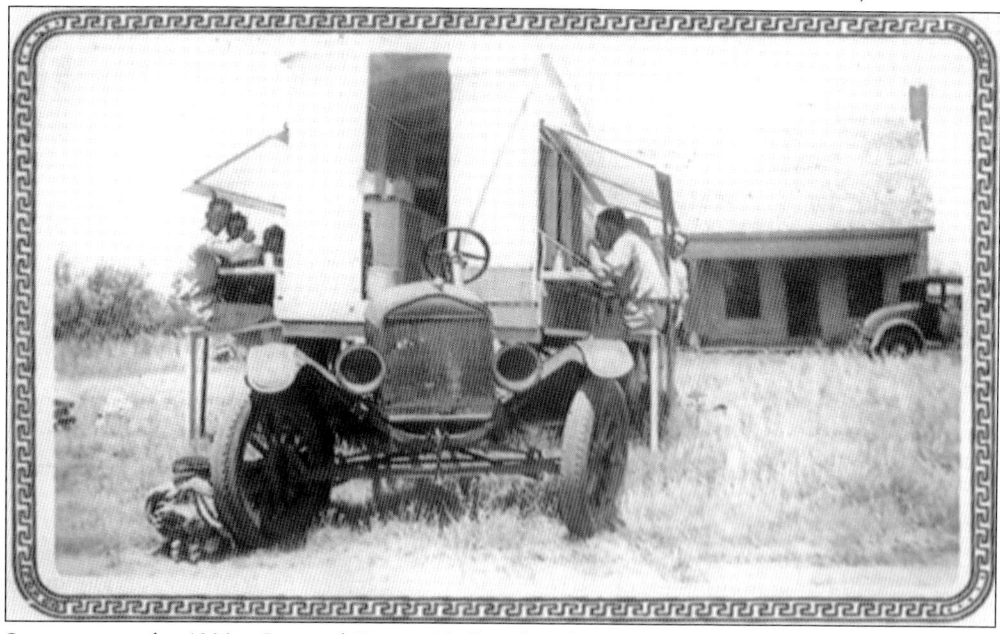

Sometime in the 1930s, Osmond Dewitt Phillips bought a threshing machine, which moved to different locations to thresh people's grain. Along with the thresher was this cook shack, which provided three meals a day to workers. Two of the sides of the cook shack folded down to make a table and bench for seating.

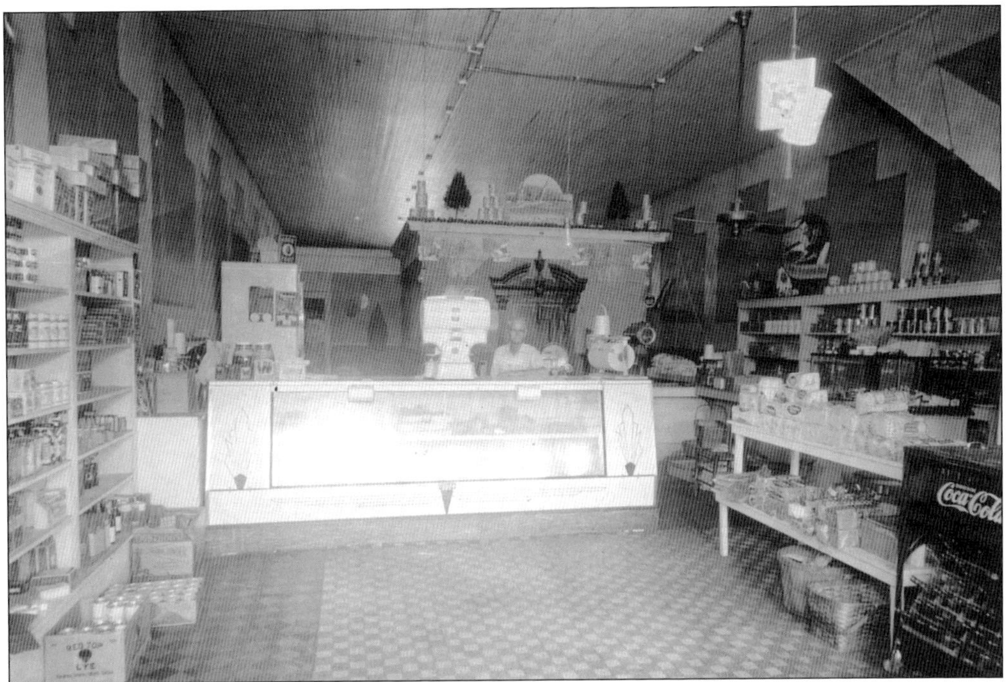

Albert Gibson and his wife, Ethel, opened Gibson Grocery in the old First National Bank building in 1934 (pictured above). Their son Ira Gibson joined the business after serving in World War II. On July 31, 1947, a fire started in the Farmers Lumber yard, which spread and destroyed Gibson Grocery. The store was rebuilt and later moved across the street to 124 North Main Street (pictured below). Albert passed away in 1958, but Ira operated the store until 1973. For nearly 40 years, Mansfield residents could buy their groceries for everyday meals and holiday feasts alike in Gibson's store. Pictured below are, from left to right, (first row) Michael Gibson; (second row) Ethel Gibson, Ira Gibson, Grady Hogan, and Red Vincent.

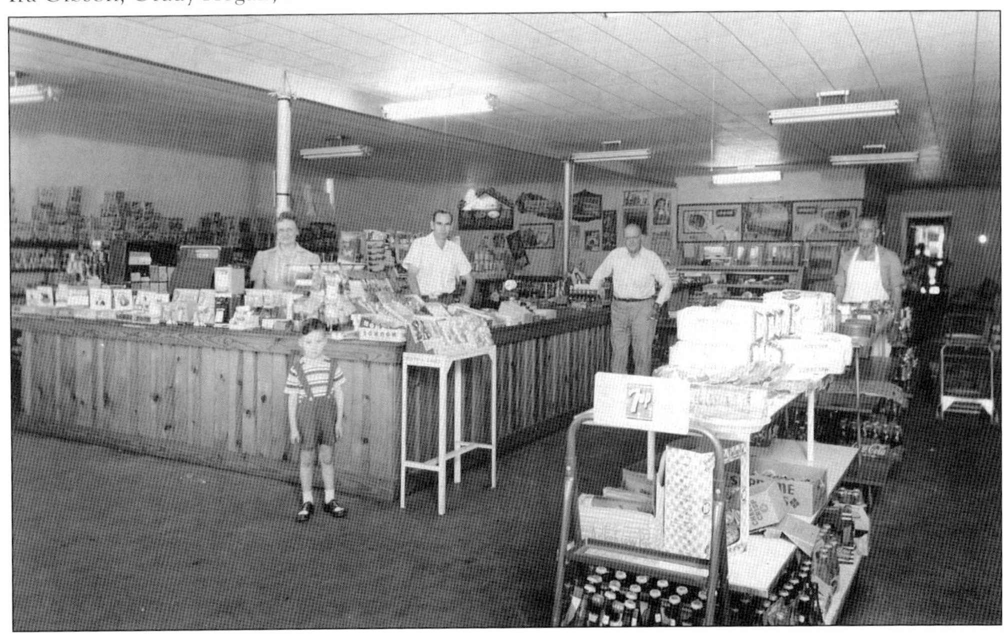

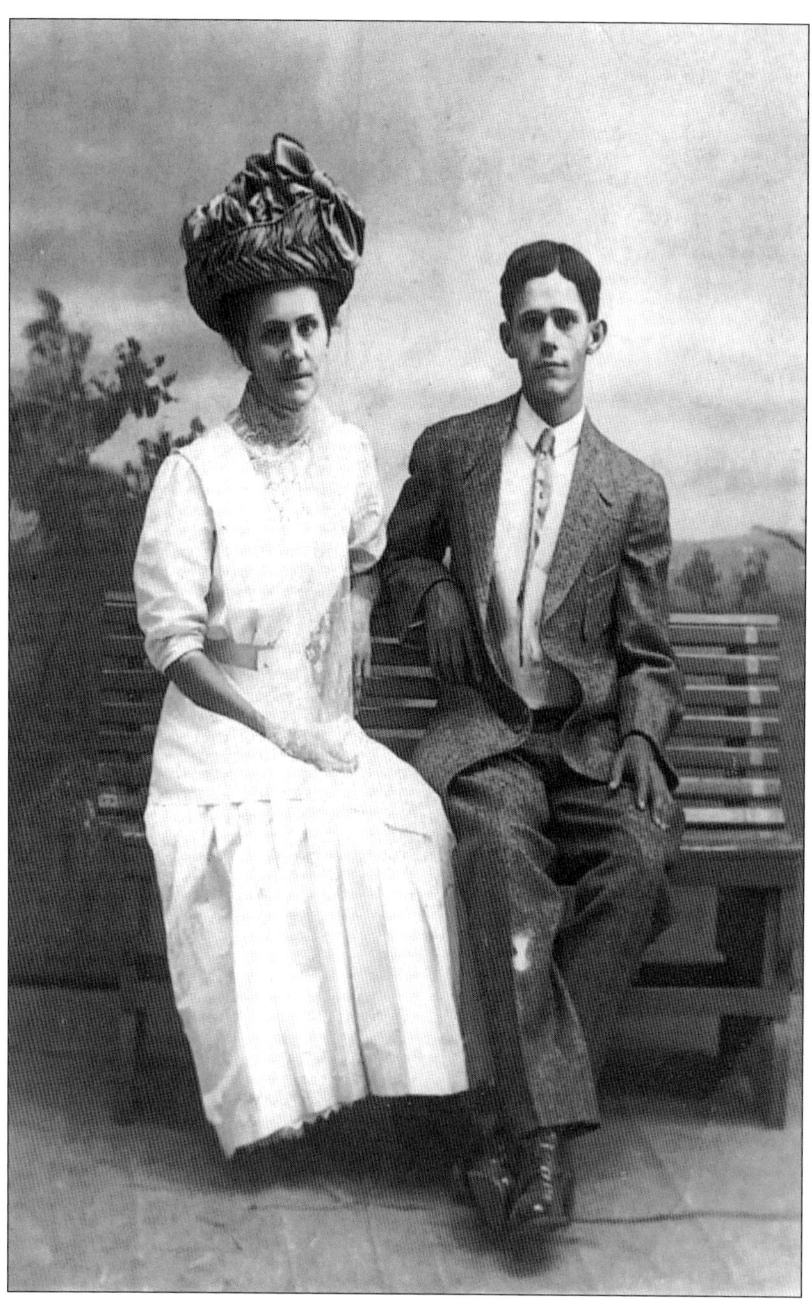

In 1926, Mildred Dalton baked pies in her kitchen in Mansfield for her husband, Jesse, to sell in his Fort Worth grocery store. She frequently used egg whites to make meringue topping for her pies. Because of this, she had leftover egg yolks. So, she used the yolks to make a sandwich spread to sell as well. The spread contained pickle relish. The pickles needed for the spread were not always readily available, which led the family to begin a pickle processing operation. This kitchen operation became Best Maid, a nationwide company still famous for its pickles. The Dalton family had owned land in Mansfield since the 1860s, and the land, including the site of the family home, became a tank farm where the pickles were processed. The tank farm is still in production today. Photographed here are Mildred and Jesse Dalton.

Dr. Harry Nifong graduated from Fort Worth Medical College in 1904 and began his practice in Britton, Texas. He was accepted into the Medical Corps in 1917 and received orders for overseas duty during World War I. Stationed in Toul, France, his hospital treated soldiers who had been gassed. Later, during his long medical career in Mansfield, Dr. Nifong delivered over 3,000 babies and was active in the community.

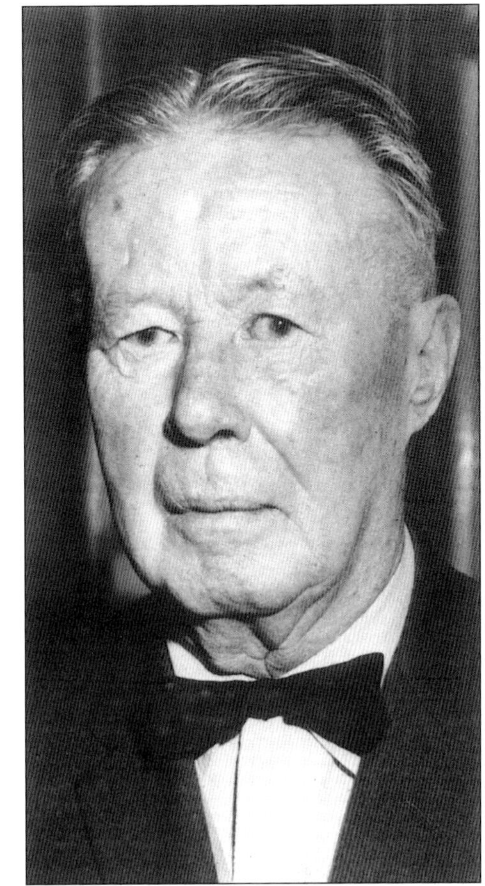

The Hopson Hotel was located near downtown Mansfield on the corner of Walnut and Broad Streets. The property changed names twice, once in 1886 to the Wallace Hotel and again in 1890 to the Mansfield House. John Hopson took ownership in 1890 and, when he died, it transferred to his wife, Telithia Back Hopson. The family deeded the property to W.J.C. Burus in 1908. The building burned down around 1919.

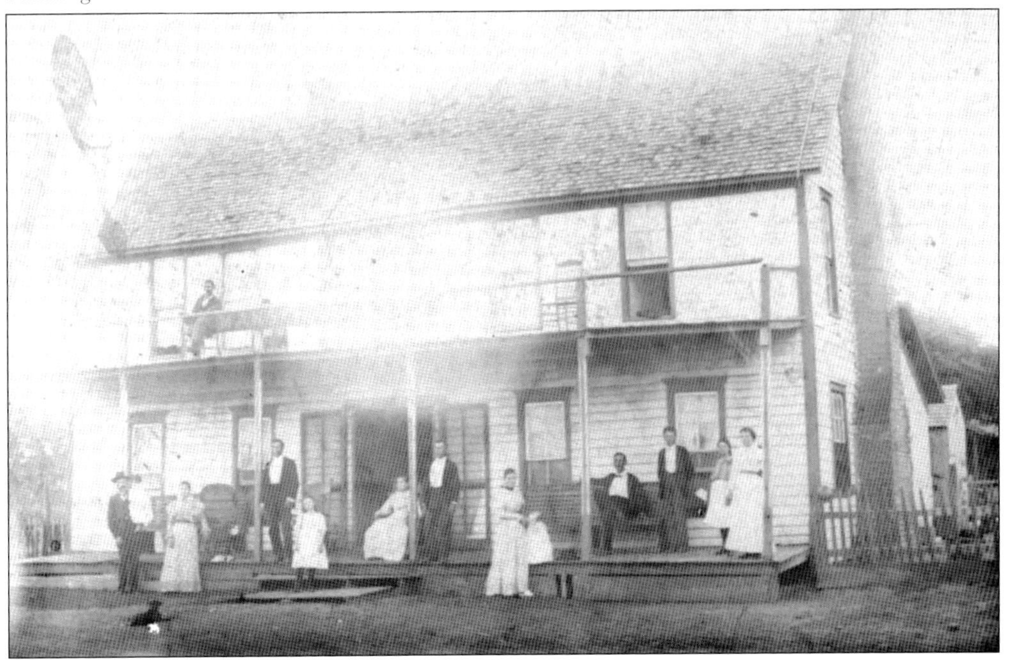

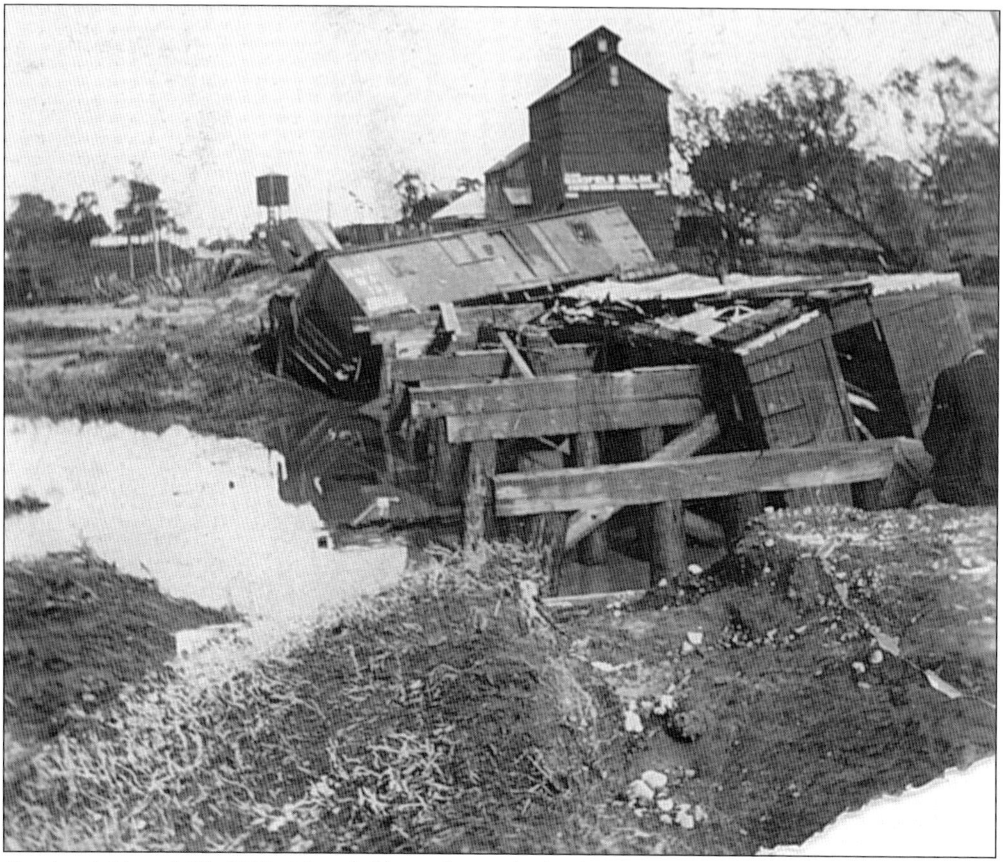

On April 24 and 25, 1922, Mansfield was hit with the largest rainfall in its history. With more than eight inches of rain falling, Walnut Creek was pushed out of its bank. Many local businesses, including the Mansfield Gin, the peanut mill, the railroad pump house, and the water tower, were either damaged or destroyed. Homes along the creek were also flooded. The pictured iron truss bridge near North Street remained undamaged. The boxcars in the foreground were where many laborers were living. The cars were pushed off the track and washed away in the floodwaters, resulting in the drowning of some of the laborers. The flood of 1922 was the deadliest natural disaster in the town's history.

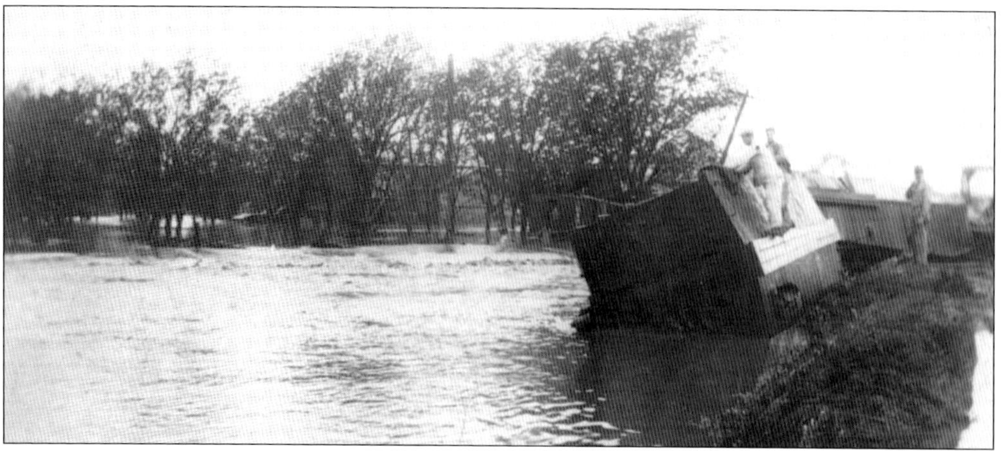

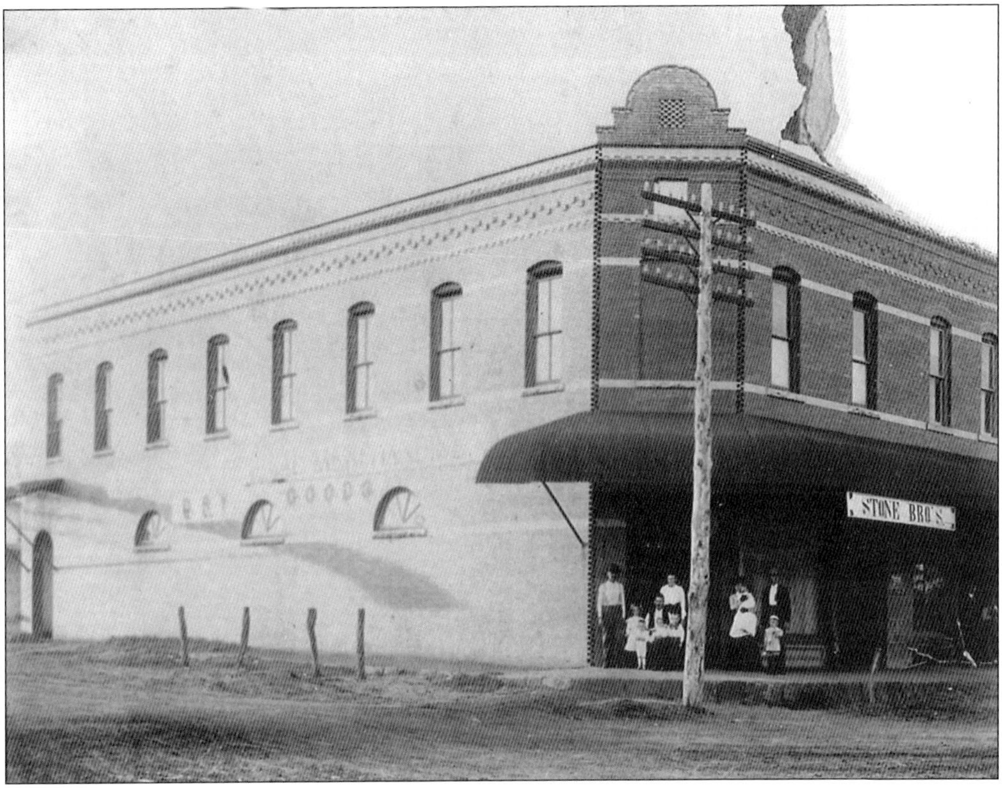

In 1904, James Clay and Albert Stone operated their mercantile store on the first floor of the Masonic Building located at 101 North Main Street after the Masonic lodge moved to the second floor. They called the shop Stone Brothers Dry Goods Store until 1906, when they decided to trade the store to the Smith family in exchange for land and cattle.

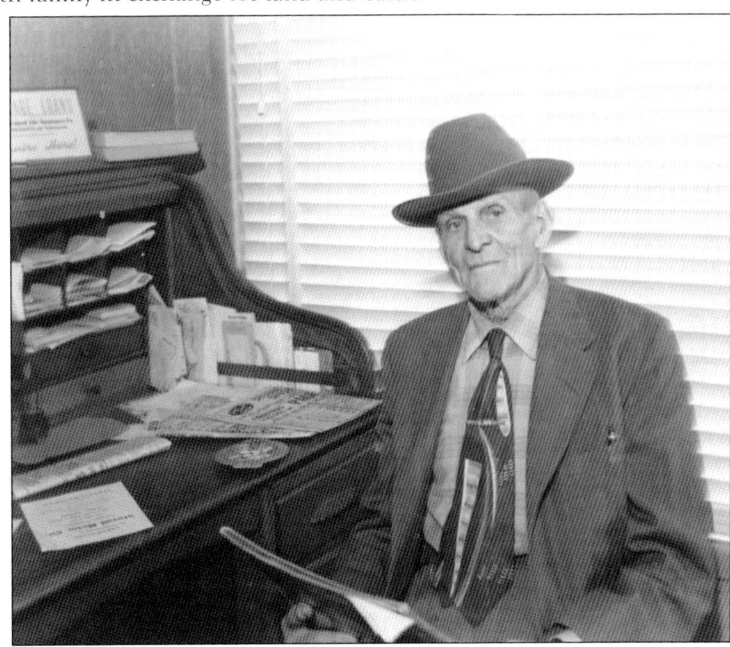

James W. Allmon practiced veterinary medicine from 1908 until 1960. He received his training through an extended education course in his native Tennessee. He settled in Mansfield because there was no veterinarian for miles. Dr. Allmon made rounds with a horse and buggy until 1912, when he bought a car. In the beginning, he treated mainly cows and horses. As people could afford it, his practice expanded to include pets.

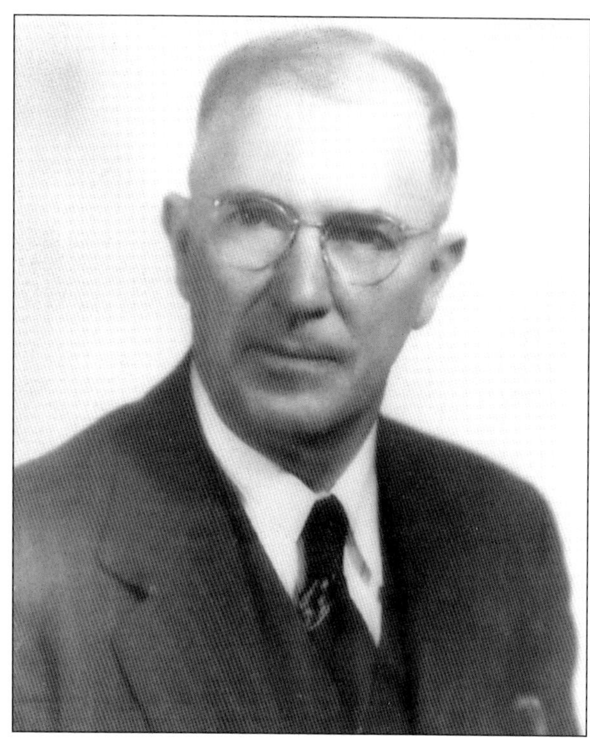

Thomas Ernst Blessing began operating the Blessing Funeral Home in 1920 in his furniture store on Water Street. In 1944, Thomas and his wife, Hattie Blessing, purchased the home of Dr. William McKnight on Elm Street. The home had been built by John Collier for use at the Mansfield Male and Female College. The Blessings, pictured, both received their funeral director's licenses in September 1935. Thomas Ernst Blessing worked for his uncle, Thomas Bratton, in his funeral home before taking over the family business. Hattie Blessing is believed to be one of the first female embalmers in the state of Texas. They ran the funeral home for 54 years before selling the business, which is still in operation today.

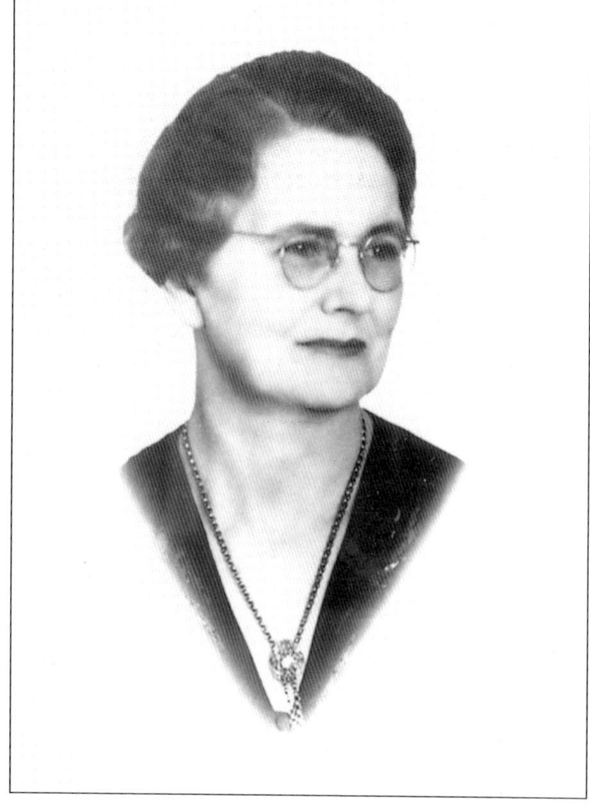

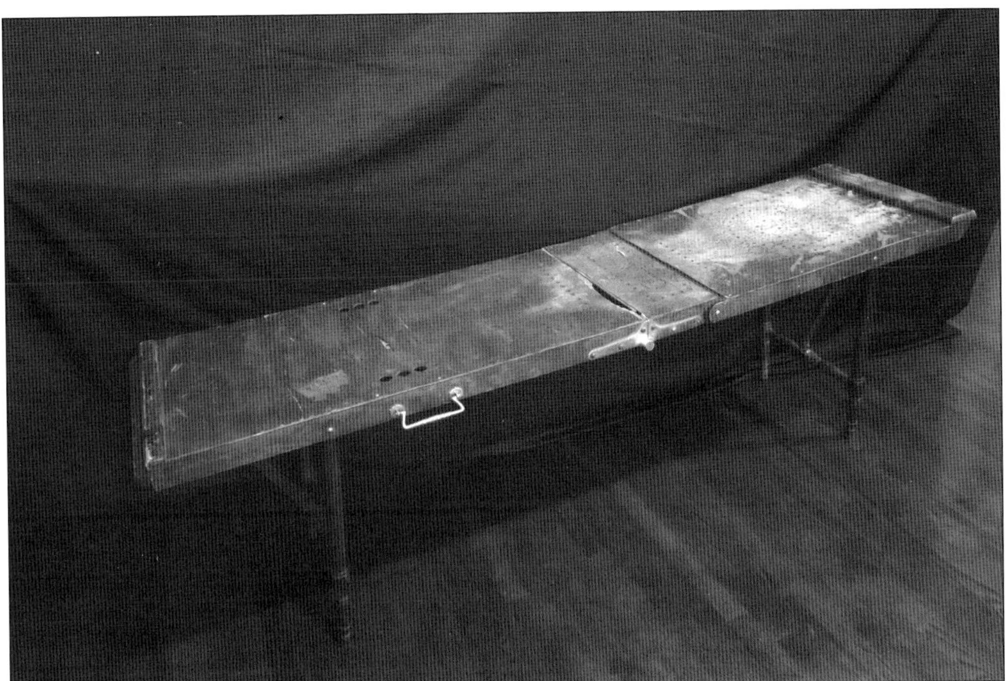

A remnant of days gone by, this cooling table belonged to the Blessing Funeral Home. Its primary use by the funeral home would be to keep a body cool while preparing it for burial or displaying the remains for a wake. Ice was placed beneath the table in order to slow the decomposition of the deceased. (Bill Thomas.)

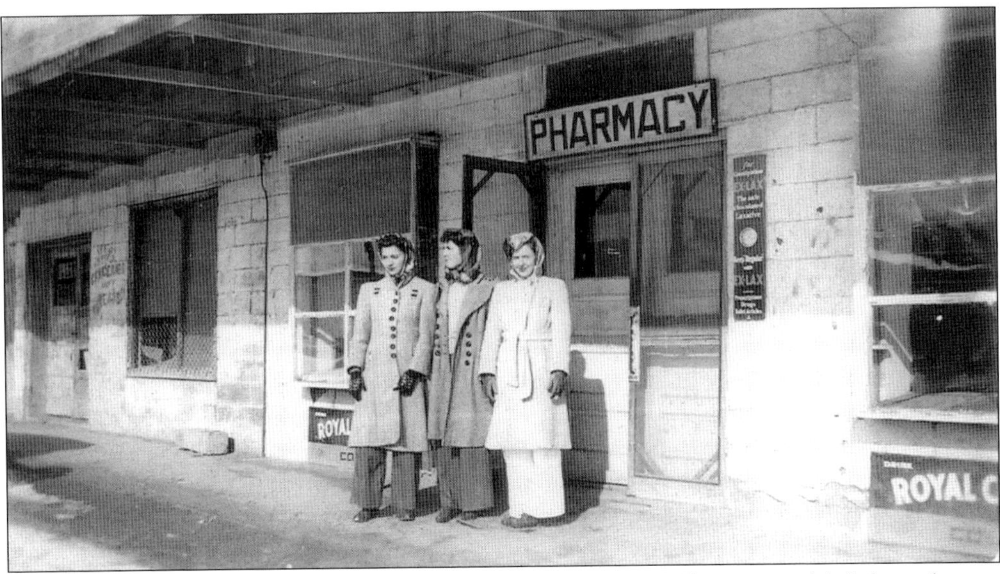

Phillips Pharmacy in Britton, Texas, was owned by Emma Sue Phillips Womack's father, who was the pharmacist. It had an old-fashioned soda fountain with small tables and wire-backed chairs. Later, it became a grocery store. Pictured in front of the pharmacy are, from left to right, Faye Louise Wilson Wynn, Emma Sue Phillips Womack, and Dorothy Helen Wilson Howell. This photograph is dated 1941.

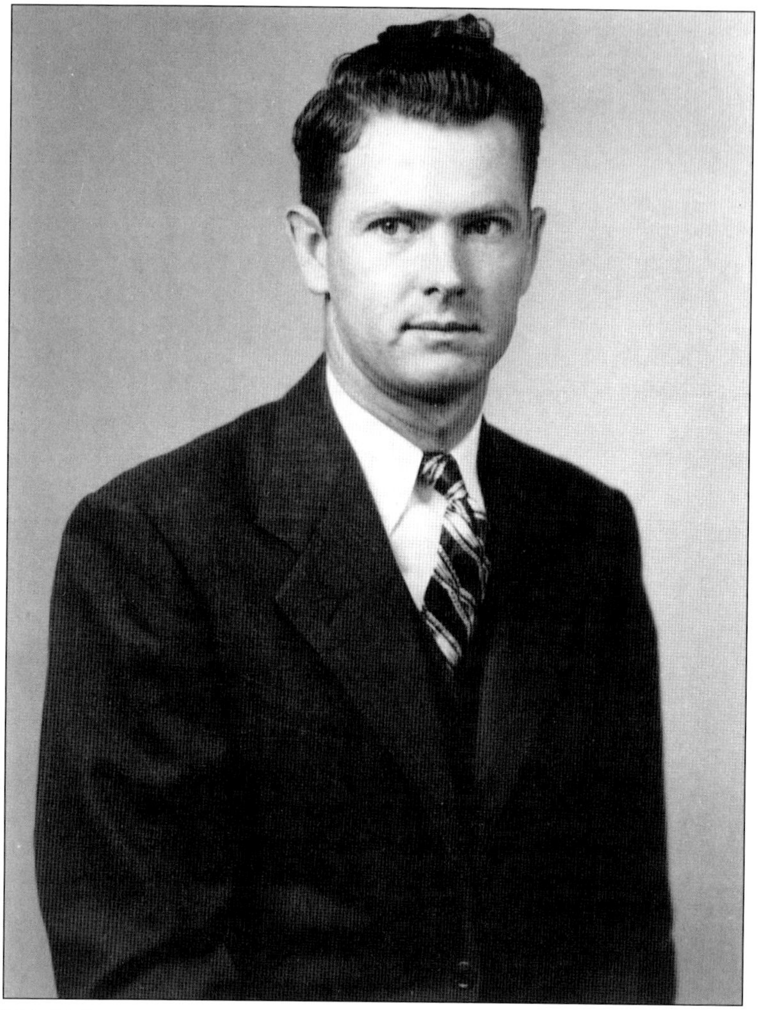

A native-born Texan, Dr. Percy Cook lived in Eustace, Texas, until he served in World War II. After the war, he studied medicine at Baylor University, among others, and upon completion of his medical internship at John Peter Smith Hospital in Fort Worth, he took over the practice of Dr. Raymond Thomas in Mansfield. He practiced in this community for many years and was one of the people responsible for opening the first hospital in town. Cedars Hospital opened in 1959. The facility had 27 beds and had an X-ray laboratory, operating room, and delivery room. Dr. Cook retired in 1987. (Below, Carol Cook Cooper.)

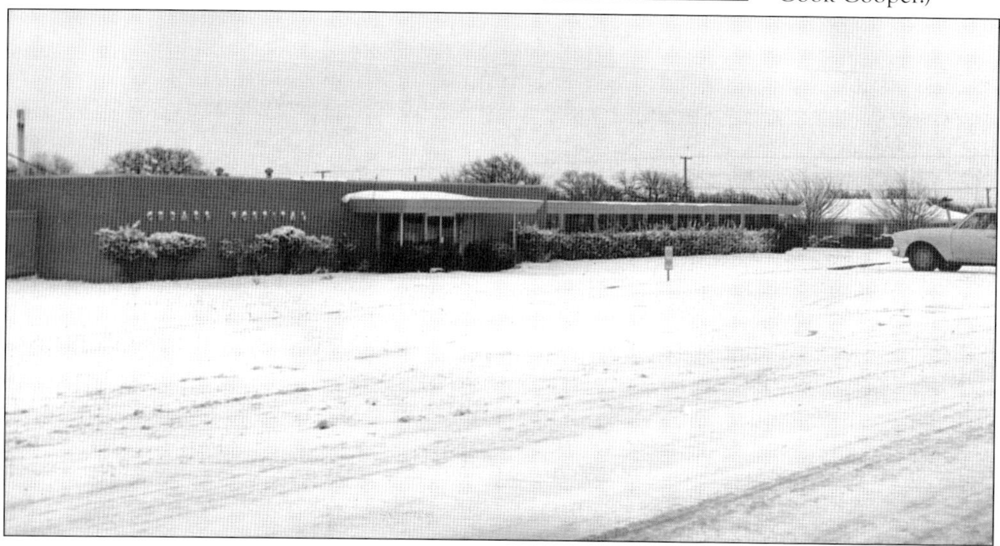

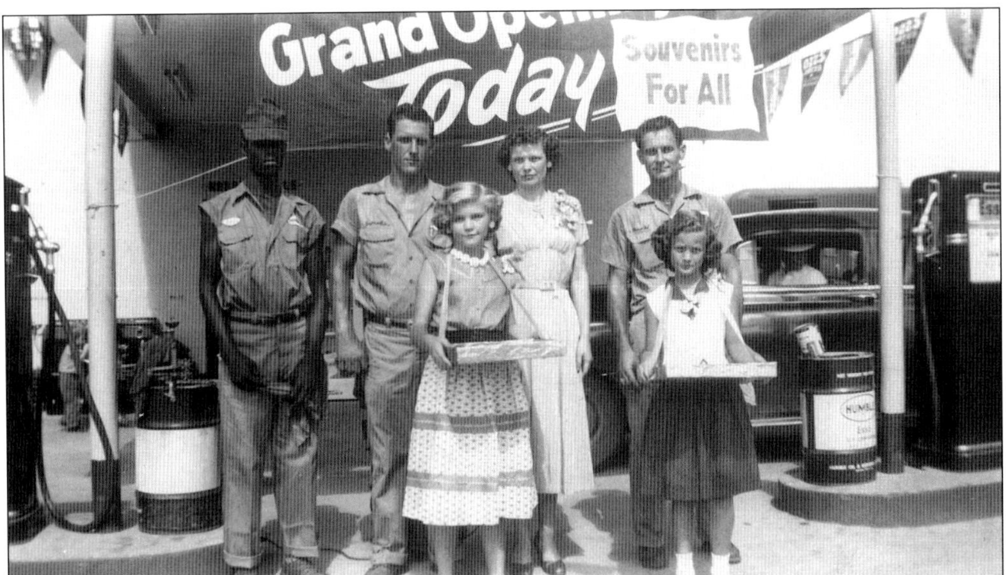

On July 17, 1953, Harold and Mary Sells opened their Humble Oil Station on the corner of Main and Broad Streets. Harold and Mary ran the business together for 35 years. In January 1988, they turned the station over to their son. Bill and his wife, Brenda, continued to run the station until 2014.

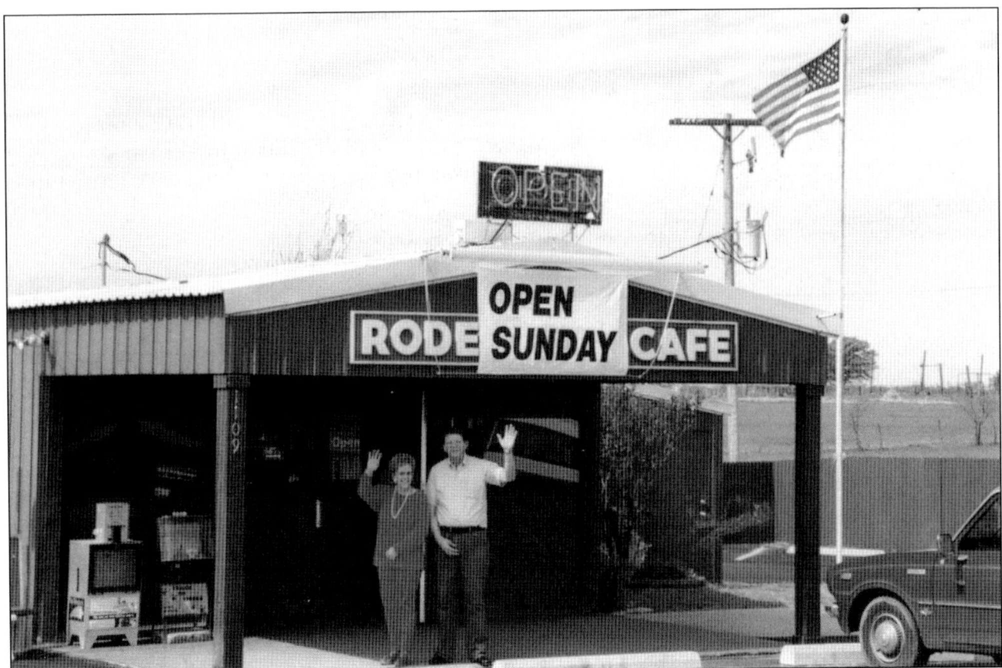

In the 1970s and 1980s, Rodeo City Café was situated across the road from the Kow Bell arena. Friday afternoons would often see the Mansfield High School football team eating chicken-fried steaks, and on Friday nights, people gathered for the "all you can eat shrimp." On Saturdays, the restaurant would be busy with people stopping in for a bite before the rodeo.

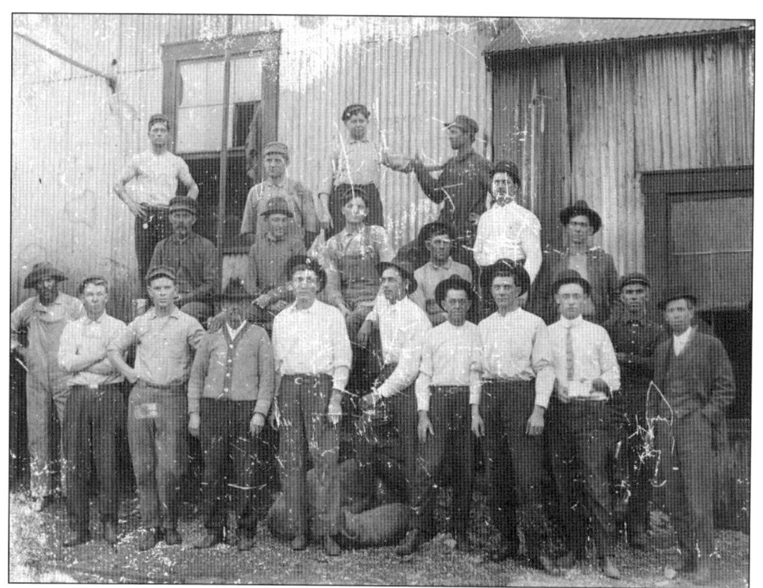

Pictured here is the old cotton gin on Cardinal Road (now North Street), next to the railroad. While the names of most of the men pictured are unknown, the man on the first row, fourth from the left, is a Mr. Balch and on the third row, third from the left, is Shorty Berryman. Also in the first row, ninth from the left, is Arthur Wallace, and on the far right is Joe Edwards.

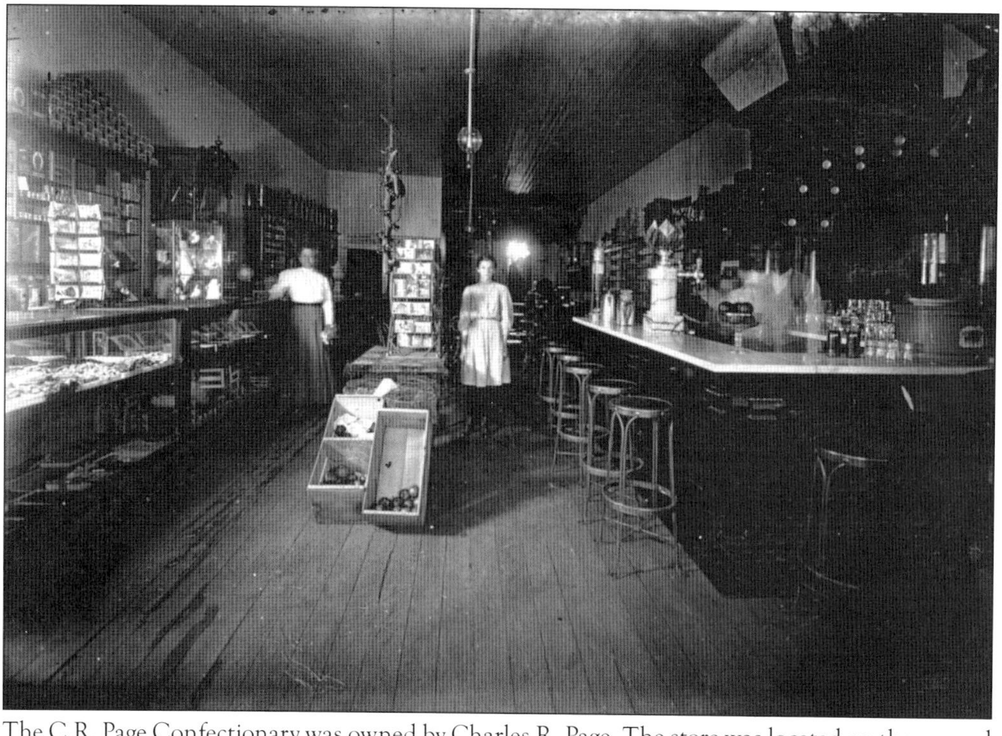

The C.R. Page Confectionary was owned by Charles R. Page. The store was located on the ground floor of 118 North Main Street. This photograph of the shop was taken in 1910. Pictured are, from left to right, Georgia "Sis" Maclin Page, Charles's wife; Lillian Maclin, who was the half-sister of Georgia and lived with the couple; and Charles Page.

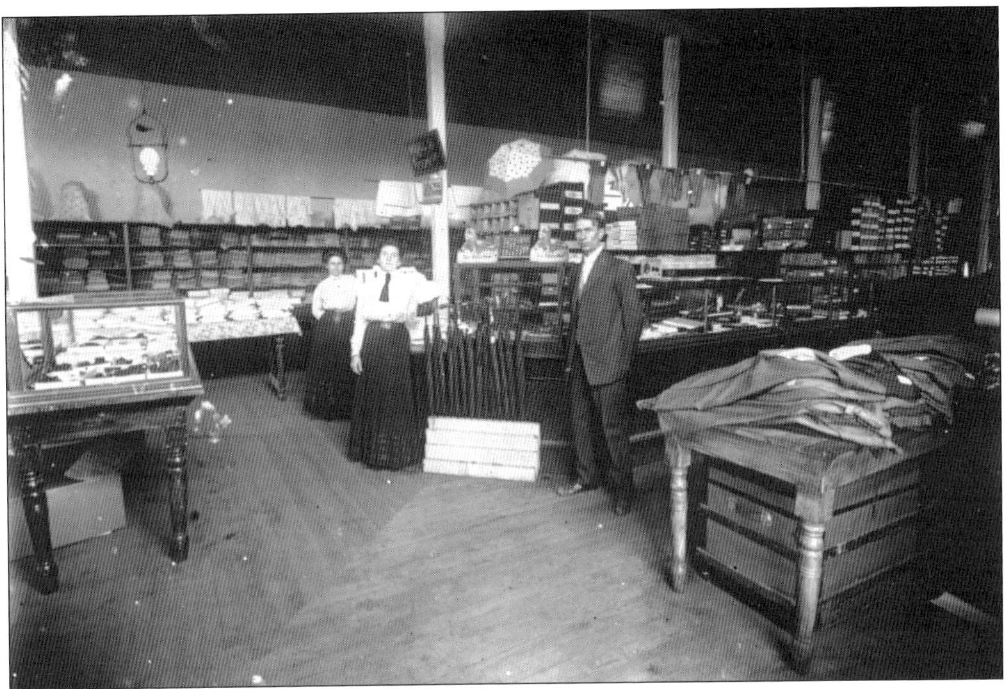

Fitts-Rogers General Merchandise Store was located at the southwest corner of Main and Broad Streets. The building was a two-story brick structure. Pictured in this photograph from around 1900 are, from left to right, unidentified, Ellen Fitts, and Austin Fitts. The location served as a skating rink before it opened as a general store.

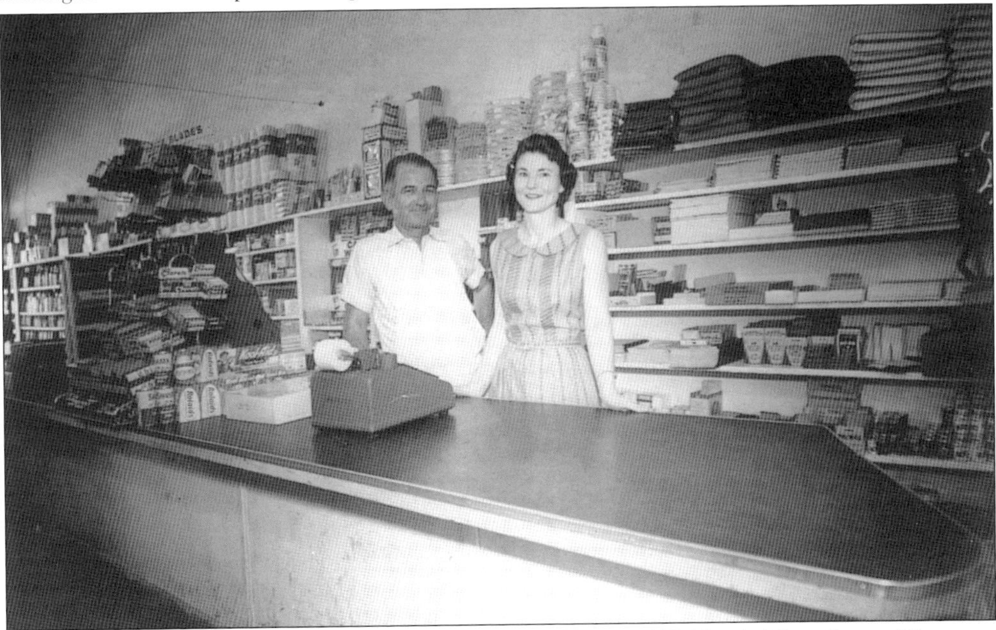

Sells Grocery Store was located in the McKnight Building at 102 North Main Street. The store operated at this location from 1938 to 1965, and the owners lived above the shop for the first decade. Pictured here in the 1940s are owners Troy Vestus Sells and his wife, Elsie Sprinkle Sells. The couple moved the shop to a new building directly behind the old location in 1965.

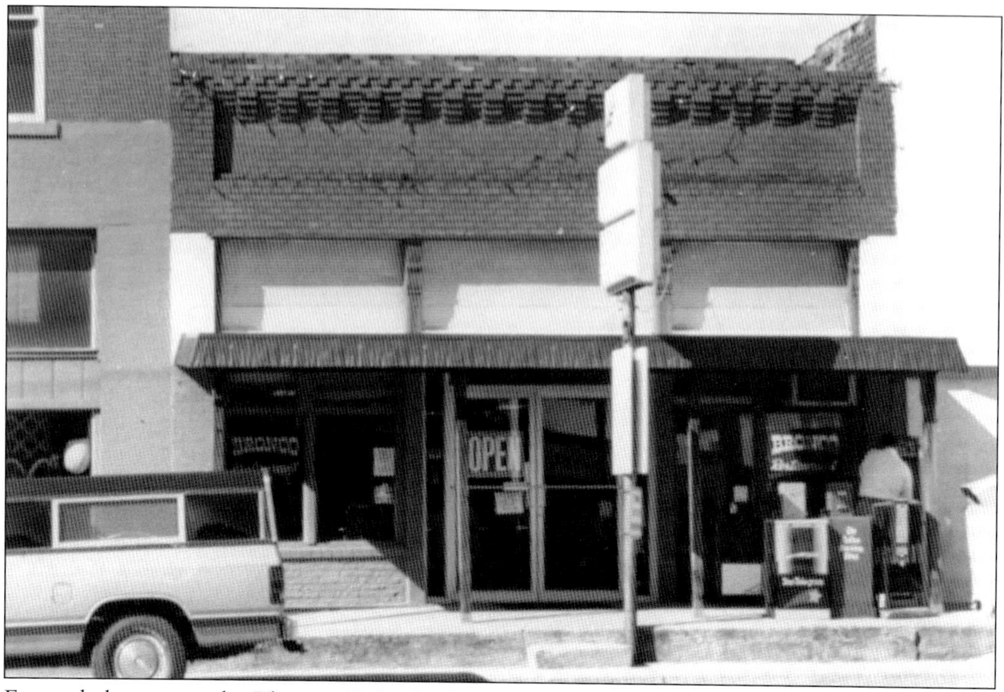

Formerly known as the Theater Café, the Bronco Café was established in the mid-1970s when Jean Huggins took ownership. It was known for its homemade food and pies. Huggins asked her friend Margaret Smith to help until a new waitress could be hired. Smith ended up working at the café for 30 years. The restaurant was known for being where Mansfield movers and shakers met to conduct business.

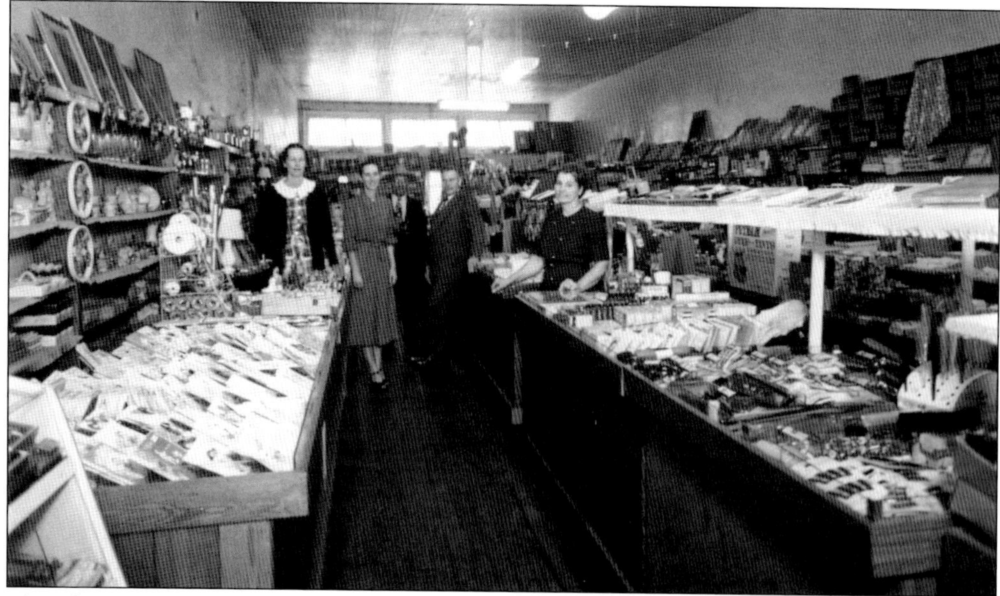

This photograph is of the Boteler Variety Store in 1946. It was owned by B.R. and Jo Boteler and was located on the east side of North Main Street. The shop moved to 114 North Main Street in 1948, and the name changed to Boteler Dry Goods. Photographed here are, from left to right, Bonnie Stone, Jo Boteler, B.R. Boteler, and Edna Brown. An unidentified man is in the background.

Five

GOVERNMENT AND CIVICS

When this area was first settled, the small community was simply known as the Walnut Creek community. Once the Man and Feild Mill was established and the community began to grow, it also needed to be organized. The town was platted in the 1870s as a condition of John Collier before establishing his school, the Mansfield Male and Female College. The post office began operating in 1860, with Julian Feild serving as its first postmaster. An election was held in 1890 to determine the future of the town. The vote passed, and the town was officially incorporated in 1890. Shortly after the incorporation, the first municipal election was held, with Newton C. Pyles elected as the town's first mayor. Early law enforcement came from Tarrant County. The constable was responsible for keeping the peace in Mansfield. The police department was formed with one person in 1954. A radio was installed in his car, and local citizens called the home of the police captain, where his wife would then radio him in his car. The first fire department was an all-volunteer fire department that was formed in 1901.

Citizen groups also played an important role in the development of the community. Civic organizations provided a way for men and women to socialize with like-minded citizens. They provided a sense of belonging to their members. The groups also took on projects to improve the town. Mansfield has had chapters of Odd Fellows, Knights of Pythias, Masons, Jaycees, Kiwanas, and others. The chamber of commerce was formed to help local businesses.

The earliest census record in Mansfield shows the community had 249 citizens in 1880. In 2025, it is estimated that the city will have a population of about 80,000. As Mansfield continues to grow, the city government has provided other amenities for the community's citizens. The library, museums, cultural arts events, and parks provide Mansfieldians with places to learn and play.

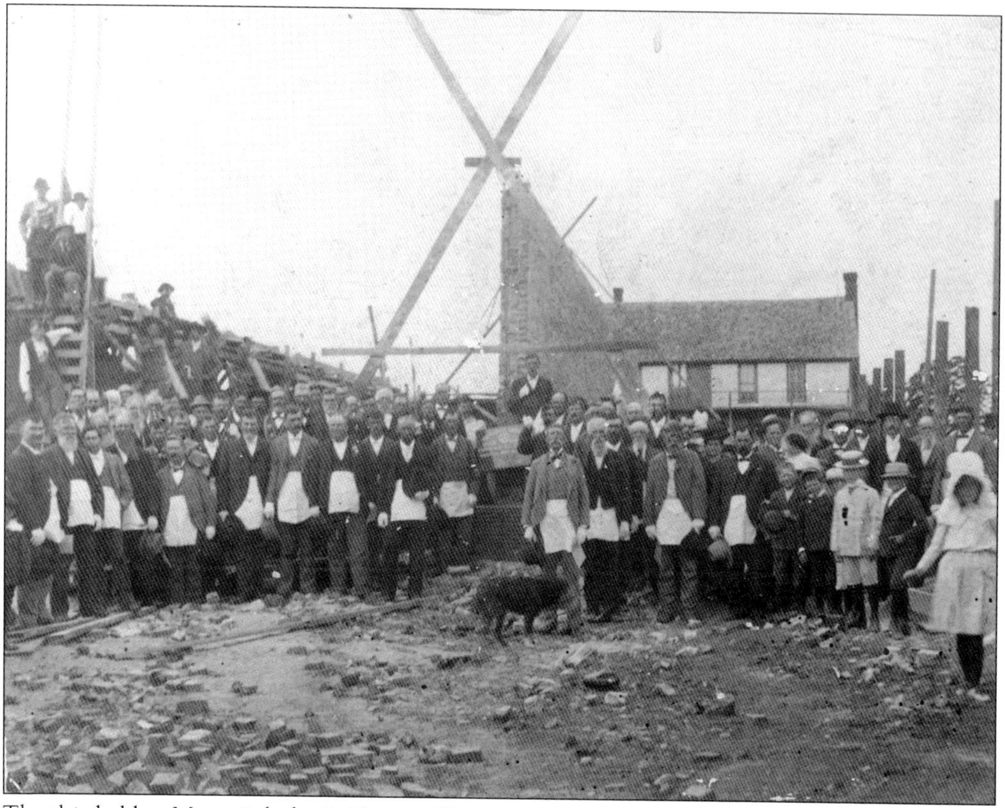

The third-oldest Masonic lodge in Tarrant County got its start on July 9, 1870, when a group of 13 local men petitioned the Grand Lodge of Texas for permission to form a local lodge. The group was headed by T.O. Moody. Within a year, membership had increased to 51 members. The site of the original lodge is unknown, but in 1873, a cornerstone was purchased and a frame building was erected at the corner of Broad and Main Streets. In 1900, this frame building was replaced with a two-story brick structure, which stands today. In 1984, the lodge sold the downtown building and constructed a new lodge on US 287. Above, the Masons gather at the site of their new building. Below is the Masonic Building at 101 North Main Street.

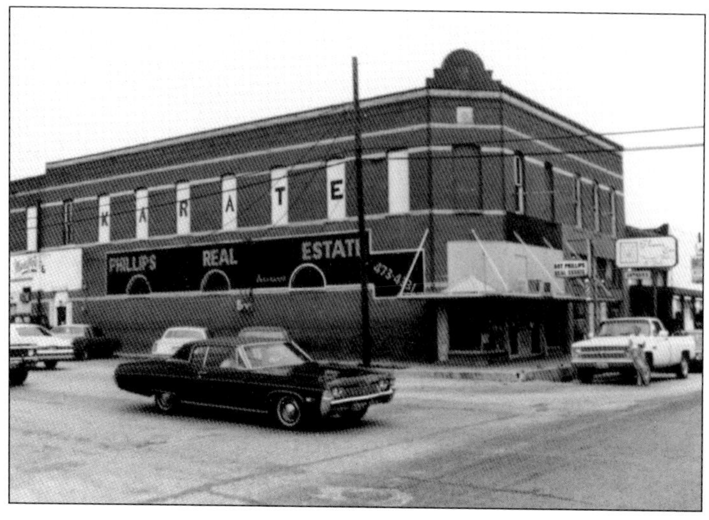

The Independent Order of Odd Fellows Lodge No. 138 was chartered on August 29, 1871, and located at 118 North Main Street. Charter members of the lodge were C.H. Welch, A.B. Pyles, W.C. Pyles, R.A. Gaulden, A.J. Botts, and A.W. Balch. Photographed here are members of the lodge in 1927 sitting on the awning of the C.R. Page Confectionary, which was built in 1892.

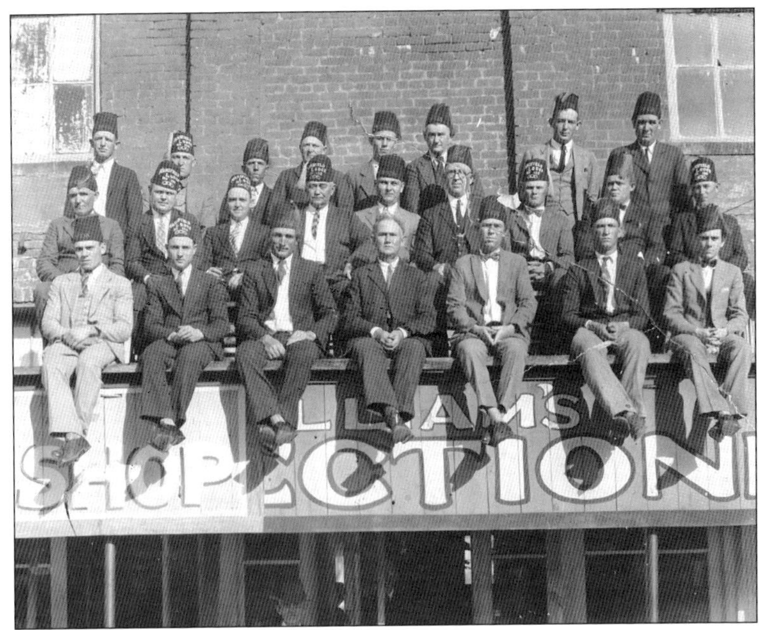

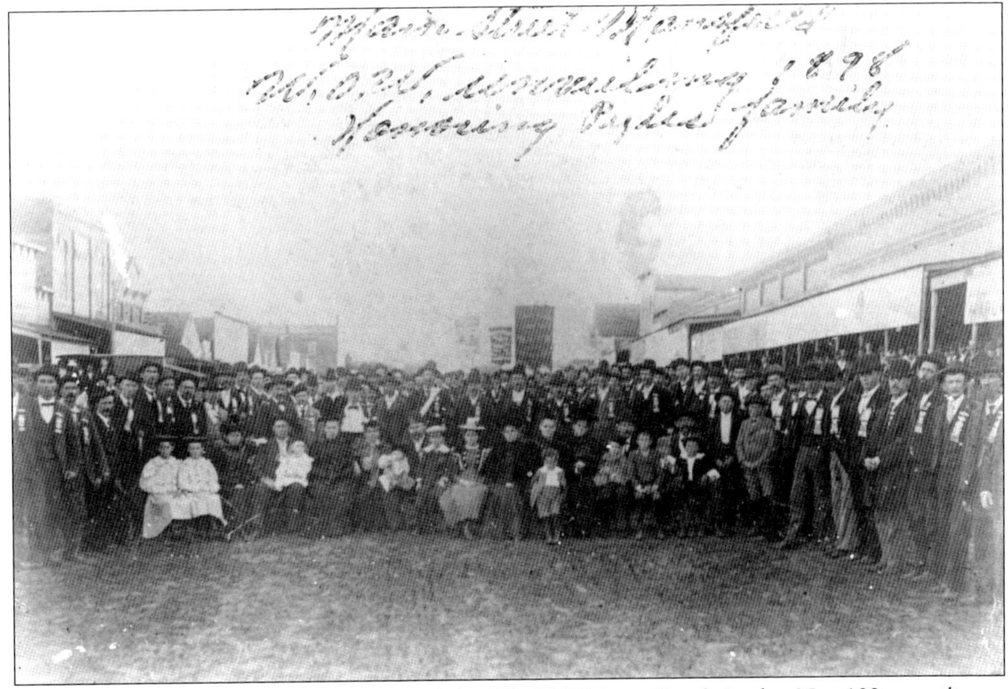

This photograph is of the Woodmen of the World Walnut Creek Lodge No. 132 unveiling a memorial to Abner Pyles. The photograph, taken on Water (now Main) Street, includes lodge members standing behind members of the Pyles family, who are seated in the front. The Woodmen of the World is a fraternal organization and life insurance company.

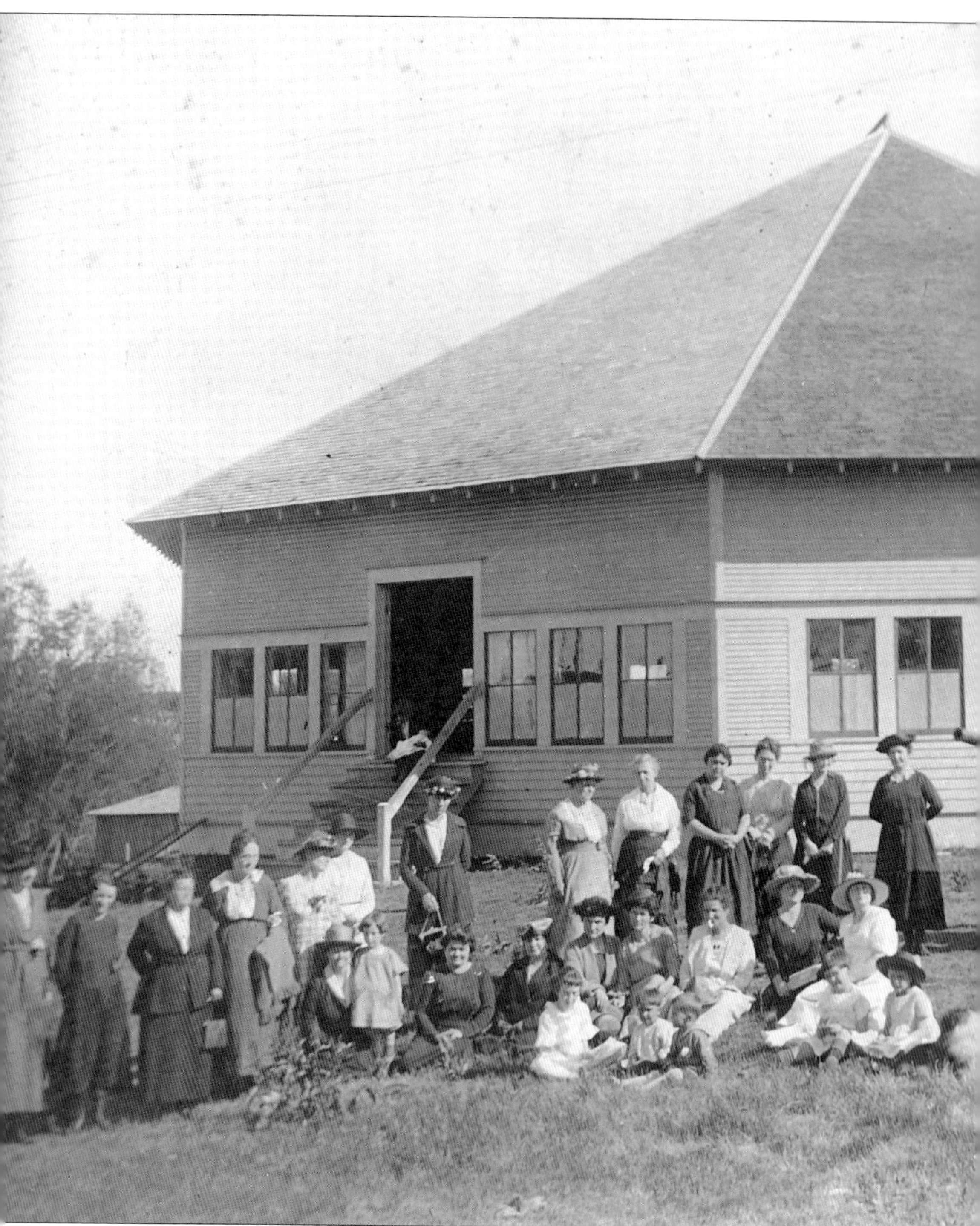

In 1918, local citizens touched in various ways by World War I looked for a way to pay tribute to those who served. Sponsored by the American Legion Auxiliary, Mansfield built a hall to serve the community. The structure was built on the site of the razed Man and Feild Mill on the southeast corner of Water and Broad Streets. Ward Bratton served as the chief architect, contractor, and

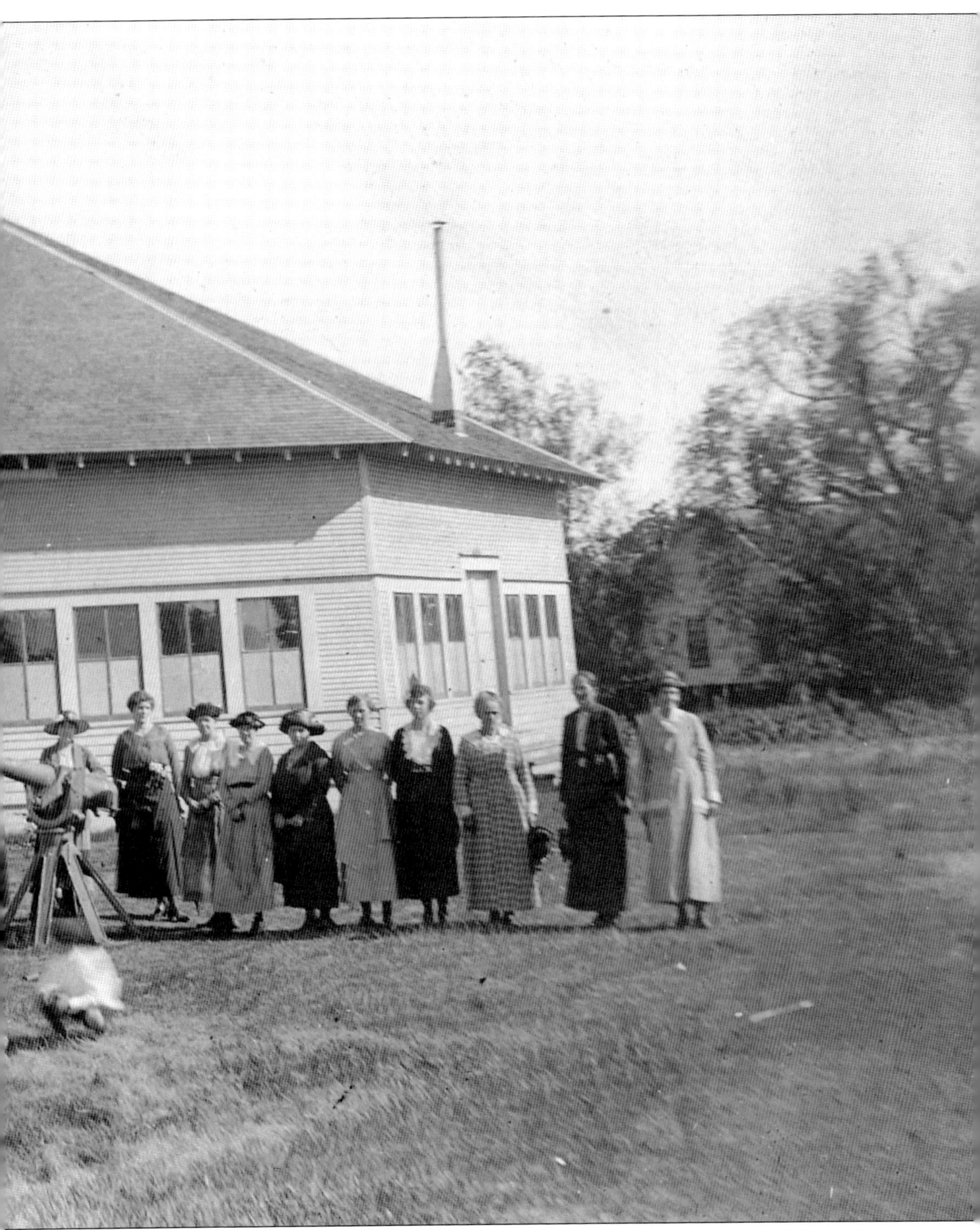

carpenter. The building was octagonal, and the design was based on the Chautauqua Building in Waxahachie, Texas. This photograph, taken in 1919, is of the building, known as Memorial Hall, with a women's group posing in front.

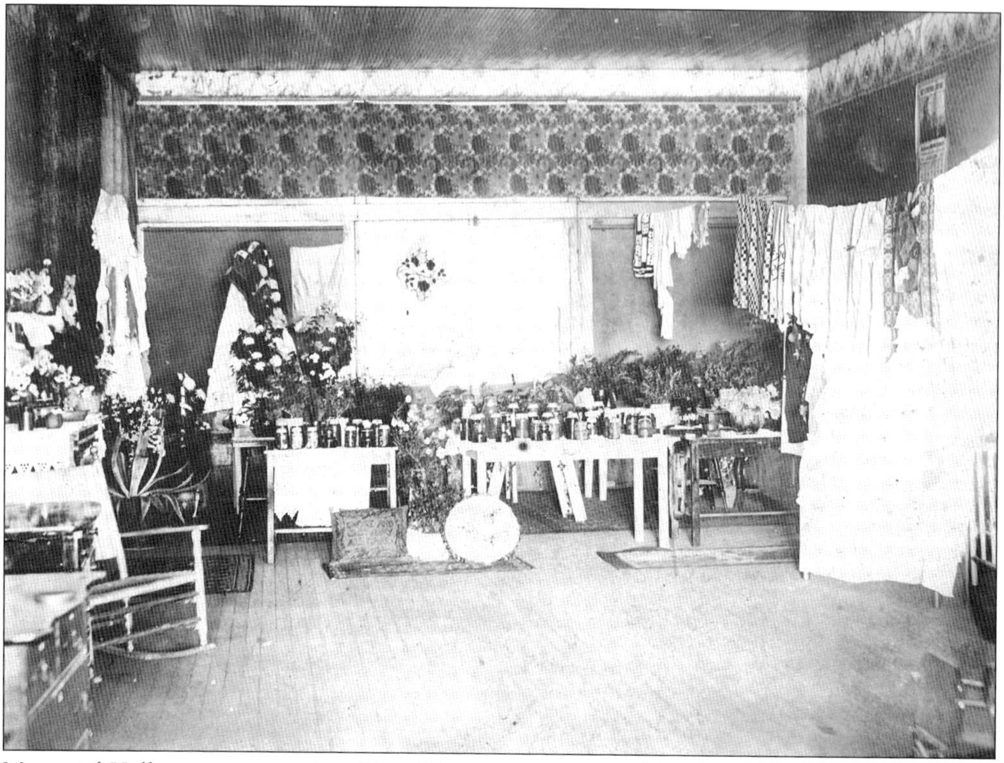

Memorial Hall was a community effort. The money was raised by donations from local citizens. It was built using lumber removed from the Mansfield Male and Female College's dormitory, and the labor for construction was from volunteers. Memorial Hall accommodated community needs and was used as a community center for church functions, school programs, club meetings, and civic activities. It was also used to house city offices and functions. The building contained a stage and dressing rooms for performances. Eventually, change and progress took their toll. In 1956, Memorial Hall was demolished and replaced with Mansfield City Hall. The photograph above is of items submitted to the local Mansfield Fair, which took place in the hall. The image below is of an Old Settlers Reunion, which took place in 1937.

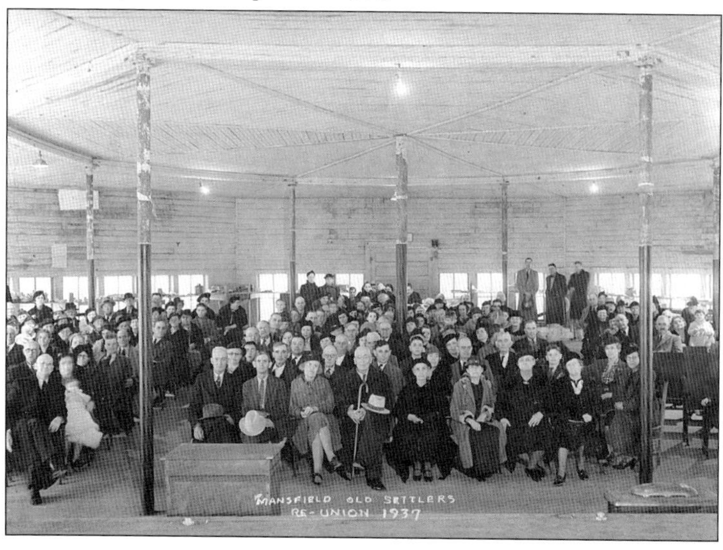

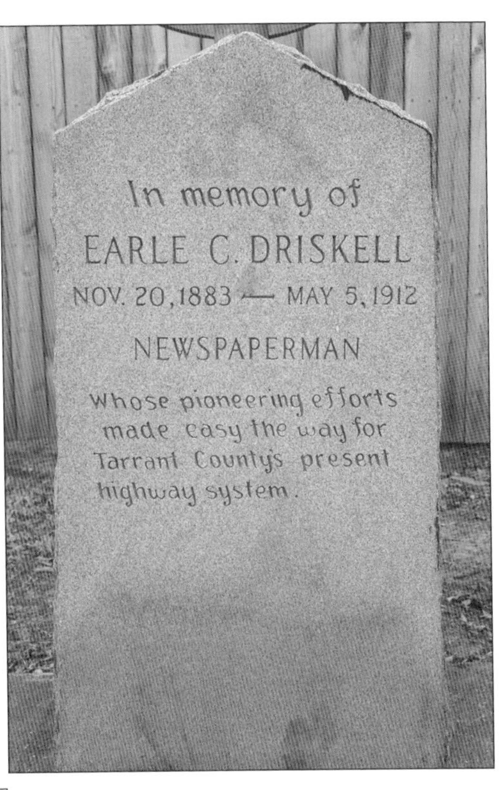

Earle C. Driskell Sr. moved to Texas from Indiana with his family in 1887. They settled on a farm north of Mansfield in the early 1900s. Earl Driskell Jr. worked as a reporter for the *Fort Worth Star-Telegram*. In 1911, traveling the dirt road from Fort Worth to Mansfield was difficult on his motorcycle. He started a campaign for a bond issue to build a paved road. With the bond approved, the Cardinal Road System began. This led to the formation of the Texas Good Roads Association, which became the Texas Highway Department. Unfortunately, Driskell never had a chance to ride on the highway he championed. He died of smallpox shortly after the bond passed in 1912. Seen here are photographs of the memorial and marker located along North Main Street. (Both, Bill Thomas.)

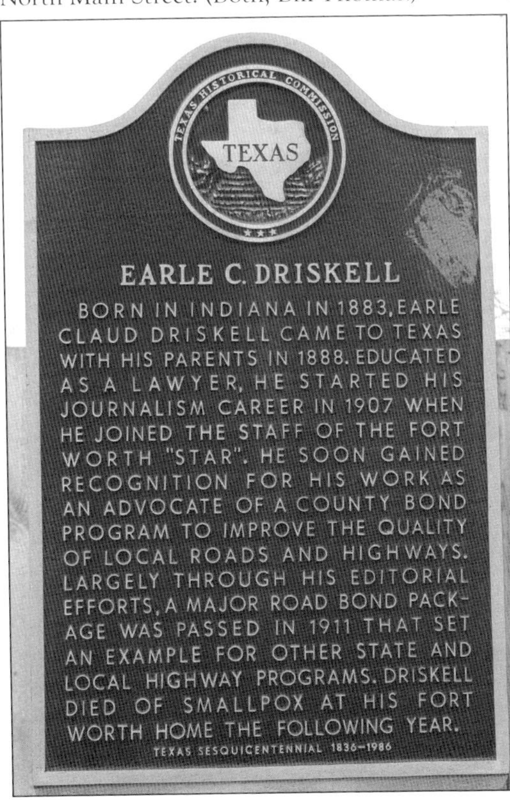

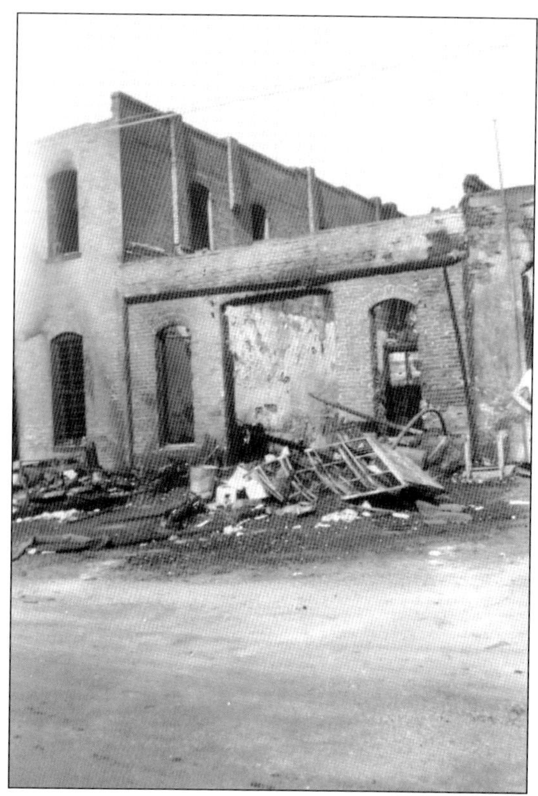

Initially, a bucket brigade of volunteers was used to fight fires in Mansfield. Following a downtown fire on January 5, 1901, a volunteer fire department was organized. Its equipment consisted of 250 feet of hose wrapped around two pieces of pipe. After another devastating fire in 1947, the first factory-built fire truck was purchased in 1948. In 1964, a new fire station was built with volunteer labor.

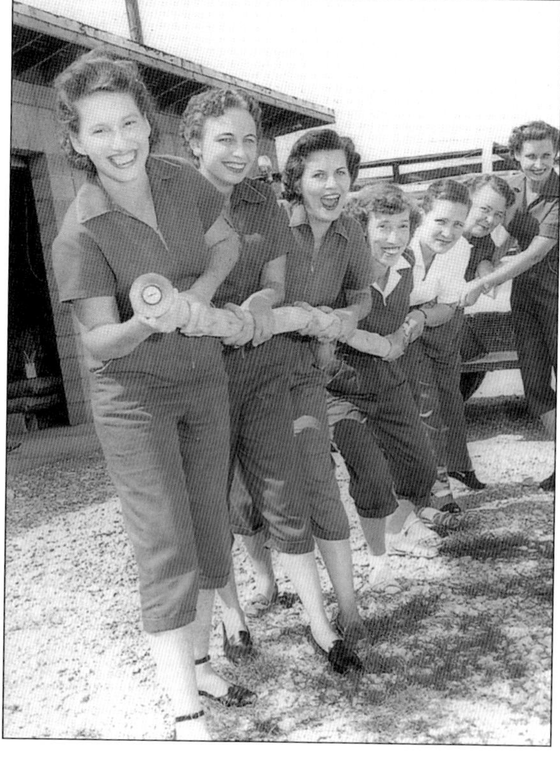

While the men in Rendon fought the fires and answered the calls, the women formed an auxiliary and did all they could to help. The women of the pumper team carried water, fought fires, drove the trucks, and held fund drives of all kinds. The pumper team members are, from left to right, Inez Davis, Lillie English, Imogene Criswell, Claudine Sellers, Myrtle Cogburn, Marion Hall, and Lavern Daugherty.

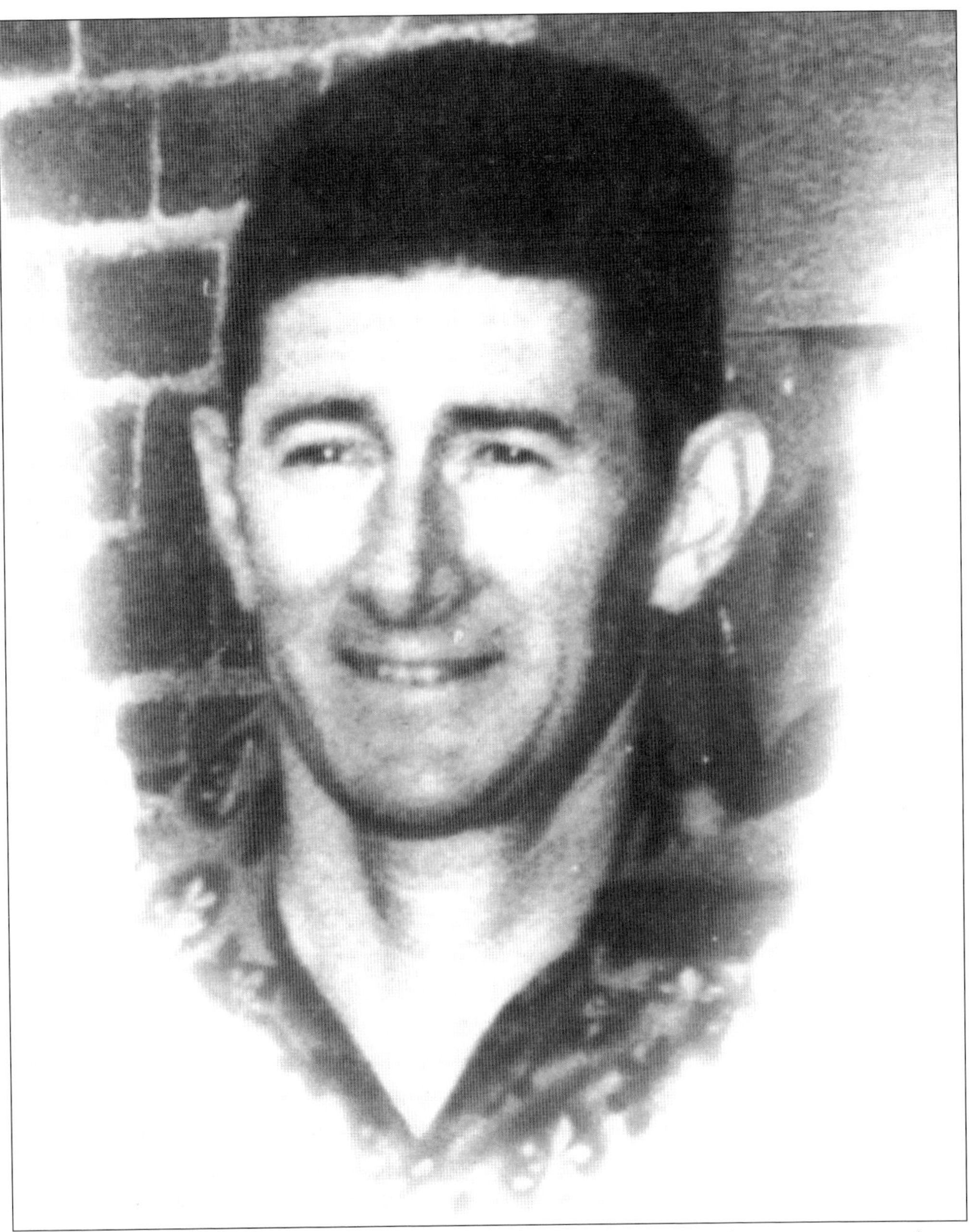

On July 31, 1968, the Red Ball Gas Station in Kennedale, Texas, exploded. As a pumper truck was pumping gas into a tank, an overflow of gasoline sparked, causing a fire. Mansfield firefighters responded to the call. As they were attempting to put out the blaze, vapors streaming from under the aboveground tank acted as a fuse, and a great ball of fire exploded, spewing tank parts 150 feet into the air and 200 feet in diameter. Firefighters from several communities eventually put out the fire. Mansfield firefighter Shirley Copeland (pictured) and Fire Chief Harry Blissard were killed in the explosion.

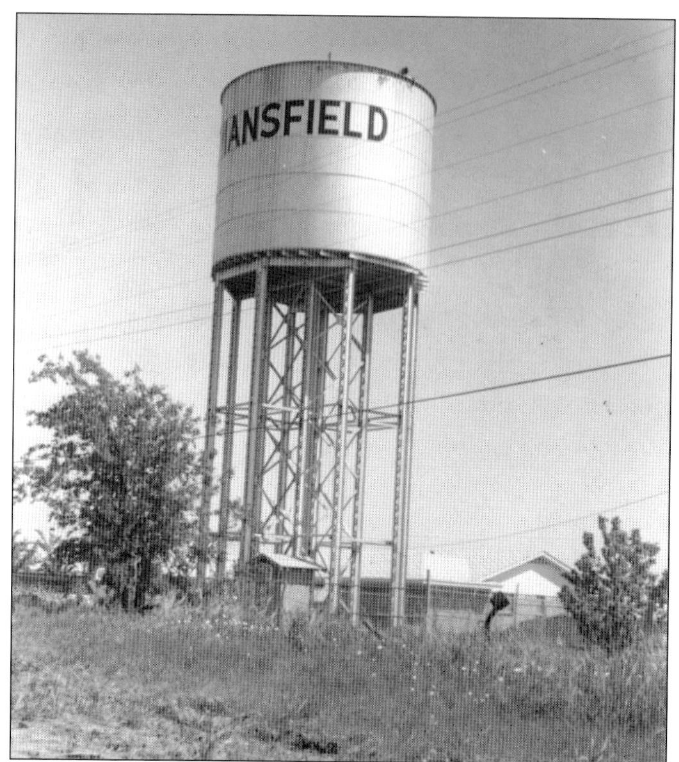

The 1909 water system for Mansfield consisted of a pump and an old cypress tank located by the old mill on Water Street. The tank leaked water constantly, causing the dirt road to be muddy and filled with holes. This proved to be a large problem for wagons and automobiles. As the water system modernized, a water tank, pictured at left, from the rail line was repurposed and moved to the Hillcrest addition. Another modern water tower, pictured below, was located between Alvarado and Kimball Streets and between First and Second Avenues. It was 90 feet tall and had a capacity of 55,000 gallons. It is remembered for being a tower that local kids enjoyed climbing.

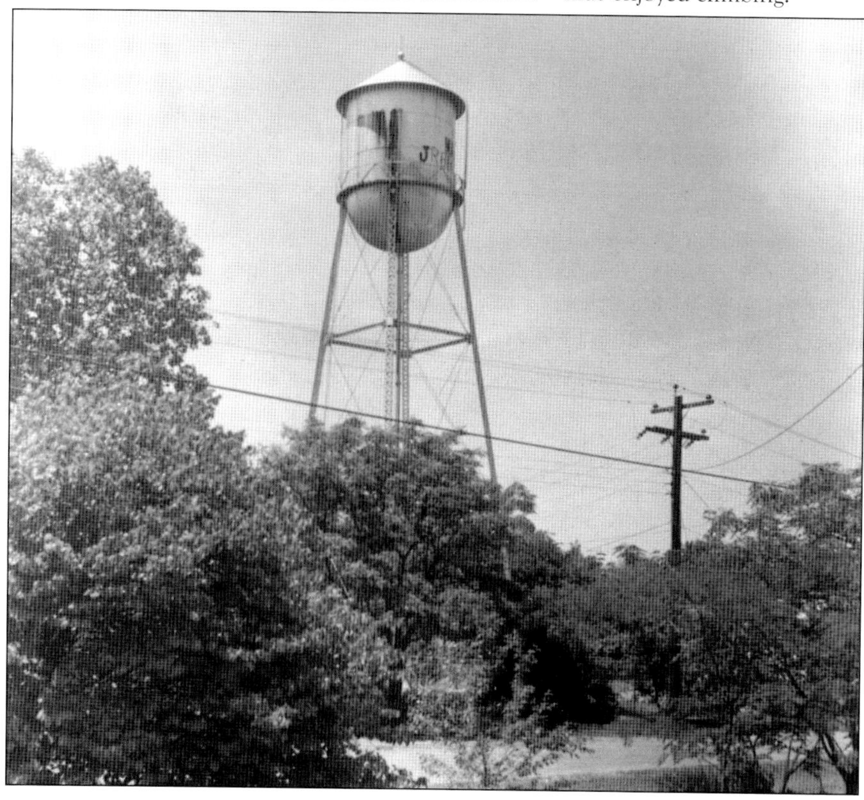

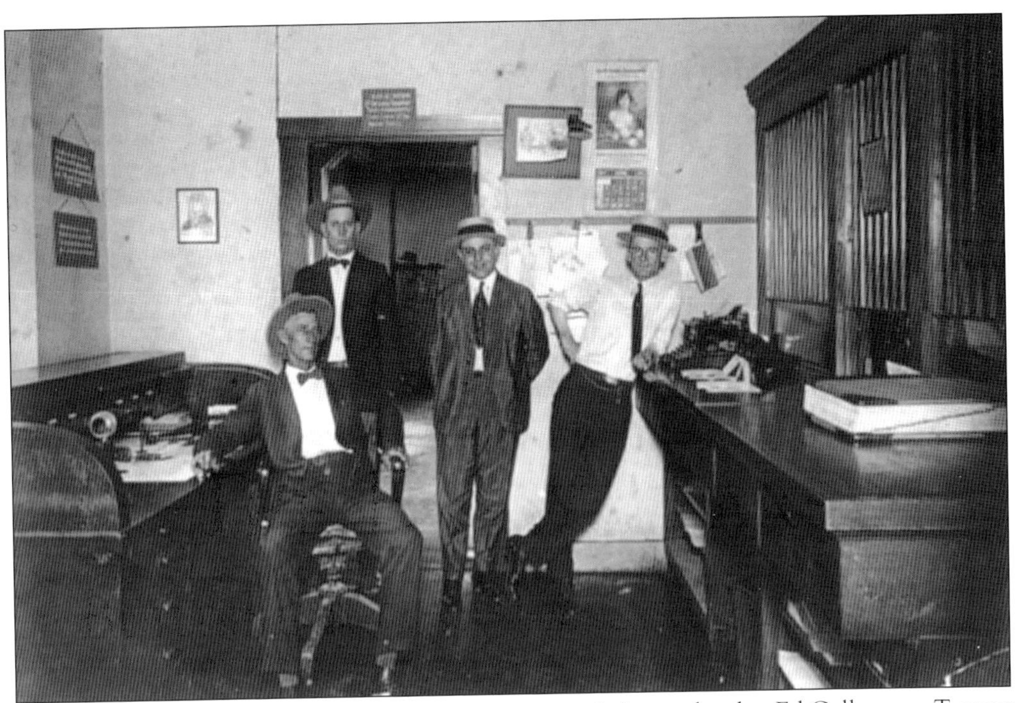

For many years, Mansfield relied on the county to provide law and order. Ed Galloway, a Tarrant County Sheriff's deputy from Mansfield, is seen here in 1929 with his fellow deputies. Galloway is standing on the left in a western hat. He is most remembered by locals for having once chased the famed outlaws Bonnie and Clyde.

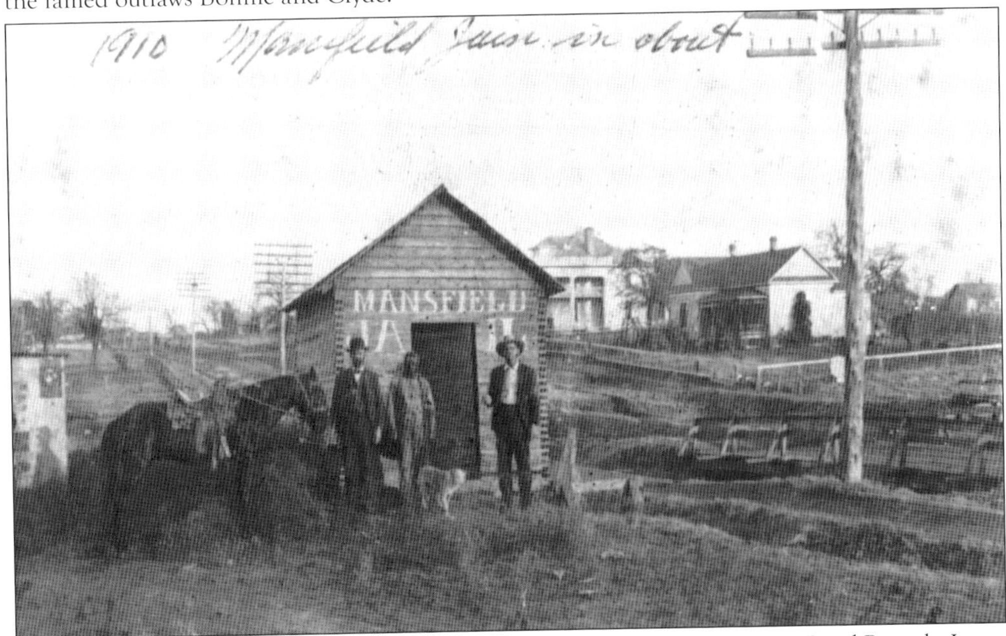

The early Mansfield jail was located by the footbridge on East Broad Street at Pond Branch. It was a small, makeshift building that could only hold three prisoners at a time, and the only furniture inside was a mattress. The bars were low on the ground, requiring prisoners to lie down in order to look outside. Most arrests at the time were for repeated drunk and disorderly individuals.

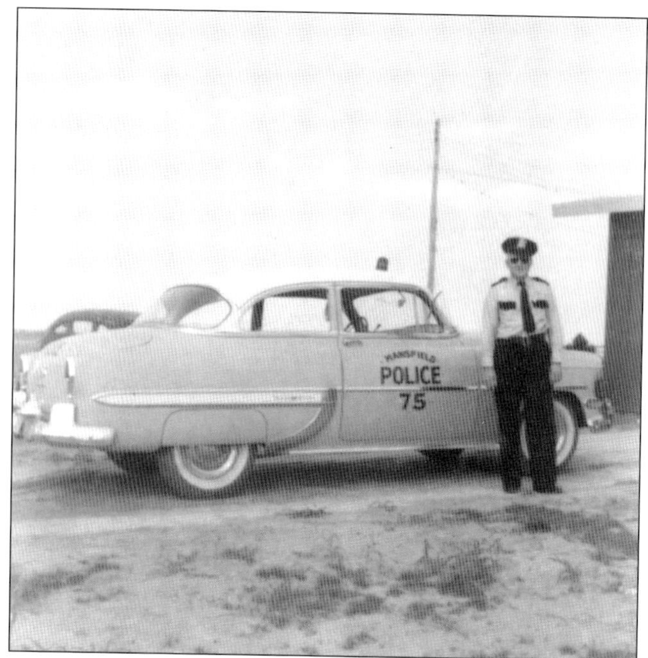

Law and order in early Mansfield was provided by the city marshal and the justice of the peace. In later years, it was the constable. In June 1954, the city council hired the first police chief. Initially, there was a large turnover for two reasons: low salary and the need to furnish his own vehicle. Pictured is Chief Louis Stricklin standing by the first police car—his own vehicle.

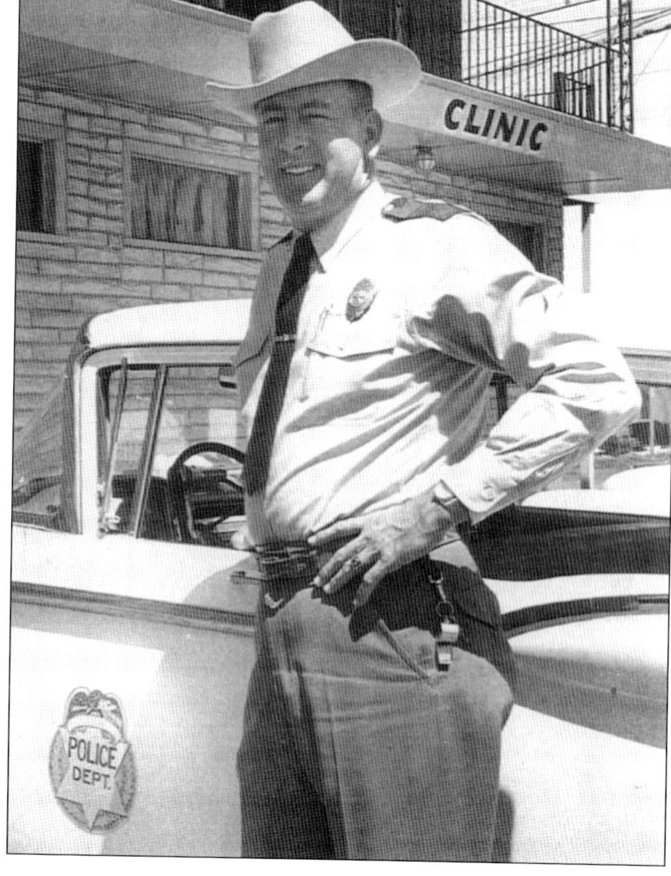

In 1956, the city purchased its first police car—a 1956 Chevrolet four-door sedan—at the cost of $1,542. A few months later, the first police radio was installed. Dispatching was done by the police chief's wife from their home. By 1964, the city had hired two full-time and one part-time officers, three reservists, and a full-time dispatcher. Pictured is Lee Seeter, the police chief from 1961 to 1964.

The first post office was created in 1860, with Julian Feild serving as the first postmaster of Mansfield. In those early days, postmasters had to purchase their own supplies, and it was a position that did not have a large amount of continuity until E. Otho Driskell, pictured, took the position in 1914. He held the position for a record 34 years, working through both world wars before retiring in 1948.

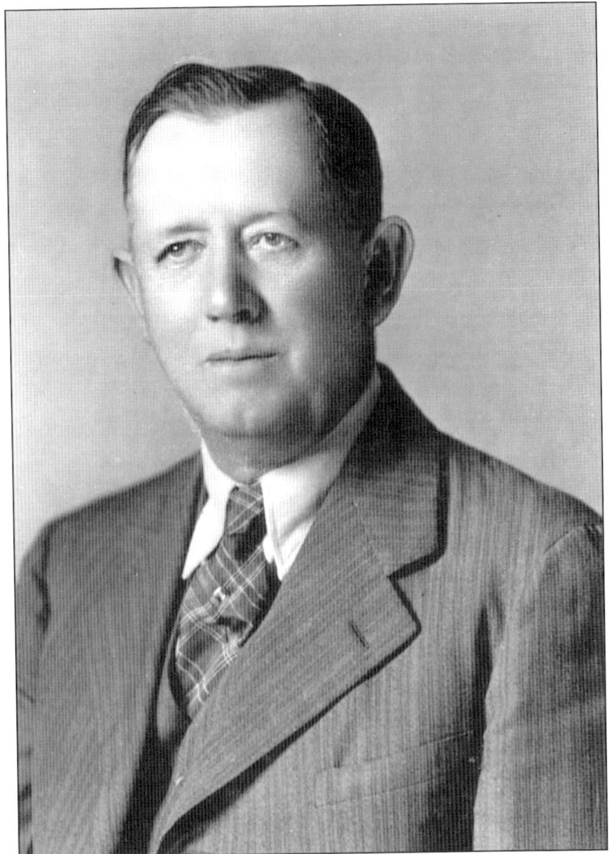

Mansfield City Hall, located at the corner of Main and East Broad Streets, was built on the site of the original gristmill erected by Ralph S. Man and Julian Feild, around which the town was founded. The new city hall was built in 1956 when Memorial Hall was torn down.

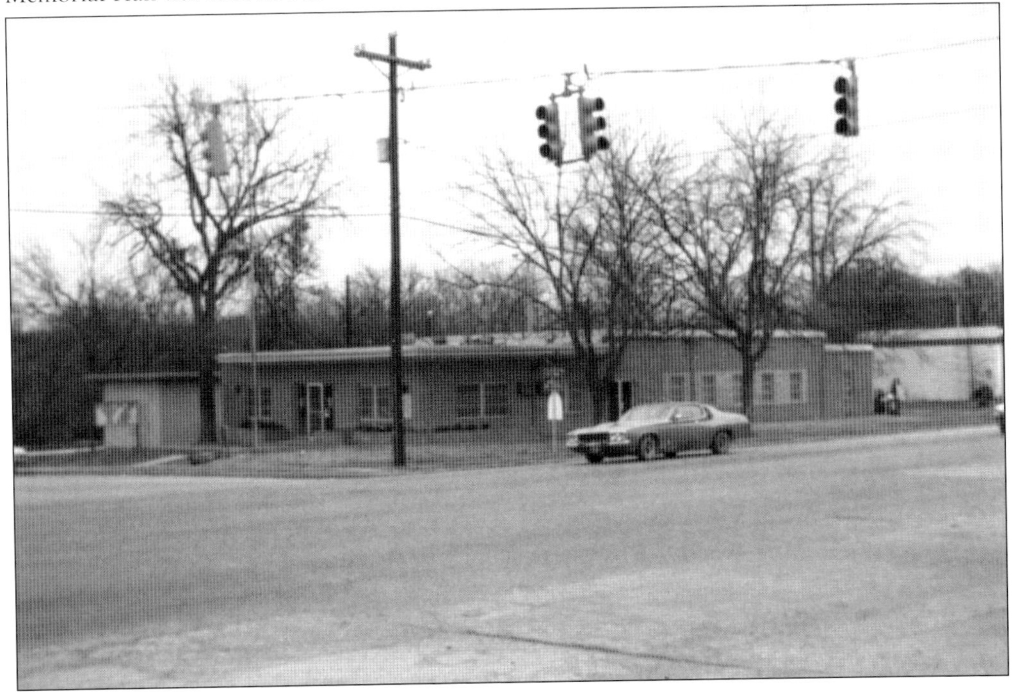

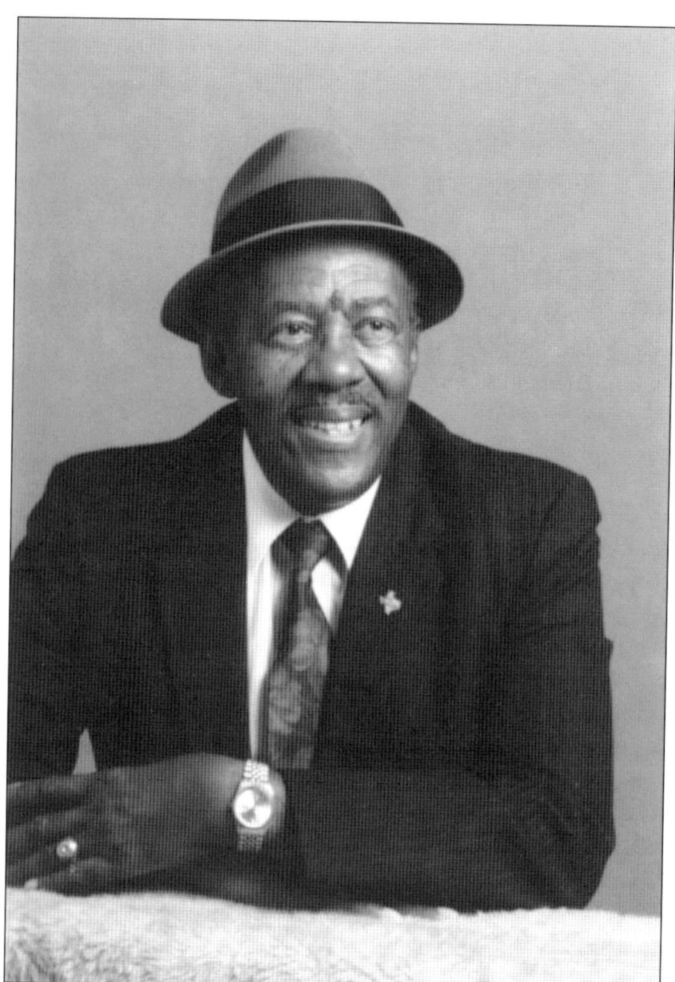

McClendon Moody was born in 1932. He was well known in the community for his work in the bakery at Buddy's Food Store and Winn-Dixie. With the encouragement of his wife, Cleo, in 1979, Moody ran for and was elected to the city council, where he served as the first Black council member for 15 years.

Charles Hubbard Harrison was born in Mansfield in 1891. Harrison was well known throughout the town as the owner of the Blue Goose Confectionery. He was elected mayor in 1947 and served until 1955. Under his tenure, the street signs were changed to steel, and the first traffic light was installed. He coined the city motto, "Welcome to Mansfield: where you are as welcome as the flowers in May."

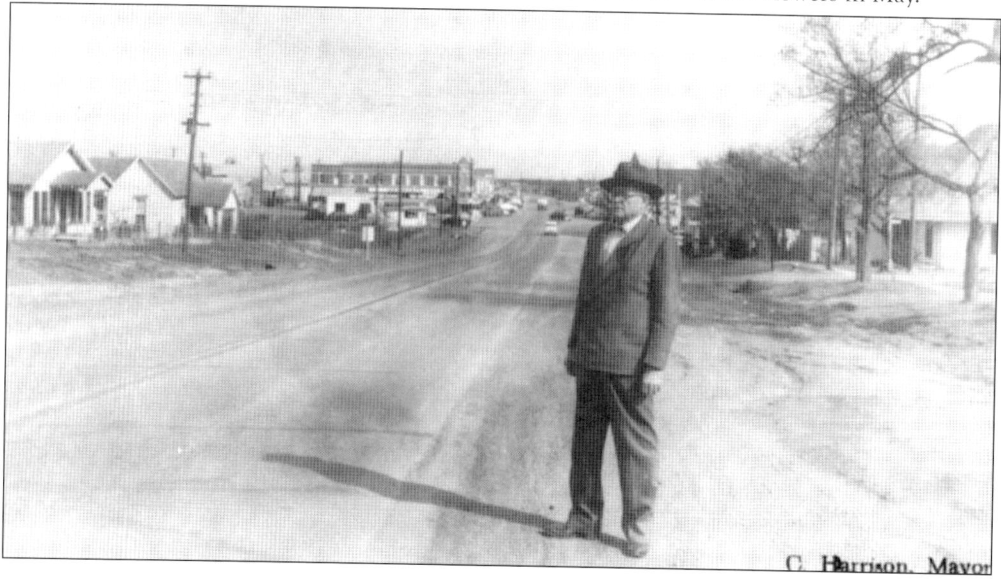

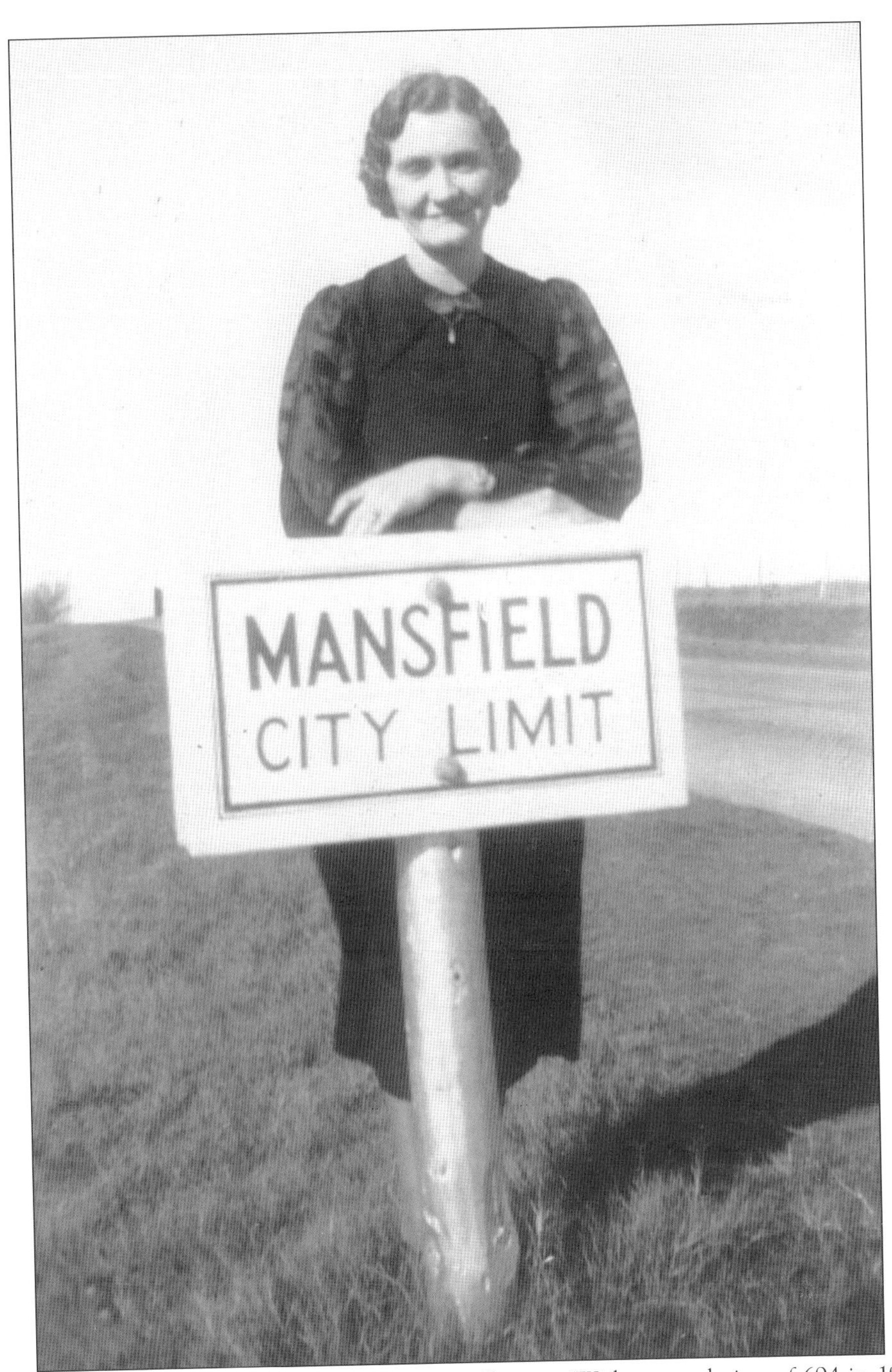

For most of its history, Mansfield has been a small town. With a population of 694 in 1900, it fluctuated only slightly over the next few decades to 627 in 1910, to 719 in 1920, and to 635 during the Great Depression in 1930. Mansfield annexed additional land in 1943 and continued to expand during the coming decades. By 1950, the town had grown to 964 residents. In 1970, the population was 3,658. From that time forward, the city has been growing rapidly. The population was 8,102 in 1980, 15,500 in 1990, 28,324 in 2000, 57,091 in 2010, and 73,094 in 2020. This photograph shows Clara Howell standing by the Mansfield city limit sign in 1937.

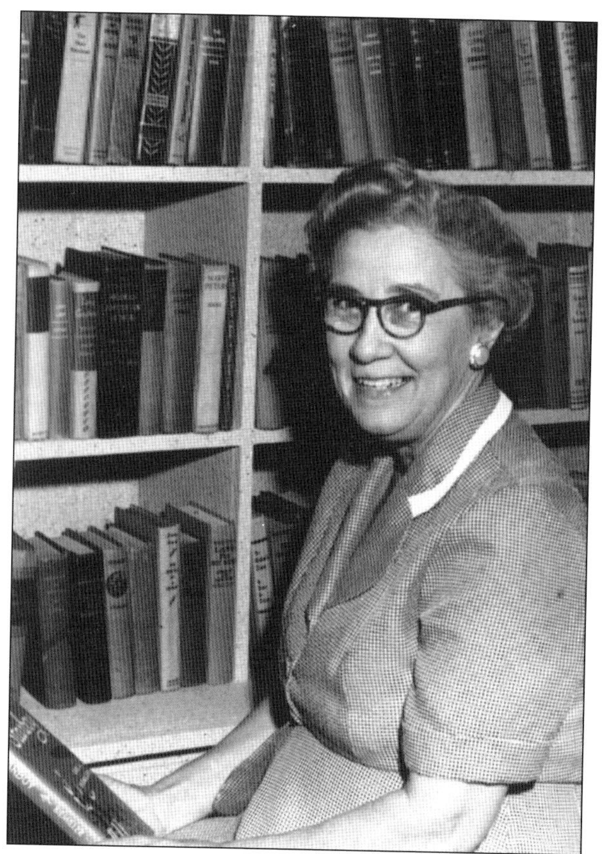

Ida Nichols served as Mansfield's first librarian when the building opened in 1929 and continued in that capacity until 1960. However, the library did not possess a long-term home for many years. Mansfield citizens checked out their books from the corners of stores, cramped spaces of city buildings, and for a while, in the waiting room of a doctor's office. Eventually, the books, shelves, and Nichols herself were moved into Memorial Hall, where they stayed for 37 years. From there, the library moved to McGaha's Variety Store. It is currently housed in a purpose-built structure on Wisteria Street, next to the Mansfield City Hall complex. Pictured at left is Ida Nichols, and below is a photograph of the library.

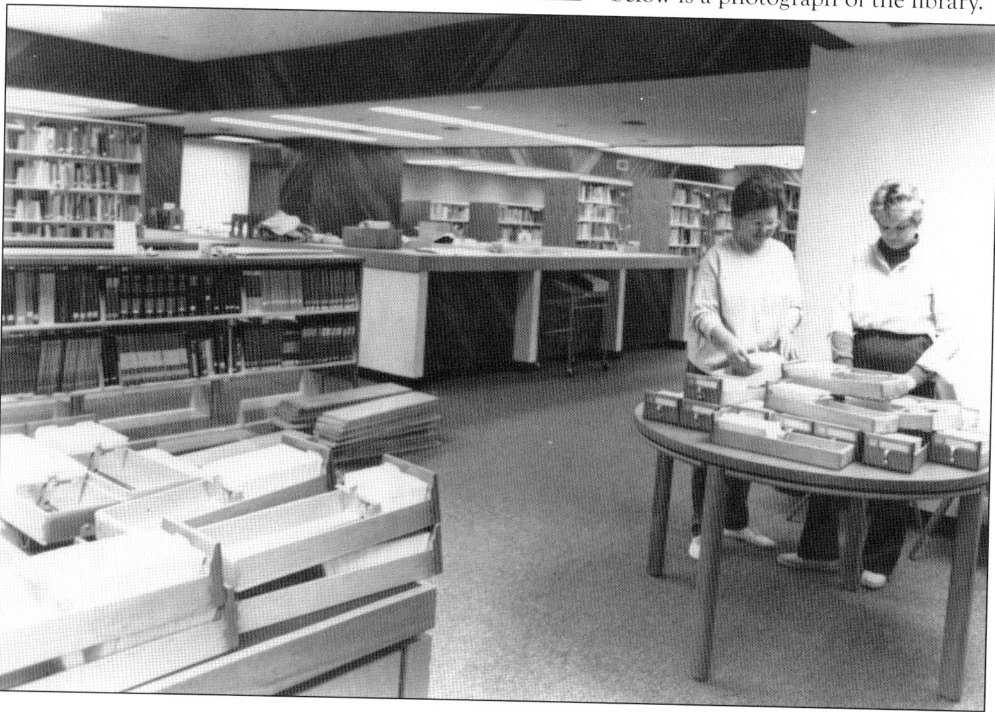

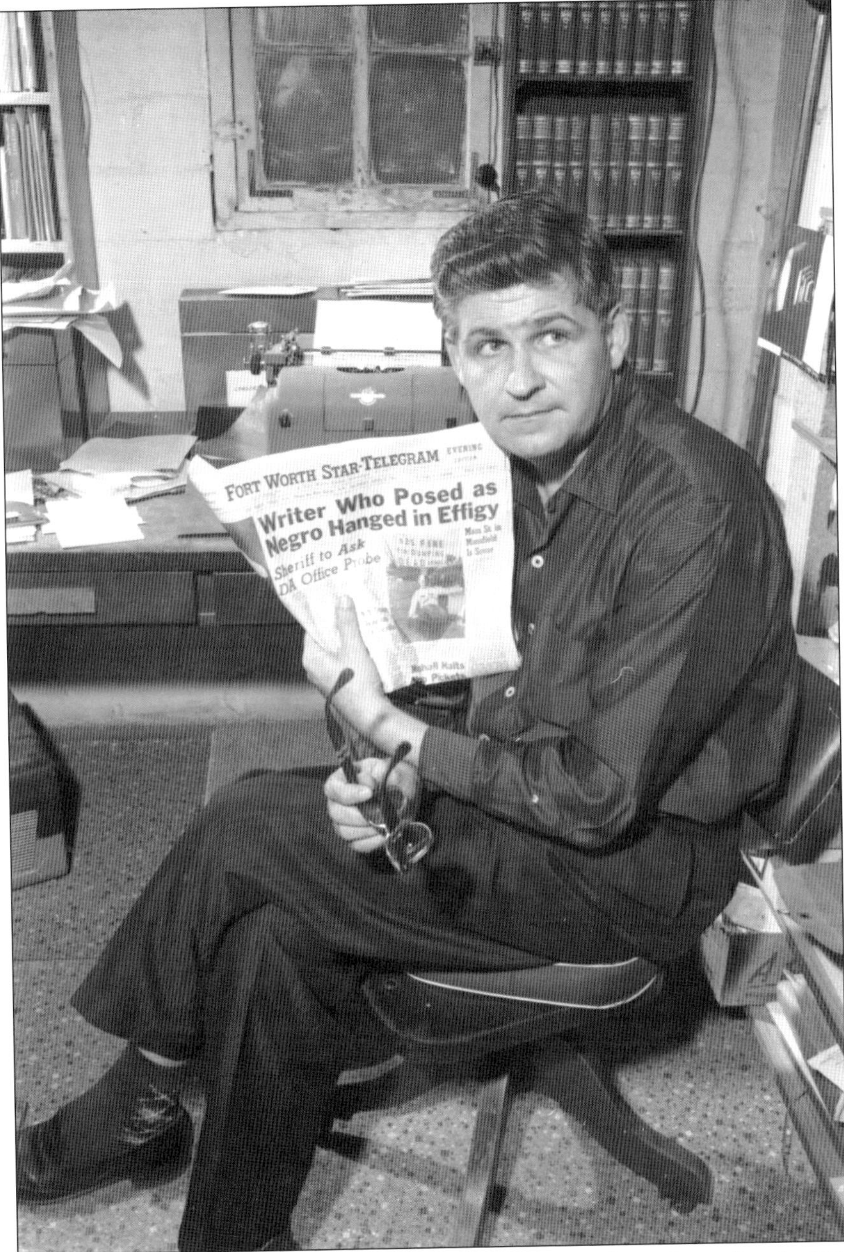

Author of *Black Like Me* (1961), John Howard Griffin championed racial equality. In 1959, over a period of six weeks, he temporarily chemically darkened his skin and traveled through the Deep South to experience segregation through the eyes of a Black man. While he thought his experience chronicling the troubling dynamics of the Jim Crow South would only interest sociologists, his book was a runaway success. In a 1975 essay, he recounted the hostility he encountered on the trip and threats to himself and his family in his hometown of Mansfield. In 1975, he was severely beaten by the Ku Klux Klan. He moved his family to Mexico for a time before returning to Fort Worth. In 2011, the Mansfield Public Library was designated a National Literary Landmark in honor of the contribution Griffin made to literature in a ceremony officiated by First Lady Laura Bush. (The *Fort Worth Star-Telegram* Collection, Special Collections, the University of Texas at Arlington Libraries.)

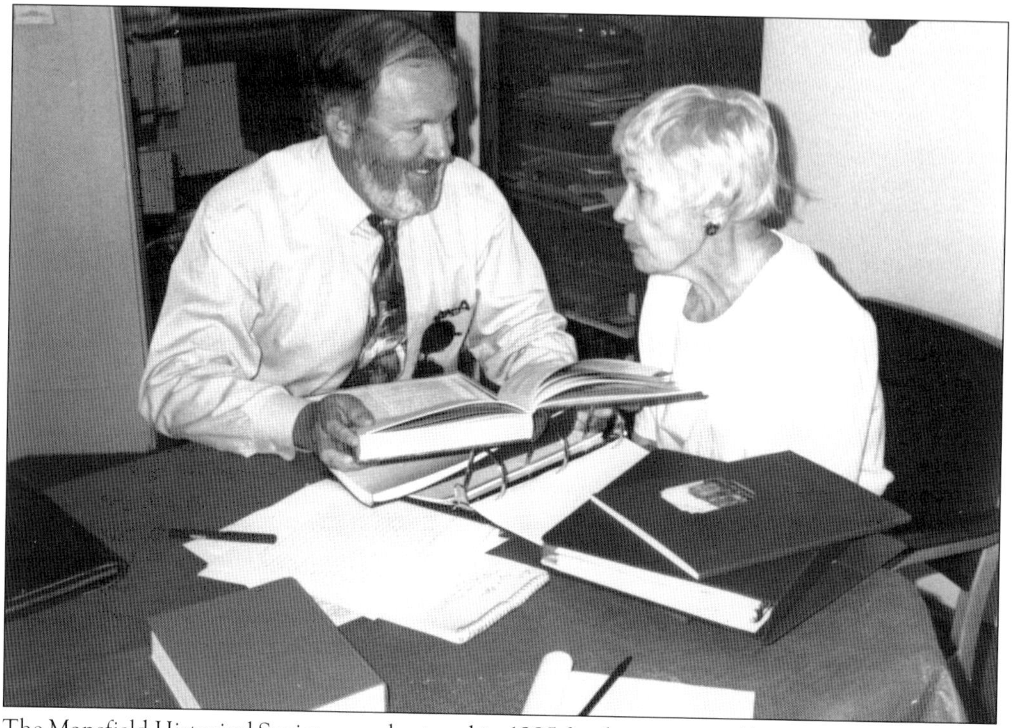

The Mansfield Historical Society was chartered in 1985 for the purpose of bringing together people interested in the history of the area. It collected and preserved photographs, printed materials, and physical items that represent the history of the Mansfield community. Beryl Steele Gibson was one of the founding members. She worked faithfully for many years to preserve information regarding the history of Mansfield. The historical society had two major benefactors: James S. McKnight, who bequeathed the organization a 99-year lease on the W.B. McKnight Building, and Ira D. Gibson, who established a trust to help with the operating expenses. Pictured above is Beryl Gibson and O.K. Carter working on a Mansfield history book in 1986. Pictured below are members of the historical society at the 1987 annual meeting.

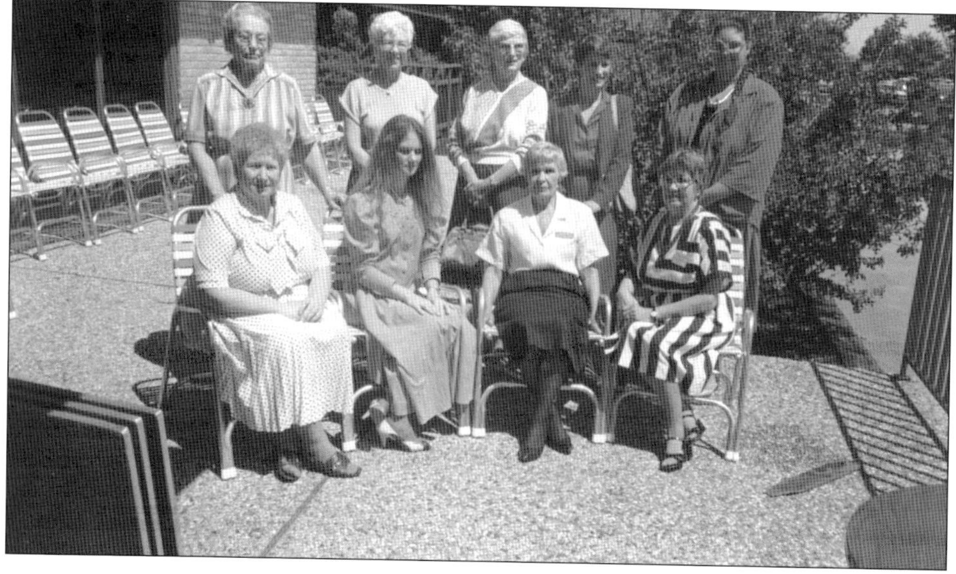

Six

Entertainment

From Mansfield's early days in the 1850s through today, local people have always sought ways to entertain themselves. Hunting meant time to get off by oneself as well as to provide for the family table. For young people, climbing down to Red Bluff to the local swimming hole in Walnut Creek was a way to cool off and have fun. City bands and baseball teams also provided ways to get together for social activities. As time passed, conveniences allowed for more free time. For women, that might mean joining a home demonstration club. There were also clubs to play dominoes or bridge. The Farr Best Theater provided entertainment in the form of movies and other performances. Young couples often chose seats in the balcony, where hand-holding was not as easily observed. In the mid-1900s, the Kow Bell Arena was more than local entertainment. People came to Mansfield from all around to ride the bulls and horses or to watch the action. It was a much-anticipated Saturday night event. Parades have also been a great cause for celebration. From early Fourth of July parades to today's popular Pickle Parade here in "the Pickle Capital of Texas."

Today, Mansfield is also renowned for its award-winning parks. Katherine Rose Memorial Park, Elmer Oliver Nature Park, and the Walnut Creek Linear Trail are all beloved spots for enjoying nature. There are also water parks, sports fields and courts, ice hockey facilities, and a dog park.

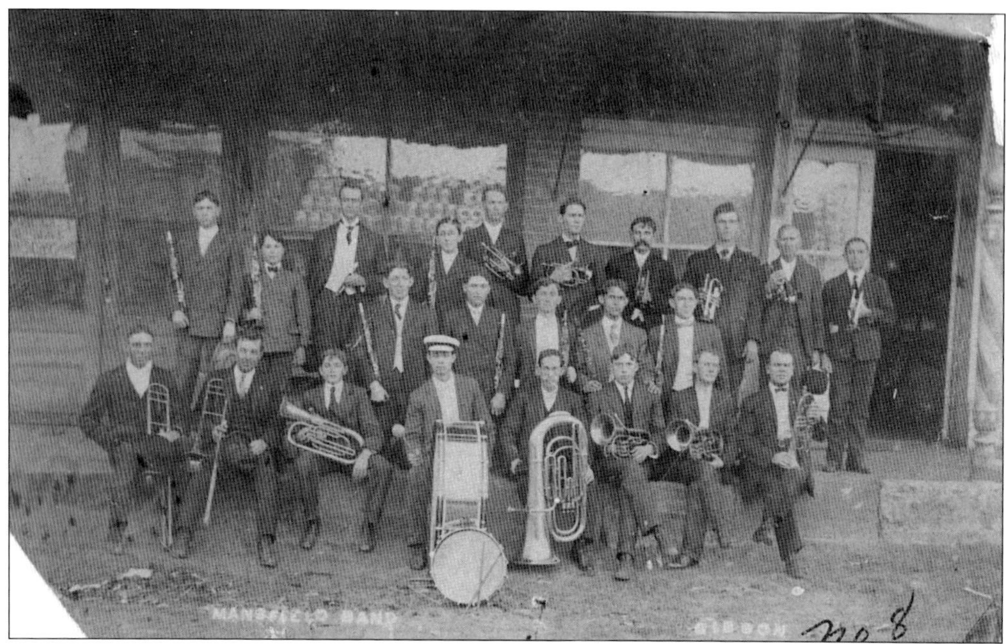

The 1908 city band played at various events. From left to right the members are (first row) Elmo Davis, Marcus Tims, Claude Ellis, Ed Dalton, Ned Man, Hayden McElvaney, Henry Buttrill, and Jake Hopson; (second row) Raymond Thomas, Hodges McKnight, unidentified, Robert Tims, and Herbert Wilson; (third row) E.A. Rosier, unidentified, Cleo Wilson, W.H. Bowman, Fred Caldwell, unidentified, Allen Wade, Joe Hopson, Jim Yeates, and Bob Smith.

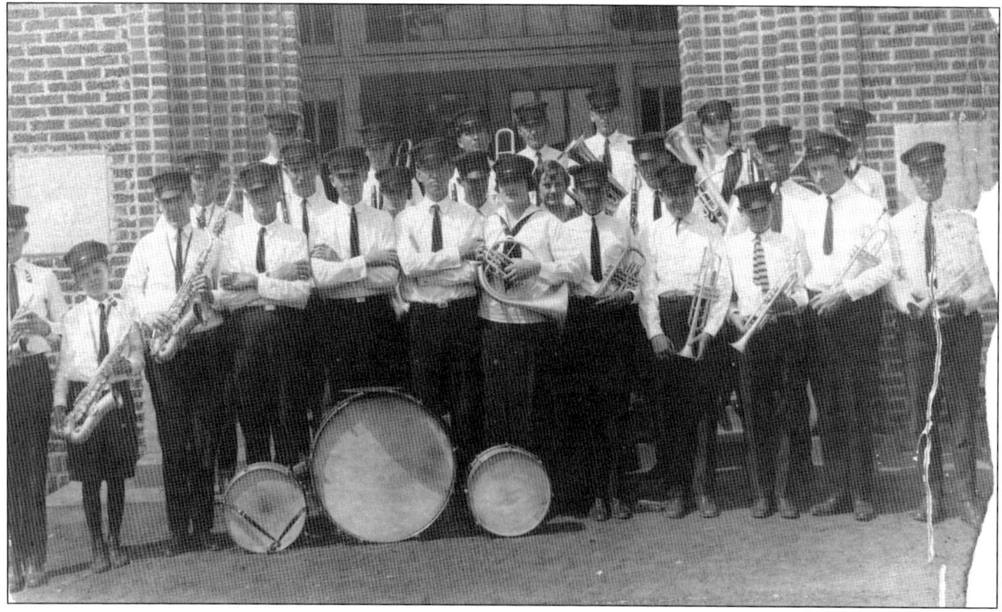

The city band continued into 1924. Pictured here are, from left to right, (first row) Thomas Carroll, Hardy Allmon, Bob Keith, Charley Hart, Ben Wilson, W.O. Hurwood Jr., Jennie Baker, Toby Greer, Elbert Farr, Ira Gibson, Wilbur Upchurch, and Newman Baker; (second row) Terrell Kelly, John Jordan, Katie Mae Stone, Eula George, Bernie Owens, Fred Smith, and Jim Malone; (third row) Jack Collins, ? Allmon, Eric Lawson, W.O. Hurwood Sr., Fount Carrell, Velma Upchurch, and unidentified.

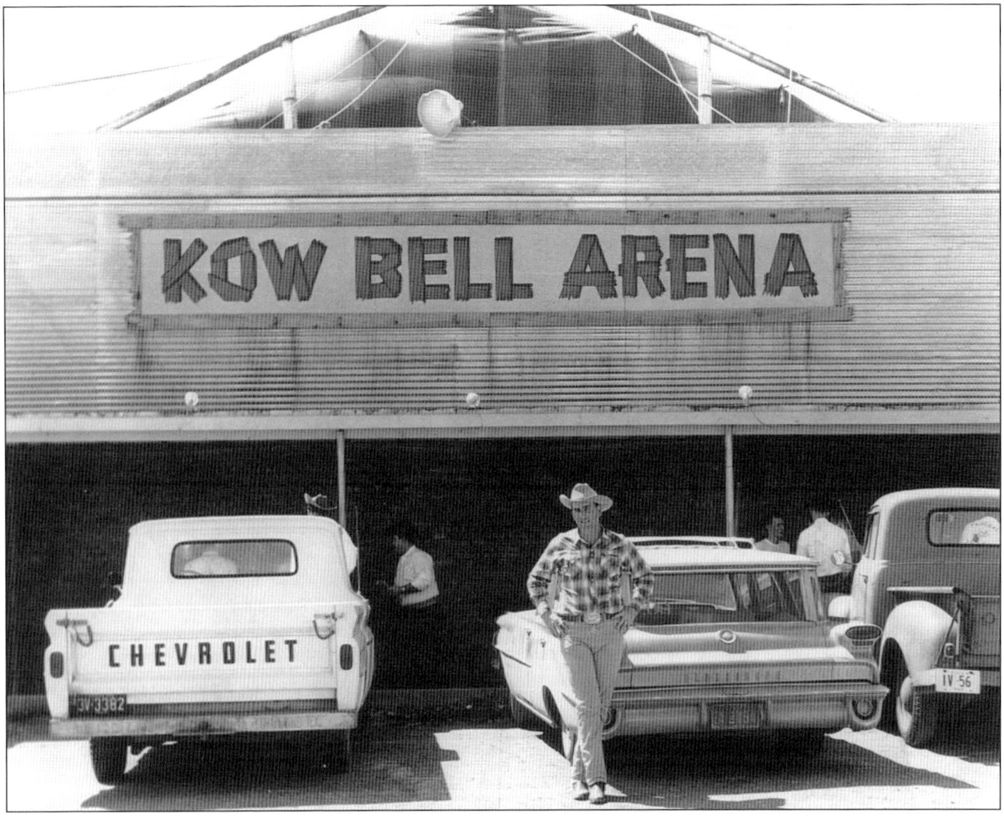

The Kow Bell opened in 1958 as a rodeo arena owned and operated by Bill Hogg. On Saturdays, it drew in people from around the country who enjoyed watching bull riders and barrel racers. Some professionals got their start at the Kow Bell. However, it was not just for the experienced; many locals have stories about paying a fee to try their hand at one of the events offered at the rodeo. Though the structure was demolished in 2004 to make way for Legacy High School, many still remember the Kow Bell's legacy as a source of entertainment and the original home of many professional and amateur riders.

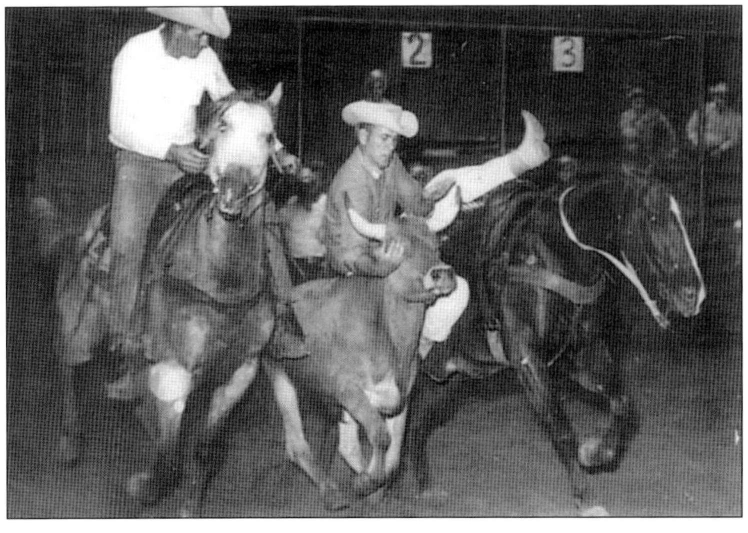

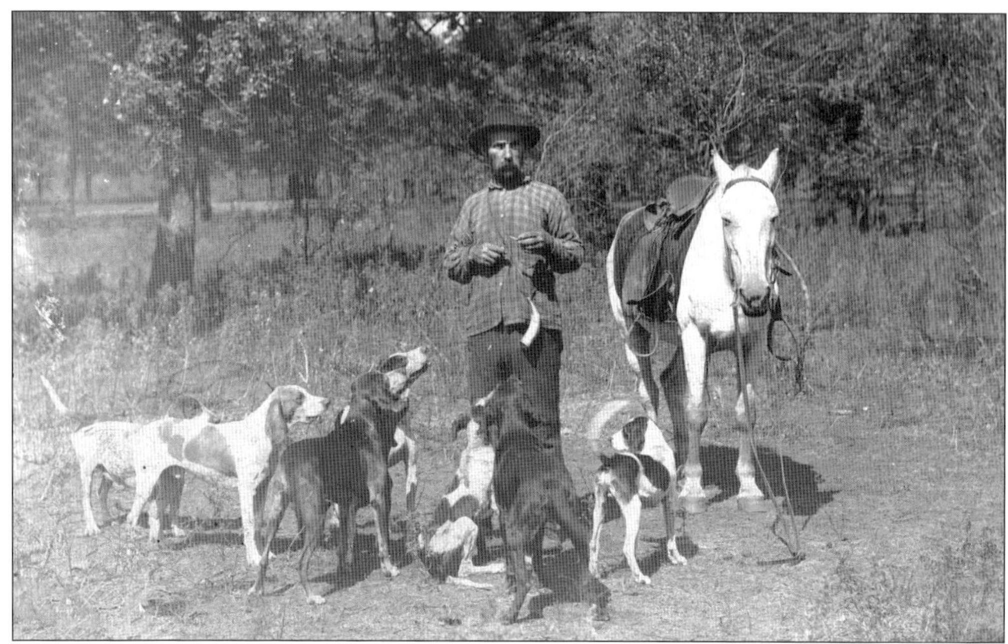

Thomas Henry Cope lived east of Mansfield, near Webb, and hunted with his dogs as far away as Cedar Hill. The dogs would corner their prey, then bark to signal to Cope. Rowdy, one of Cope's favorites, was remembered for having a distinct bellowing bark that could be heard from long distances away. When the hunt finished, he would blow his horn to call the dogs and head home.

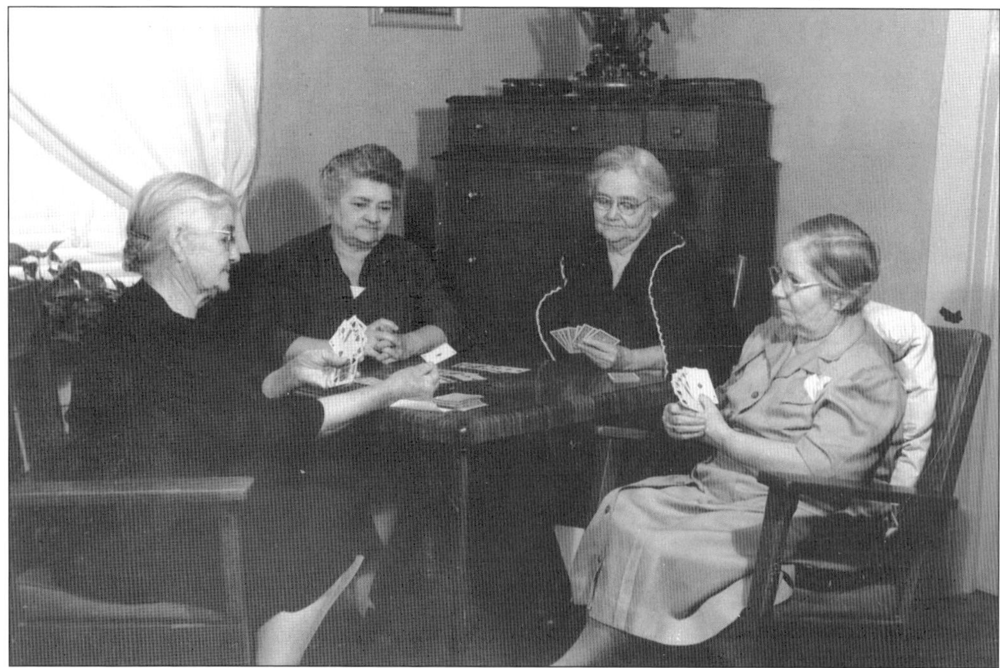

This Mansfield weekly bridge club met for over 30 years. The women pictured here—Duanna House Smith, Lela Ramsey House, Gula House Graves, and Stella House Smith—took turns hosting and played cards all day, stopping only for a quick sandwich for lunch. While bridge was a popular pastime for many decades, it is believed that this is the longest-running group in Mansfield's history.

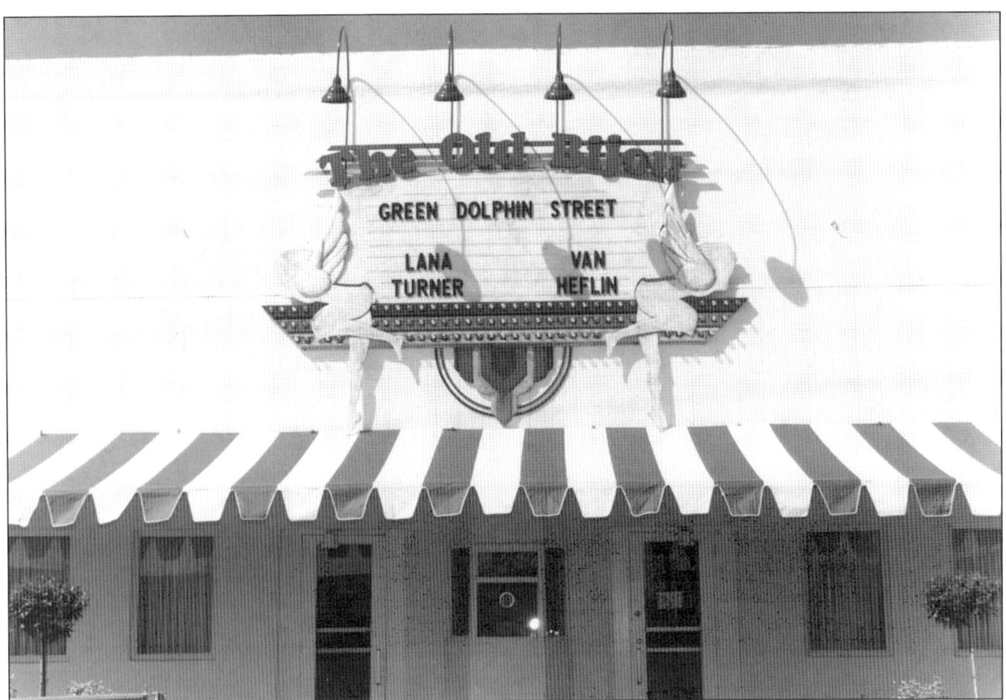

Milton Farr came to Mansfield in 1917. Believing Mansfield needed healthy entertainment, he rented a building at 109 North Main Street. On October 10, 1917, the Farr Best Theater was born. The name was selected by a citywide contest. Tickets were a dime for adults and a nickel for children. Shows, of which 90 percent were Westerns, were on Thursdays, Fridays, and Saturdays and were hand-cranked and silent until 1929. In 1936, an adjacent building was purchased to double the size of the theater. In 1975, the theater was sold and renamed Old Bijou. In 1980, it was purchased by St. John's Lutheran for church services, and then in 1988, the theater became Main Street Theater. On September 13, 1996, a nonprofit group bought the theater and renamed it Farr Best.

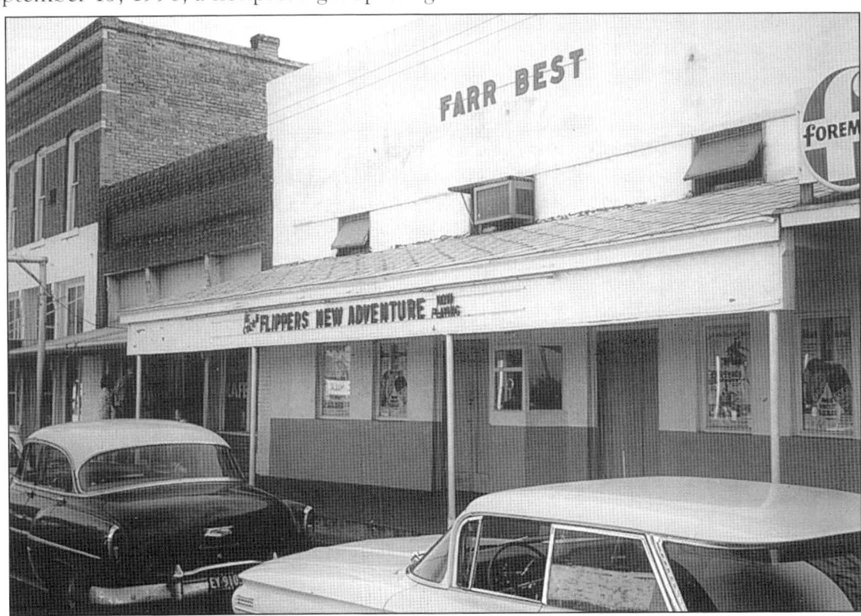

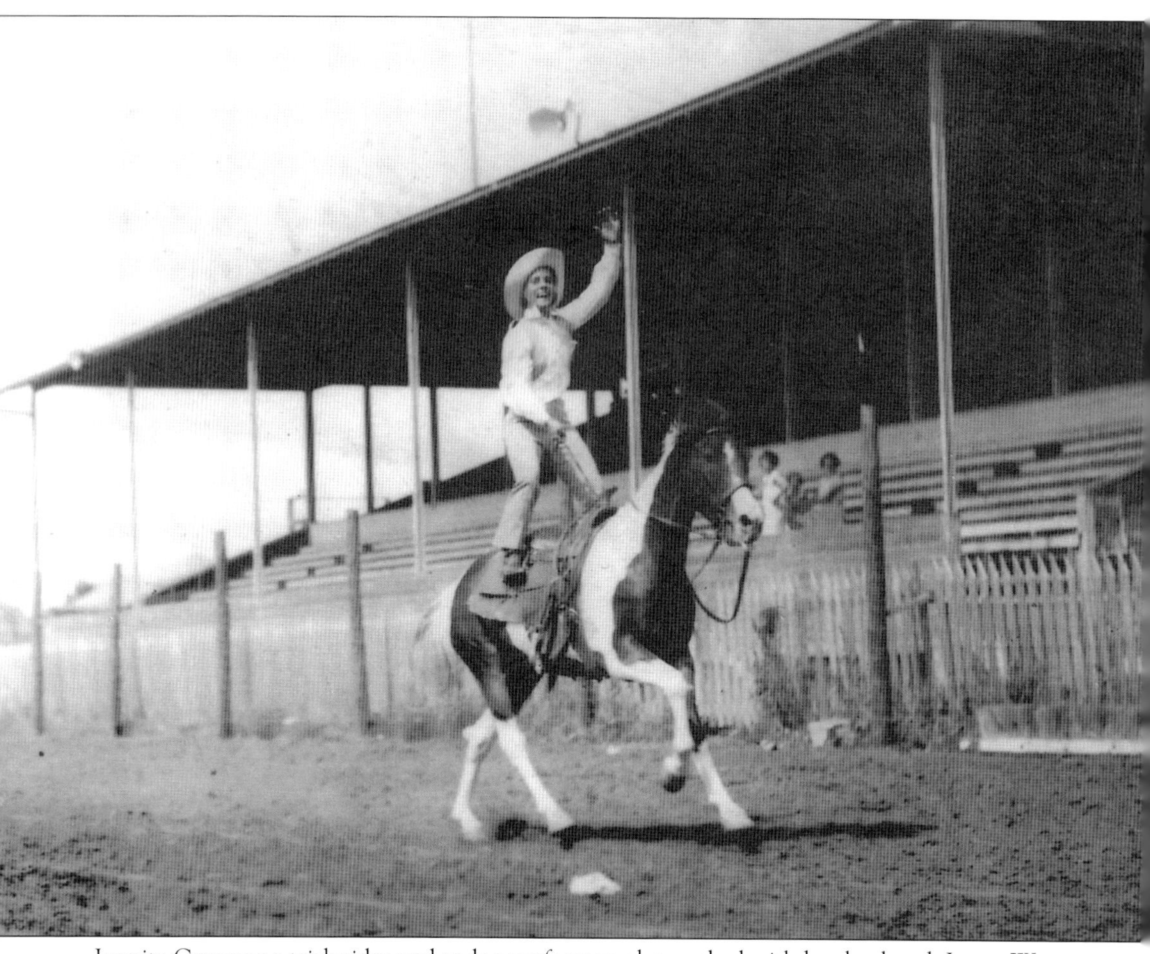

Juanita Gray was a trick rider and rodeo performer who worked with her husband, James Weaver Gray. She and Weaver held street shows in Mansfield on Smith Street during the Depression. In those days, show people found it hard to get work. They were often paid with whatever merchants could afford, such as a loaf of bread, a can of tomatoes, or a small amount of money. The Grays left Mansfield in 1952 and went on to perform in all the leading rodeos and tour around the country. Weaver could throw three ropes at a time and catch a horse and rider in three different places. Juanita's most famous trick was standing on horseback, falling backward over the horse's hips, and going under the horse's belly, all while the horse traveled at top speed. In 1966, they returned to Mansfield to be among friends.

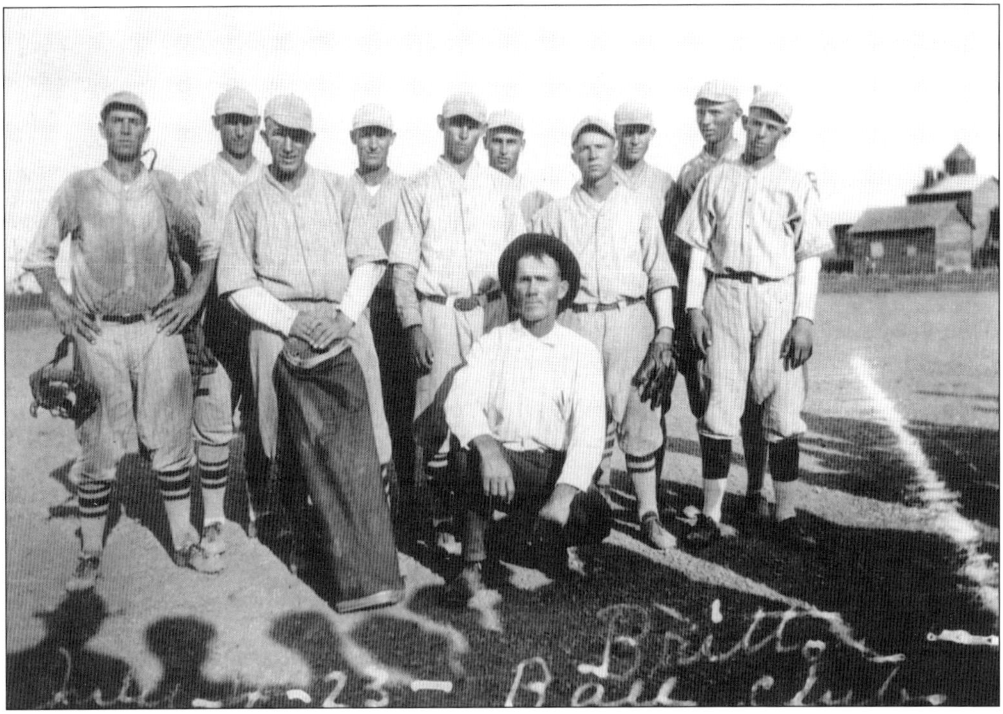

Mansfield's baseball rival was Britton, which won the championship every season they played. Kneeling in front of the players is their manager, B.B. "Boss" Cope. From left to right are (first row) Jodie Cooper, Albert Regan, Clarence "Booz" Speck, and T.A. Nichols; (second row) Cecil "Duck" Brown, Verne Wilson, "Nubbin" Chorn, Elmer Wilson, Jum Beckum, and Cave Gilstrap. Many of these men played with Mansfield on the 1928 men's baseball team.

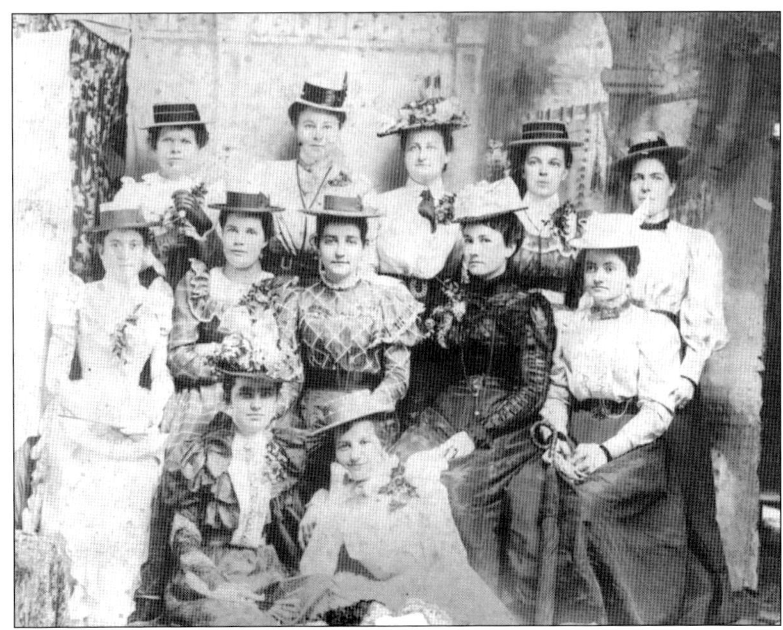

This group of young women became known as the Mansfield Belles of 1896. Pictured are, from left to right, (first row) Eula Pyles and Jessie Lou Hamil; (second row) Norma Man, Mat Helms, Hattie Times, Annie Dotty, and Lela Ramsey; (third row) Moreland Smith, Allie Chorn, Bell Chrisman, Kate Helms, and Delia Lowe.

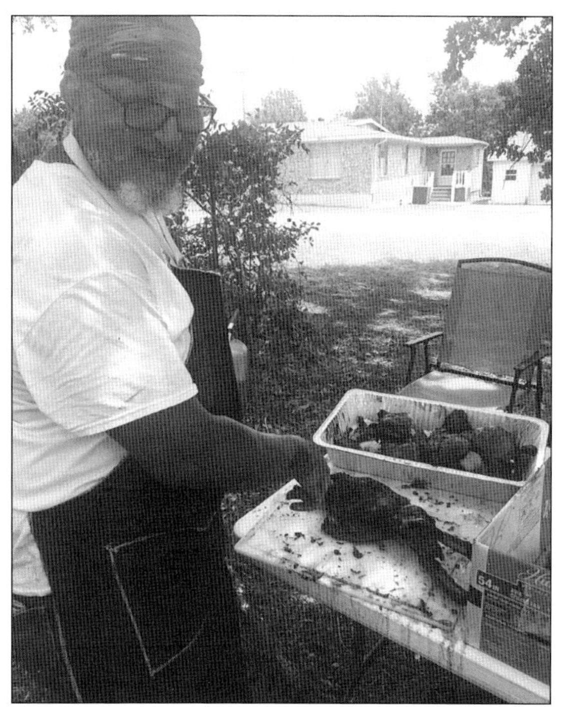

Juneteenth, a holiday commemorating the announcement that enslaved African Americans in Texas were free, has been celebrated in Mansfield for decades, long before it became a federal holiday. For many years, Bethlehem Baptist Church has put on an event for the community. Eventually, Norman and Brenda Norwood began hosting a picnic that features lots of good food and fellowship. Everyone is welcome, and hundreds of community members come out each year to celebrate. The photograph at left is of Norman Norwood cooking at the grill. In the image below, from left to right, Brenda Steele, Shyla Taylor, and Carolyn Smith are dancing at the picnic. (Both, Brenda Norwood.)

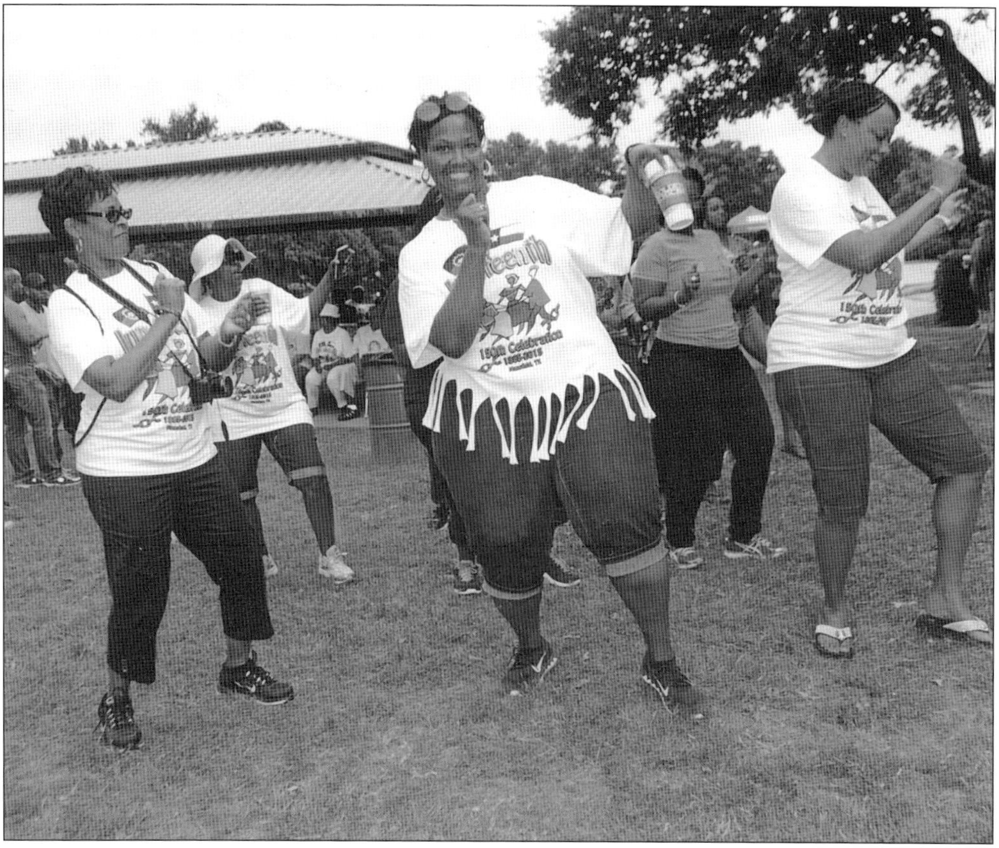

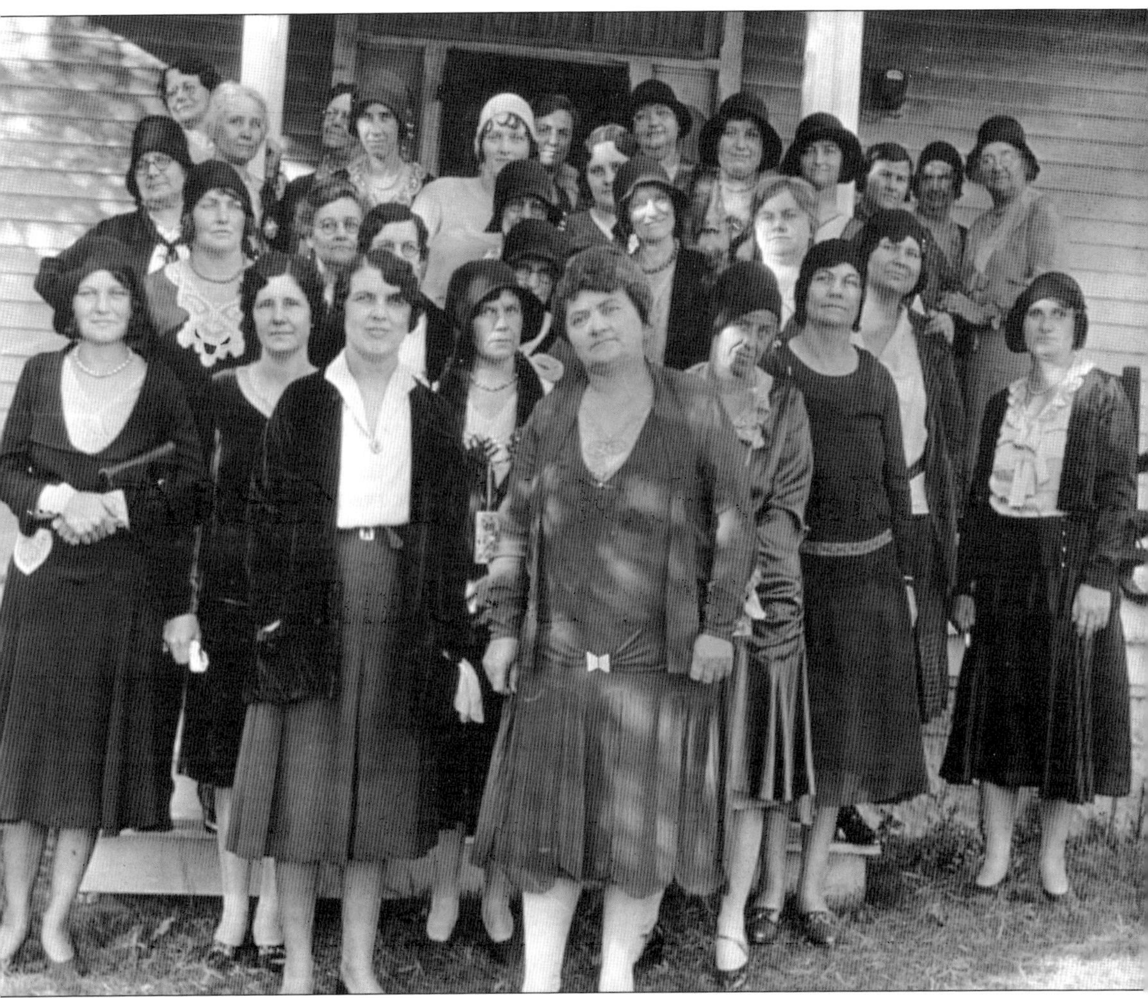

The game 42 was a popular card game with Mansfield's women through the years. This photograph, taken in 1928, shows members of the 42 Club standing in front of the Holland House. Some of the women pictured here are Una Lamb, Bess Holland, Flossie Stewart, Lelia House, Ester Wilson, Lula Back, Billie Walker, Sudie Sims, Gula Graves, Jessie Lou Mamil, Ted Nifong, Dora Halbert, Duanne Smith, Nora Ward, Jennie Patterson, Grace Galloway, Margaret Mayfield, Hattie Blessing, Kate Smith, Earl Gilstrap, Carrie Mills, Pearl Galloway, Annie Guest, and Mrs. Bart Smith.

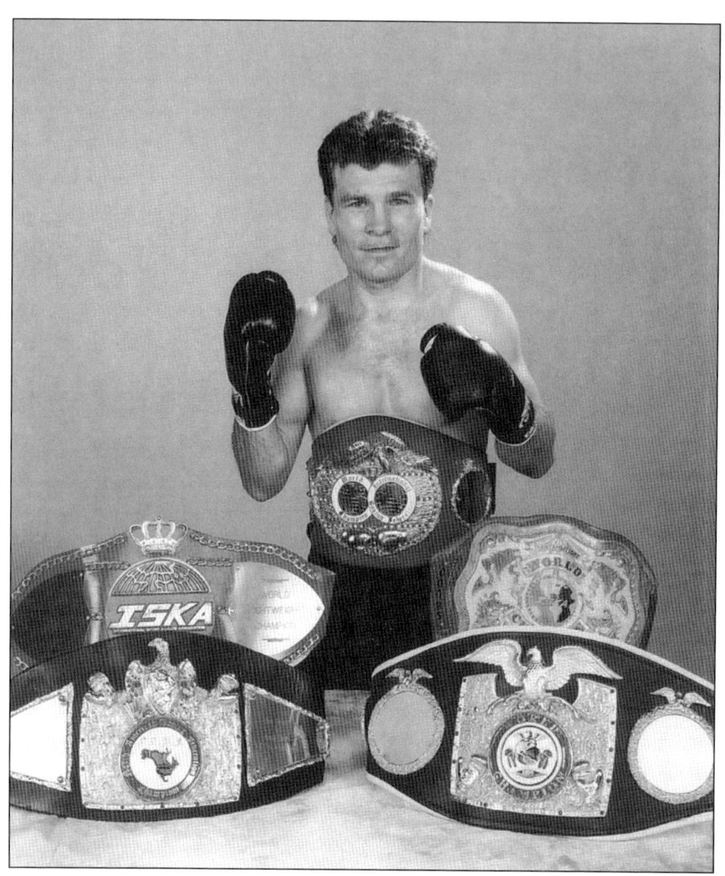

Troy Dorsey was born in Mansfield in 1962. He began his training in karate and taekwondo at the age of 10, eventually attaining a 10th-degree black belt in karate and a black belt in taekwondo. He later made the switch to kickboxing. Turning professional in the early 1980s, he fought in the bantamweight, featherweight, and lightweight classes. He is the only man to hold a boxing world title and a kickboxing world title at the same time and has eight world title belts. He was known as "the Destroyer" because of his aggressive style of fighting. In June 1999, he opened Dorsey's Karate and Fitness in one of the city's oldest buildings in downtown Mansfield.

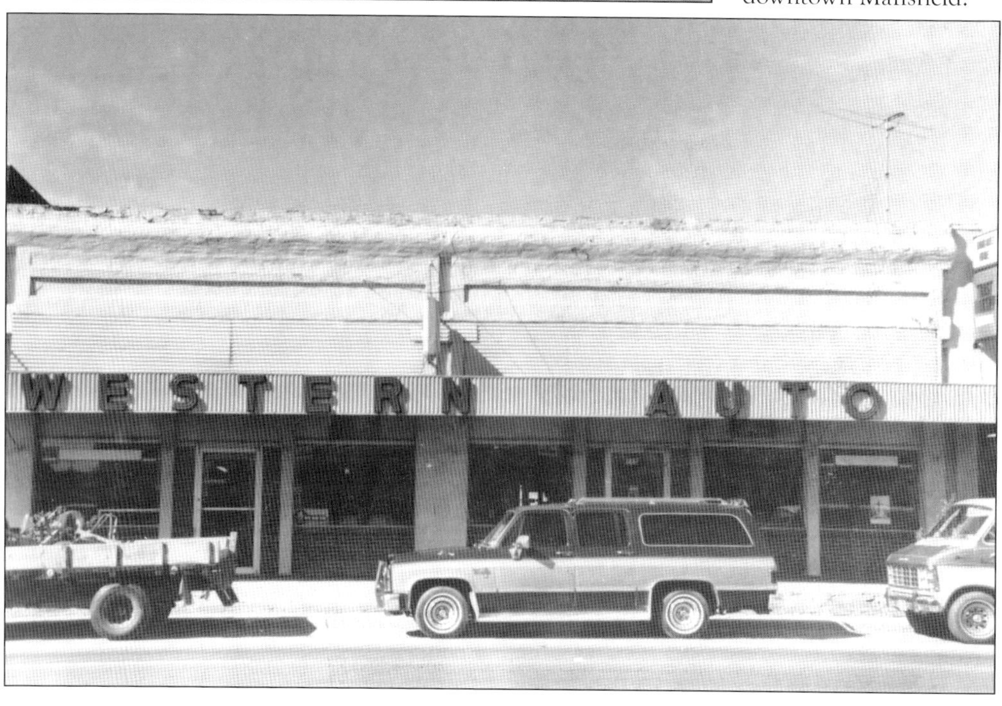

Nathan Thomas Smith lived in Mansfield in the late 1800s and early 1900s. He attended Mansfield Academy, received a teaching certificate, and spent his career as a rural school teacher. Smith met his wife, Katherine, at a teacher's association meeting. They had five children. Here, Katherine (far left) and Nathan (far right) Smith stand in front of the State Bank of Mansfield.

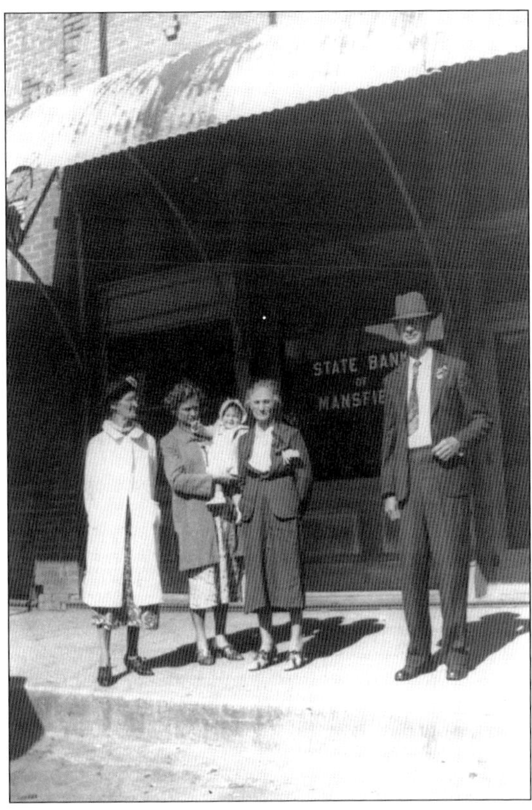

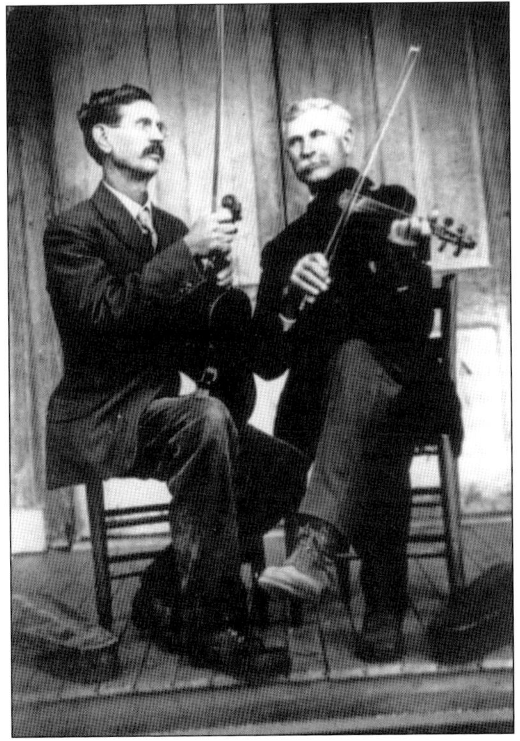

One of Nathan Smith's prized possessions was a fiddle that he bought in Fort Worth in 1876. He made his first fiddle when he was 10 years old, using a gourd and horsehair for strings. Here, Nathan and his brother Lewis tune up for a performance. They often played their fiddles at home or for social gatherings.

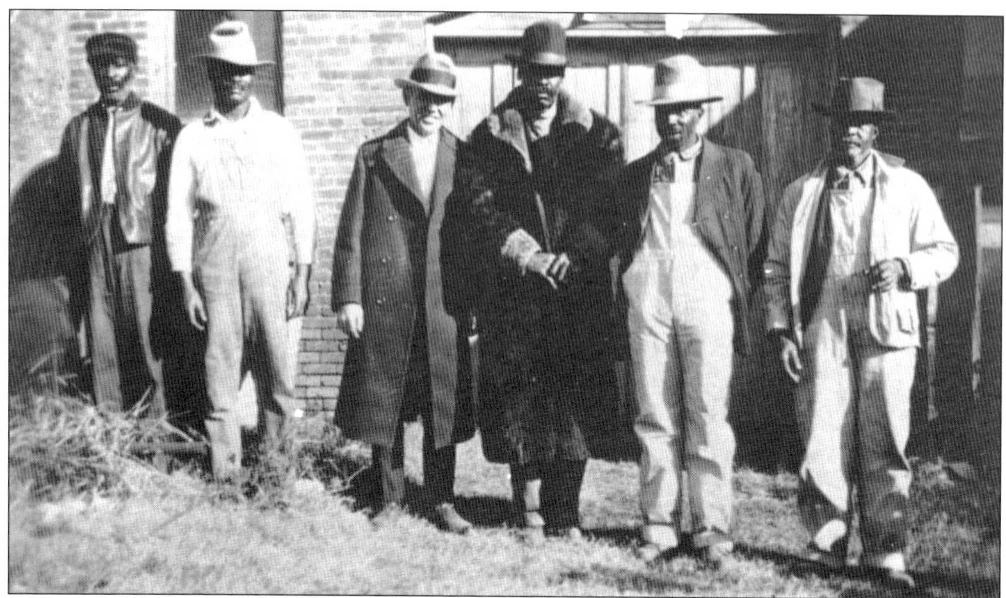

Pictured here are Mansfield residents strolling downtown on a Saturday afternoon. From left to right are Charlie Moody, John Moody, Bill Lamb, Tom Moody, Robert "Bird" Lawson, and Charlie Davis. The men considered this activity a good time to catch up on the news and play a few jokes on one another.

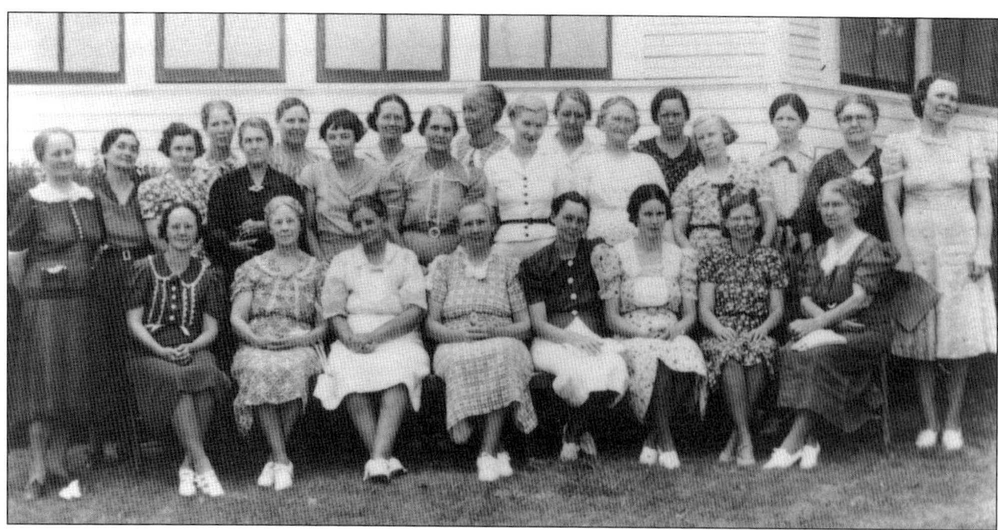

Pictured are members of the 1940 Home Demonstration Club. From left to right are (first row) Pearl Rawdon, Bonnie Gaulden, Ruth Grow, Nora Stone, Isabell Gibson, Ellen Clack, Odessa Sullens, and Mattie Watson; (second row) Mrs. Stahl, Mrs. Cone, Una Spears, Bertha Stone, Mrs. Bowlin, Julie Hamel, Miriam Wendell, Nora Gothard, Sallie Braton, Mary Stone, Ruby Turner, Minnie Justice, Alta Stone, Hattie Turner, Elsie Jamil, Mrs. Browning, Sudie Stewart, and Leona Hamil.

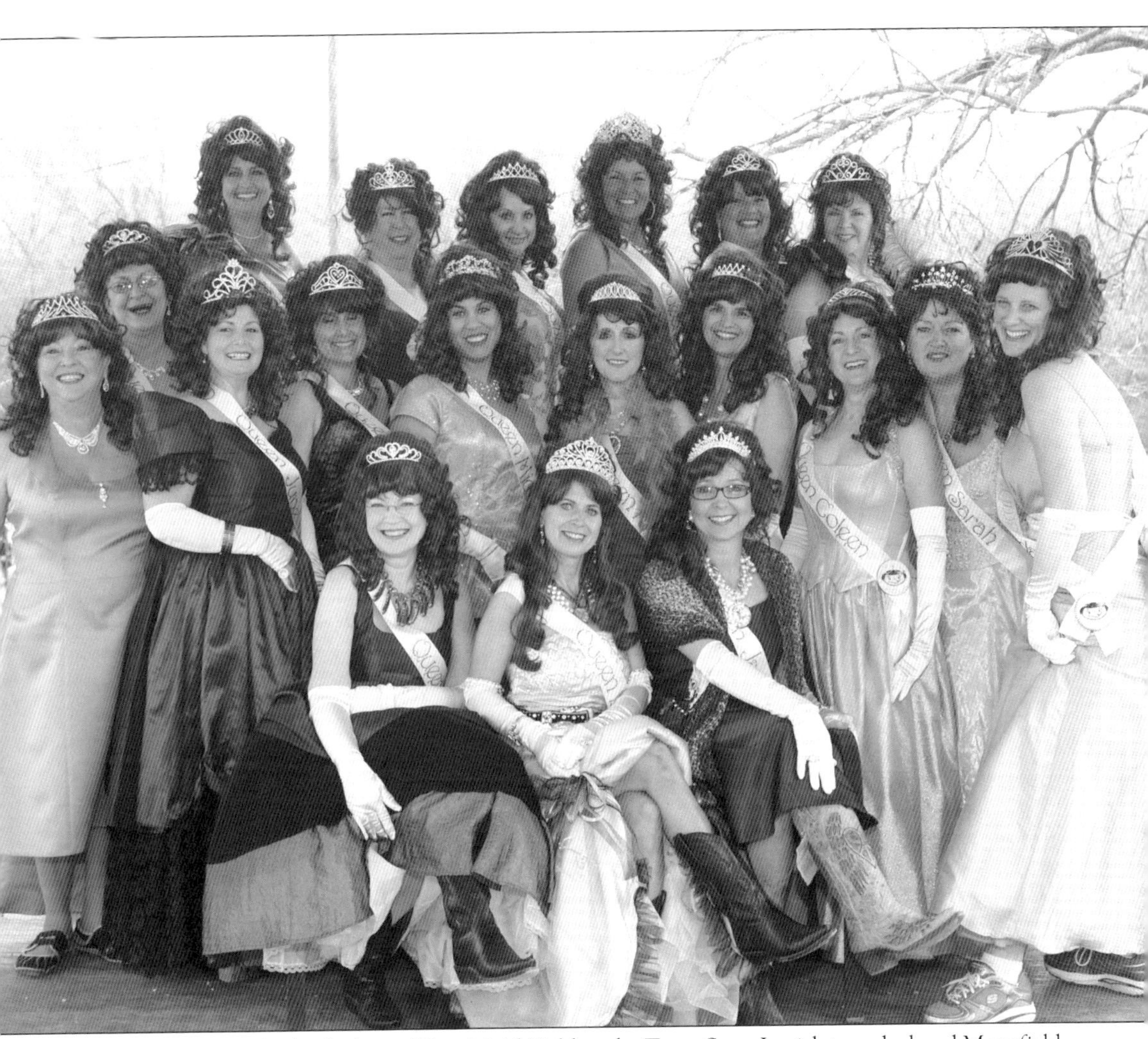

Since Mansfield is the birthplace of Best Maid Pickles, the Texas State Legislature declared Mansfield "the Pickle Capital of Texas" in 2013. The annual "World's Only St. Paddy's Pickle Parade and Palooza" brings thousands of spectators to Mansfield for musical performances, parades, and 5k runs. Other activities through the years have included pet parades, baby parades, beer barrel races, cornhole tournaments, and live music. The parade each year features homemade floats from local businesses and organizations, car clubs, churches, children's groups, marching bands, sports teams, and more. The last float always carries the women who organize the event each year, who are known as "the pickle queens." These ladies are easily identified by their green dresses, red wigs, and tiaras. (Dave Goodwin.)

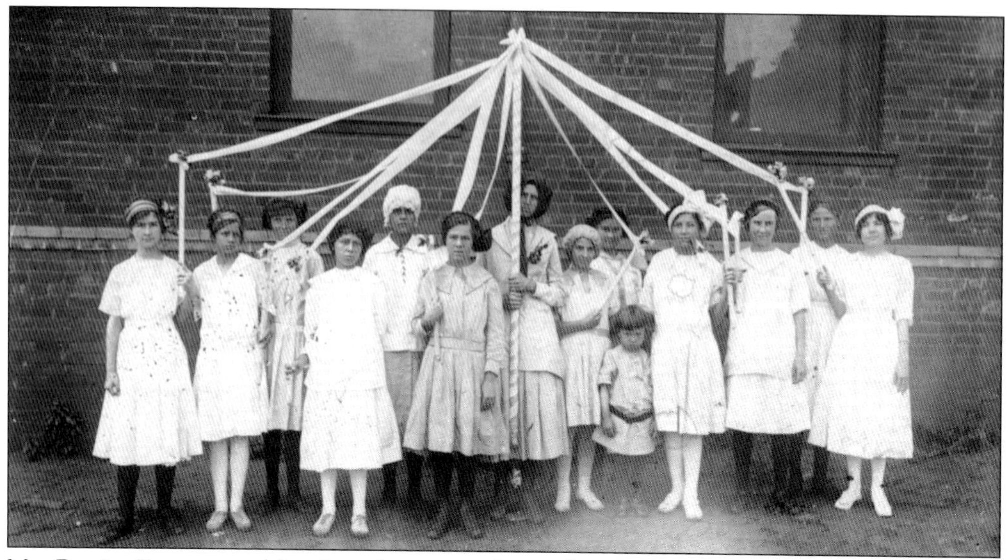

May Day is a European celebration of spring, traditionally celebrated on May 1. In the 1800s, many Americans chose to revive May Day with local festivals, including activities such as dancing around a Maypole decorated with ribbons. This photograph shows early-20th-century Mansfield children preparing for their own Maypole dance at the Mansfield Academy.

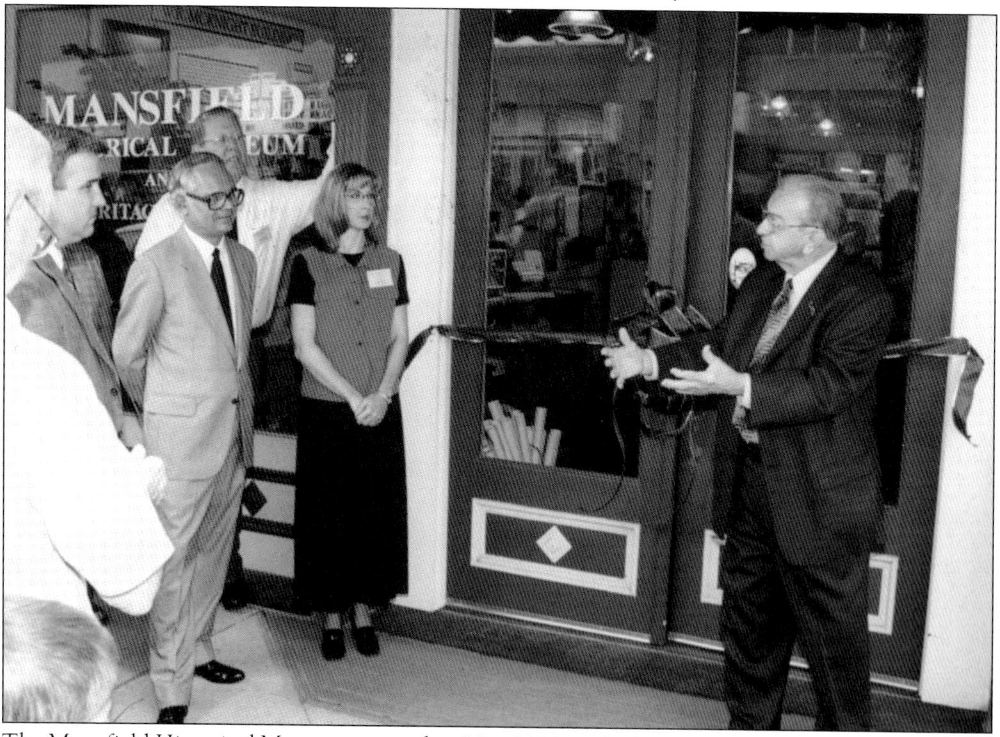

The Mansfield Historical Museum opened in May 2002 in the historic W.B. McKnight building at 102 North Main Street. It was originally owned and operated by the Mansfield Historical Society, but the City of Mansfield gained ownership in 2019. Visitors to the museum view exhibits about the history of the community and the people who lived in what is now modern Mansfield. This photograph was taken at the museum's grand opening.

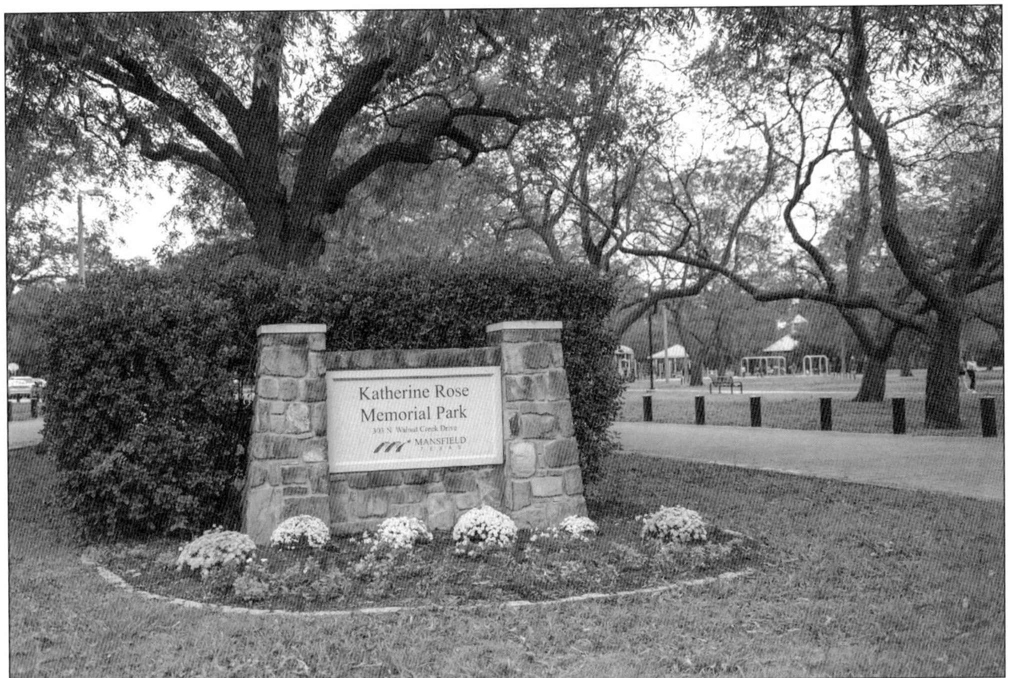

In 1960, volunteers from the Mansfield Jaycees cleared a vacant lot on East Main Street. They built picnic tables, benches, and a playground. This became Mansfield's first public park, named Julian Feild Park. The next park established was Katherine Rose Memorial Park. It was developed on land that had been a pecan orchard and was paid for by Mansfield's newly approved half-cent tax. A long-discussed Linear Trail is being created in stages. The trail follows Walnut Creek and will eventually span the entire city east to west. Since the spring of 1960, the Mansfield Parks Department has grown into 20 parks, plus five public-private partnerships, with plans for more in development. (Both, the City of Mansfield.)

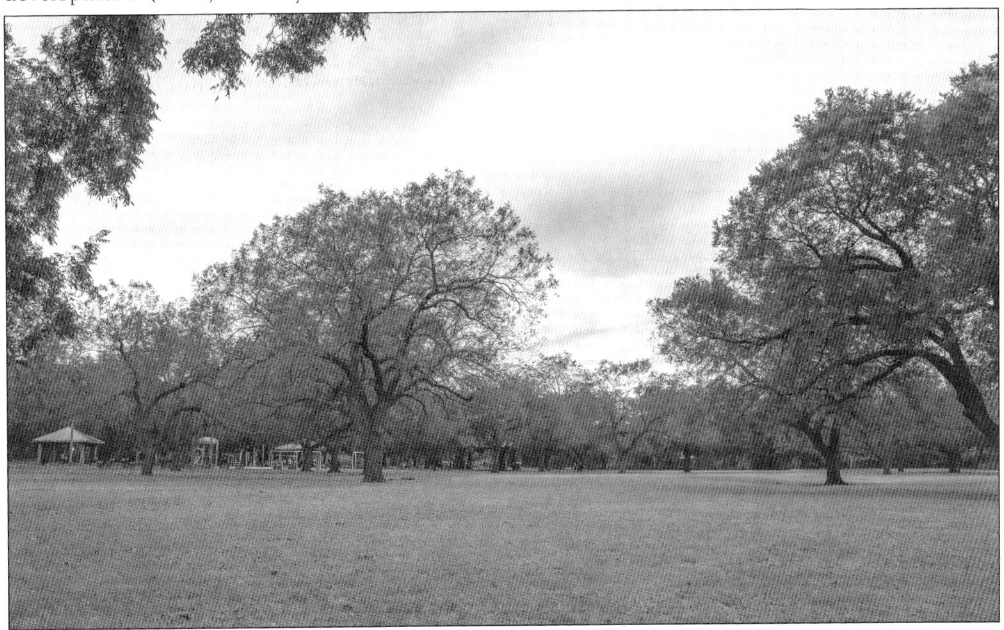

Consistent with our mission to preserve history on a local level, this book was printed in South Carolina on American-made paper and manufactured entirely in the United States. Products carrying the accredited Forest Stewardship Council (FSC) label are printed on 100 percent FSC-certified paper.

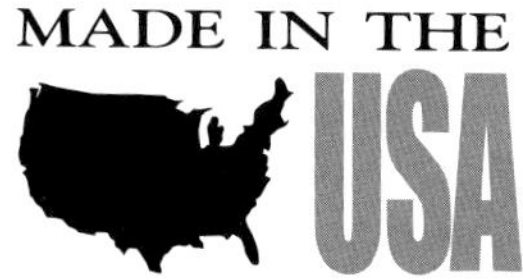